# BECOMING GOD'S CHILDREN

# BECOMING GOD'S CHILDREN

## Religion's Infantilizing Process

M. D. Faber

 PRAEGER

AN IMPRINT OF ABC-CLIO, LLC
Santa Barbara, California • Denver, Colorado • Oxford, England

**Library of Congress Cataloging-in-Publication Data**

Faber, M. D. (Mel D.)
    Becoming God's children : religion's infantilizing process / M.D. Faber.
        p. cm.
    Includes bibliographical references and index.
    ISBN 978–0–313–38226–0 (hard copy : alk. paper) – ISBN 978–0–313–38227–7 (ebook)
1.  Christianity—Psychology. 2.  Christianity—Controversial literature. 3.  Emotional maturity—
Religious aspects—Christianity.  I. Title.
BR110.F33   2010
261.5′15—dc22                    2009050949

ISBN: 978–0–313–38226–0
EISBN: 978–0–313–38227–7

14  13  12  11  10      1  2  3  4  5

This book is also available on the World Wide Web as an eBook.
Visit www.abc-clio.com for details.

Praeger
An Imprint of ABC-CLIO, LLC

ABC-CLIO, LLC
130 Cremona Drive, P.O. Box 1911
Santa Barbara, California 93116-1911

This book is printed on acid-free paper ∞

Manufactured in the United States of America

For Erin Faber

# Contents

# Preface

What follows is the culmination of an inquiry undertaken some 15 years ago when I found myself drawn to the psychology of religion (mainly the occidental creeds) as well as to the psychology of what was then called the New Age (shamanism, channeling, witchcraft, psychic healing, among others). My journey led to the writing of several books, two of which obliged me to pay close attention to the particulars of Christian doctrine and rite. Although I wasn't concentrating specifically on Christianity in these works, I was learning a good deal about it. Eventually I realized that I had reached conclusions on the nature of the Christian faith sufficient to guide me, and hopefully the reader, toward a better understanding of the alleged supernatural realm. Permit me to emphasize that my aim here is not to pick on Christianity but to conclude a project on the psychology of religion that turned out to be a central, defining task of my working (or writing) life. Christianity for me discloses fundamental information on the whys and wherefores of the willingness among people everywhere not merely to believe in a supernatural domain but to give the very direction of their lives over to invisible spirits, including above all, for Christians, the Holy Spirit or, as many Christians used to say, the Holy Ghost. I would like to think that the reader keeps in mind as he or she moves through the text both the underlying nature of current Christian theology and the underlying nature of the human animal that invented the world's supernatural creeds in the first place.

## Acknowledgments

I wish to express my gratitude to the staff of the library at the University of California, Irvine, for assisting me in a variety of ways as I strove to complete the project. I want also to thank Jack Rattelman for his many valuable comments on the analysis as it began to take shape in earnest. Finally, I must commend Ms. Jaina Kennedy for her splendid preparation of a manuscript that was not always easy to decipher, and Ms. Diana Marsan for her outstanding editorial assistance.

# Introduction to the Issue of Infantilization

## Thematic Vignettes

Dressed entirely in white and kneeling solemnly before the administering priest, a young male stockbroker in Manhattan is undergoing the rite of Holy Baptism. "I baptize you in the name of the Father, and of the Son, and of the Holy Spirit," pronounces the cleric as he pours water three times over the candidate's head. Shortly thereafter, the priest anoints the supplicant with sacred chrism, a perfumed oil consecrated by the bishop and signifying the gift of the Holy Spirit to the newly baptized one who is now, officially, free of sin and reborn as a child of God. "Baptism is the sacrament of regeneration through water in the Word," says the priest as the ceremony draws to a close. "It is the basis of the whole Christian life."[1] Glowing with the completion of the rite as he turns to family and friends, the young stockbroker thinks to himself, "I'm reborn, actually reborn! My life is commencing all over again, through Christ!" Glancing at his father and mother specifically, he feels a bit confused as he recalls the Biblical injunction that he is now obliged to love Jesus more than he loves his own biological parents (Matt. 10:37).[2] He resolves to ask a priest about that in the coming weeks.

~

Sitting silently in a pew of Toronto's Episcopal Church of St. Luke, a middle-aged schoolteacher prays ardently for the recovery of her young grandson who has been seriously injured in an automobile accident. "Dear Lord," she says inwardly, addressing an all-powerful Deity whom she alternately calls her Father, "grant Your healing energies to this boy, so that he may recover and live a full, rewarding life." She goes on, "I ask You this submissively, humbly, helplessly, as I depend fully upon Your goodness and mercy, upon Your unconditional love for all Your children, and I beseech

You faithfully in the name of Your only begotten Son, Christ Jesus. It is written in Your Book, Father, that if I ask I shall receive. Please, let it be so." A moment later as the woman exits the church and makes her way to the nearby hospital where her grandson lies injured, she experiences the sweet, unmistakable sensation of having "made contact." She can feel the Lord manifesting His divine presence within her through the working of the Holy Spirit. "He's there," she remarks to herself. "He's heard my prayer."

Strolling tranquilly through her sunny backyard located in a suburb of Kansas City, Missouri, a young housewife and mother of three dwells in her mind on the lovely old hymn she sang in church the previous Sunday.

> I walk through the garden alone
> When the dew is still on the roses,

she warbles softly to herself,

> And the voice I hear
> Falling on my ear,
> The Son of God is calling.

And then, savoring the famous refrain she liltingly renders,

> And He walks with me
> And He talks with me
> And He tells me I am His own.
> And the joy we share
> As we tarry there
> None other has ever known.[3]

"How beautiful are these words," she thinks to herself. "And how true! How often have I heard the Lord Jesus calling to me; how often have I felt I was walking with Him, talking with Him, listening to Him as He told me I belonged to Him." Her radiant feelings of closeness and security, of connection and love, remain with her during the next few hours as she goes about her daily chores.

Ensconced within a chapel of Paris's colossal Cathedral of Notre Dame (Our Lady), an elderly, retired French physician is about to experience Holy Communion, a religious ceremony in which he has participated many, many times during the course of his long life. He is not alone. Kneeling with a dozen other worshipers who have come to receive the holy sacraments, he listens attentively as the priest gives thanks to the Father, through Christ, in the Holy Spirit, for all His works: creation, redemption, and sanctification. He listens as the priest proceeds to ask the Father to send his Holy Spirit onto the bread and the wine so that they may become, actually become, the body and the blood of Jesus Christ. As the priest raises the Host aloft while reciting the Lord's Prayer, our elderly communicant awaits patiently his turn to take the body of his God into his mouth and swallow Him down into his stomach. Walking along the banks of the Seine later in the day, the good doctor reminds himself theologically that he now has within his own body the body of another Person/God, namely, Jesus who became a person 2,000 years earlier and also that he is now *in* the body of another person; he is now *in Christ* just as Christ is within him. The divine, mysterious relationship fostered by the Eucharist is fully reciprocal, a two-way street doctrinally. In addition, he calls to mind the familial relationship he enjoys with all those who have taken the Person/God into *their* bodies, with all those who participate in the Christian family, in the Christian Church, his spiritual "mother" who embraces him as Her own, according to the Catechism that resides upon his bookshelf at home. Resonating emotionally with all these spiritual affiliations and unions, he feels well prepared for another week of retirement in his beloved Paris.

᷉

"Just do it, just take a deep breath and do it," a young businessman is instructed by a Leader in Van Nuys, California, as he struggles to speak in tongues for the first time. He is sitting in a Pentecostal Church that has among its congregation several individuals of both sexes who possess and who manifest this gift of the Holy Spirit. Finally, after considerable encouragement, and assurances that his successful performance of this phenomenon will bring him powerful feelings of blessedness, the young businessman holds forth: "aish nay gum nay tayo," he pronounces, and then again, "aish nay gum nay tayo." That's all he has to offer on this, his first successful try. "Thank you, Lord, thank you," cries the Leader, with his hands still upon the head of the novice who is now weeping openly and joyously as he feels God's Holy Spirit coursing electrically through his body and his mind. Receiving the congratulations of his fellow worshipers, three of whom practice glossolalia themselves, he can hardly wait to get home and break the wonderful news to his wife. "This is the best I've felt in all my 25 years," he thinks to himself.

᷉

Reclining in his study one tranquil Sunday evening in October, the pastor of a small Methodist church in southern England ruminates feelingly on the loss of his elderly mother to cancer one year earlier. They were very close, and the pastor sometimes misses his mother deeply. Yet always, at some point in his ruminations, he reminds himself consolingly that he will see her again, indeed hold her in his arms again in heaven—God willing of course. The pastor imagines the next world in the classical late Victorian and early modern fashion. Families parted by death are reunited in the presence of Christ, as the omnipotent Almighty looks on from the highest spiritual plane. Within the pastor's paradise, there is no toil, no striving, no obligation, no "progress" in an earthly sense, but only beatific visions, mystical light, and robed angels singing eternal praise while loved ones luxuriate in their togetherness. The pastor glances over to the etching on his writing desk wherein he and his beloved mother hold each other's hand and face the rising sun. "Death, where is thy sting," the man thinks passionately to himself. His eye then moves to a large, hardbound volume that recently arrived in the mail and that bears the title *Mapping Paradise*. It comprises a history of earthly paradise, starting with the early Christian era and continuing to the present day. Lavishly illustrated, it indicates the extent to which humanity has always longed for a paradise on earth, for a place of emotional and physical perfection in the here and now as opposed to the eternal hereafter.[4] Resolving to peruse this fascinating volume during the next few weeks, the pastor nods off, with visions of his departed mother still flickering somewhere in his mind.

## Psychological Inquiries

I begin with these vignettes in an effort to indicate in a lively, compelling way several of the major topics on which I plan to concentrate here. Most broadly, what are these people doing? What are the mental and emotional processes, the mental and emotional *aims*, that inform their behavior? Why would someone who has already been born and parented seek to be reborn ritualistically as the child of an invisible god whom he regards explicitly as his father, or if he follows the New Testament closely, as his "Abba" or "daddy" (Romans 8:15)? Why does Christianity consider this transformational baptismal rite to be "the basis of the whole Christian life?"[5] Again, what are Christians doing when they pray, and how are they instructed to go about the business by their theological mentors? When Friedrich Heiler asserts in his classic study of supplication, *Prayer*, that Christians are expected to adopt a "dependent, child-like" attitude as they turn to the Almighty, is he reflecting the universal or orthodox position on the matter?[6] Are Christians *always* expected to pray as "little children"? If so, why? What does it mean to claim that a "Holy Spirit" mediates the communication between the earthly prayer and the supernatural deity who presumably hears and answers? What *is* the Holy Spirit anyway? When people assert that they "feel" its "presence," what do they feel? What constitutes its presence? When a Christian hymn suggests that Jesus's "voice" finds its way to the worshiper's "ear," that Jesus "calls" upon His followers to "walk" with Him and to "talk" with Him, do the lyrics imply that worshipers actually hear Jesus's voice, actually experience walking and talking with their Savior?

Why would anyone want to eat the body of Jesus, or drink the man's blood? Remember, Jesus was an actual person when He walked on earth, and it is the actual person, Jesus, whom billions of earthly communicants consume when they participate in the Eucharist. Jesus also was, and is, a God of course, and the notion of Godhead is always firmly tied to the ritual. But worshipers don't consume a Godhead; they consume the sacrificial Redeemer of the fallen human race, the Lamb of God. Permit me to ask again, why do they wish to do this? Surely such behavior invites close psychological scrutiny. Were we to visit some faraway island in some faraway ocean and find ourselves invited to eat the body of a god in the form of, say, a coconut, we would instantly put on our thinking caps and ask ourselves, what's going on? Somewhere in our minds might lurk the words "magic" or "mumbo jumbo." We would strive to *explain* both conduct and myth as inseparable facets of a peculiar cultural enactment. Why would we not do the same for the Eucharist? Were we to exempt it from such scrutiny, would we not be indulging ourselves in the "us and them" kind of thinking that characterizes former eras, the colonial, Victorian period, for example, when the "savages" ate the gods and the Christians participated in the sacred traditions of the church? Eating a god's body is exactly that whether one is naked and painted or wearing a business suit. Might the answer to the question, why do Christians wish to consume Jesus Christ? reside in the orthodox claim that such consumption triggers an actual, inward, symbiotic union between communicant and salvational presence? Those who swallow Christ immediately dwell *in* Christ, and Christ as swallowed immediately dwells *in* them. Moreover, one's feeling of being in Christ and of having Christ inside one is linked theologically to the Holy Spirit that has descended transformationally on the bread and the wine and thus awakened the worshiper's capacity to apprehend God's presence as the ritual unfolds. Accordingly, might the psychological nature of the Holy Spirit have everything to do with the feelings people experience as they participate in certain magical acts and nothing to do with the putative supernatural realm? When we further consider this rite in relation to baptism that is also tied inextricably to the Holy Spirit, we realize that one's spiritual rebirth, or the emergence of the "new Adam" from the navel of the Church, leads directly to the baptized Christian's *reentry* into the body of his divine Creator! One comes out anew in order to go back in! Even those baptized Christians who don't partake in the Eucharist believe themselves to be dwelling in Christ in some "spiritual," doctrinal sense. All this may suggest in a preliminary way that Christianity's chief aim and purpose is to bring about the *union* of humanity and God, or to express it alternatively, to end the *separation* of humanity and God that characterizes our ordinary, mortal, fallen, tragic condition as inhabitants of the planet. It's hard to feel separate when one is walking around in the body of Christ, or walking around with Christ in one's belly.

How does something as strange, indeed as bizarre as glossolalia, or speaking in tongues, find its way into one of humankind's major religions, a creed that harbors for billions of people the essence of reality? True, glossolalia has become a controversial topic among Christians during the past 50 or 60 years, yet it is doctrinally encouraged and practiced in Pentecostal and other churches throughout the world, including, of course, the United States where it currently enjoys widespread popularity.[7] What are its origins in Scripture, and, in particular, what do those origins suggest to us about the underlying psychological nature of the Holy Spirit? According to Pentecostal tradition, it is the Holy Spirit specifically that provides the practitioner with his amazing gift, with his ability to speak in tongues.

Eternal salvation through the Trinity, through the sacrifice of Christ, through baptismal and Eucharistic rites, through faith as it manifests itself in prayer, through the gift of transformational grace, and through other aspects of the Christian framework as it expresses itself on a vast, global scale, removes or at least diminishes adaptively humankind's primal, instinctual fear of death, the termination of one's existence, the dreaded, inevitable end. Writing vividly of the "profound aversion towards non-existence" that resides in people generally, Corliss Lamont comments,

> To try to realize that when once we close our eyes in death, we shall never, never open them again on any happy or absorbing scene, that this pleasant earth will roll on and on for ages with ourselves no more sensible of what transpires than a dull clod, that this brief and flickering and bittersweet life is our only glimpse, our only taste, of existence throughout the billions of infinities of unending time—to try to realize this, even to phrase such thoughts, can occasion a black, sinking spell along the pathways of sensation.[8]

Who would disagree? But death as human creatures perceive it, feel it, apprehend it developmentally and psychodynamically constitutes not only naughtment, nothingness, emptiness; it also constitutes a traumatic separation from the self and from others, both as the self extends into others and as others are internalized into the self along the way, from the inception of one's days. Accordingly, heavenly salvation for Christians is usually social in nature and tied conceptually to reunion with those they love, those upon whom they emotionally depend.[9] And in this, it harmonizes perfectly with the central enactments and symbolic representations of the creed, with baptism that rebirths the believer into eternal union with a loving, unchanging, parental Deity; with the Eucharist that positions the believer within the body of Christ; with prayer that ties the believer to the Parent-God through the workings of the Holy Spirit; with the archetypal view of the Church as mother and womb; with the congregation of worshipers as family, as brothers and sisters; and on and on it goes with dozens of related items and nuances. The whole religion is a complex, magical system for attaching people to other people ("love one another") and to a triune supernatural entity, the Trinity, from Whom the believer will never be parted (Rom. 8:39). It can hardly come as a surprise, then, that Christianity's version of terrestrial paradise, the prelapsarian Garden, the proverbial heaven on earth, is one in which there is no death, no separation crisis of mortality, for it is death precisely that humankind's parents, Adam and Eve, bring into the world when they transform themselves from innocent, obedient children of God into rebellious knowledge-seekers, lapsed immortals who deserve exactly what God gives them, expulsion from the Garden, the world's navel, the maternal matrix, an expulsion that renders mythically our original "birth" as mortals. A fundamental aim of Christianity, as every Christian knows, is restoring the fallen progeny of Adam and Eve (all human beings) to their salvational status through the mercies of Jesus Christ, the worshiper's heavenly protector and guide. Eternal salvation is ultimately *rescue* from the crisis of eternal separation.

## Methods and Theses

I intend in what follows to develop these and other ideas within a broad naturalistic framework informed by psychological, neurological, cognitional, anthropological, and evolutionary perspectives—a multifaceted, eclectic approach that sets aside entirely any and all appeals to the supernatural realm, divine mystery, the intuitive unseen, sacred inspiration, and all the rest of it. Naturalism is defined as a theory denying that an object or event has a supernatural significance and suggesting that scientific laws are adequate to account for all phenomena. There is not, in my view, one single aspect of Christianity or any other religion, not one, that cannot be fully and satisfactorily explained along purely naturalistic lines. Note the emphasis on explanation. Although I consider religious supernaturalism, whatever soothing, adaptive potential it may possess, to be a distortion of reality, an erroneous and regrettable perception of the world around us, I am determined to subordinate polemics to what I hope is clear, cogent, naturalistic analysis, the kind that persuades through painstaking empirical procedure as opposed to rhetorical passion. If readers choose to finish the book, they can simply make up their minds at the end whether or not the explanation I offer is convincing.

As for my presentation of Christian beliefs and practices, my sources of information on the creed, I plan to rely heavily on what Christians are currently writing and thinking, the books, pamphlets, prayers, hymns, devotionals, television shows, and conversations that make up the current "scene," or again in the vernacular, "what's out there right now." Why am I doing this? During the period in which I prepared myself for the writing of this book, I realized more and more deeply that the living Christian religion was speaking to me vividly, directly, through its present popular expression, through the work of Billy Graham and his daughter, Anne Graham Lotz, through Robert H. Schuller and Henry Cloud and Neil T. Anderson, through collections of Christian prayers and hymns, through pamphlets such as *Our Daily Bread*, through Christian television channels and the remarks of Christian men and women whose immediate, daily lives were inextricably bound up with their spiritual beliefs. Of course I had to focus persistently on the New Testament, and I had to pay some attention to Augustine and Martin Luther, to Thomas Merton and to the *Oxford Illustrated History of Christianity*, and to many other classical, authoritative, erudite productions past and present. But were sources such as these to dominate my discussion, the reader might never hear the voice of Christianity today, the urgent expression of contemporary people as they revealed their hopes and fears, their wishes and convictions, in simple, straightforward, and often passionate language to those who were reading or listening intently, with pressing emotional agendas of their own. I wanted to capture this accent, this contemporary slant, and I came to believe that the psychological essence of Christianity might emerge very nicely, perhaps unforgettably, if the reader were encouraged to detect that accent, that slant, as he or she moved through the text. Does this mean that I plan to subordinate the manifold historical variations and issues on the nature of Christianity as an unfolding religion to a presentation of the creed as we discover it today in our own Western culture? Yes, it does: that's exactly the kind of book I'm writing. But let me be more specific about the naturalistic approach I mean to take.

A multilayered, multifaceted system of magical behavior, Christianity as theology and rite is designed to accomplish nothing less than the veiling, or perhaps the removal, of our chief biological tormentors, namely, separation, smallness (or vulnerability), and death, and replace them with a perfectionist scheme whereby the believer enjoys loving union with a Parent-God from Whom he will never be parted, protection and empowerment through a Parent-God Whose omnipotence flows toward His dutiful followers, and immortality or an escape from death through Jesus Christ's sacrificial gift, freely offered to all those who turn to Him sincerely and ask. For everyone who cries out, "Save me, Jesus," the Lord will stand biological reality on its head and furnish the believer with a full-fledged alternate identity to replace the flawed or imperfect one he or she possesses by virtue of what the Bible terms "the Fall." These are the wishful notions that reside at the core of the creed, the ideas that fuel its theological, ritualistic engine, that drive its transformational agenda, that convince its devotees to declare both inwardly and aloud, "I believe."

The magical system is rooted overwhelmingly in *memory*, particularly unconscious memory, or implicit memory, or affective memory—*felt* as opposed to explicitly recalled, and jogged, or awakened, by a wide variety of retrieval cues embedded in Christian rite and doctrine, in the magical, religious happenings in which the worshiper is invited to participate as he actualizes his life as a devotee of the tripartite theological model, namely, Father, Son, and Holy Spirit. In this way, the *psychological* significance of Christianity is tied inextricably to specific *neurological* events occurring in the hippocampal, limbic, and amygdalic regions of the brain, as well as in the cortex, or frontal lobes, the area from which emanates the believer's rationalization, the "intellectual" or "cognitive" assent that allows the creed's supernatural framework, its inventive, imaginal claims (heaven, hell, angels, devils, and spirits of all kinds including the tripartite Godhead) to ring true. This is but another way of saying that the worshiper's *whole brain, both conscious and unconscious*, carries the perceptual weight of the religion's magical goings—on the final goal of which is to *infantilize the participant*, to restore him mnemonically and transformationally to an idealized version of his own biological beginnings, to the period in which he *was* secure in the protective, loving, salvational care of a big one, a parental shepherd after whom he followed like a bleating lamb for several crucial *years*. The magical steps of the infantilizing process that engenders the worshiper's alternative identity, the counterweight to his biological being, are clear, and I will examine each of them at some length: baptism, prayer, the Eucharist, moment-to-moment dependency on the Lord, the key New Testamental metaphors of Vine and Shepherd, obedience, glossolalia as a specialized expression of infantilization, and a number of others. If all goes well for the metamorphosed worshiper, he will, in a central part of himself, wake up as the new Adam (Col. 3:10), united inextricably with his supernatural Guide, the Big One Who leads him around every step of the way and Who saves him from extinction, from death, the ultimate separation and terror.

Let's bear in mind as we go that Christianity's reliance on the actual infancy and childhood of every believer or potential believer does *not* suggest that perfect or even overwhelmingly happy beginnings must undergird the religion's infantilizing tactics. To accomplish *all* its magical purposes, and thereby infantilize *all* its devotees, Christianity requires only "good enough" beginnings,[10] infancies and childhoods that contain for the most part normal interactional experience *good enough* to be idealized into the wondrous figures it offers the multitudes: the beneficent, mighty Father, the Parent-God; Jesus, the loving Shepherd and selfless Savior of humanity; Mary, the tender mother; the Holy Spirit Who guides the mortal heart toward the immortal Deity. The vast majority of humans with their "good enough" beginnings have no trouble at all recognizing and responding to these perfectionist entities. Even those unfortunates whose opening years are streaked with serious parental shortcomings can usually get there. It is only the very deeply disturbed, the severely neglected and abused, who are apt to be entirely shut out, and even among these tormented people miracles of grace are by no means unknown. Why do I stress this? I stress it because the Holy Spirit whose working within the worshiper establishes the veracity of the religion's doctrine and rite turns out in the final analysis to be nothing more nor less than the worshiper's implicit recollection of his own biological experience in the world.[11] Let's explore this a little further in a preliminary way that will prepare us for the full-scale discussion that occurs later on.

According to Christianity's orthodox view, the truth of the Word suffuses the seeker when and only when the Holy Spirit descends into his heart and mind. Yet *how* this transpires, precisely, is for all Christians a profound, even divine mystery, the wonder and the glory of the creed. Let's make up a typical instance as follows: a lukewarm practitioner suddenly discovers himself inspired by the teachings of Jesus Christ as they emerge from New Testamental passages. After years of floundering about, he feels deep within himself reborn, galvanized, awakened to the scope and significance of Christianity's "good news," or "Gospel." How has this come to pass? The best one can do as a Christian is attribute the whole business to the workings of the Holy

Spirit, or the Spirit-Person who miraculously finds Its/His way into the life of the quondam lukewarm practitioner. The putative "mystery" or "miracle of grace," however, resides ultimately within the nature of implicit recollection: the worshiper cannot *see* what is occurring in his own mind-brain as a retrieval cue whose provenance is some particular facet of Christian rite and doctrine (baptism, prayer, the Eucharist, the metaphor of Vine or Shepherd, or a dozen other related features of creedal literature and practice) awakens a particular aspect of his own biological beginnings and thus infuses into his present existence the affective charge of his foundational past. Remember, every major aspect of Christianity as a whole is devoted to transforming the worshiper into a "little child" of the Lord: "Verily I say unto you, Except ye be converted, and become as little children, ye shall not enter into the kingdom of heaven" (Matt. 18.3). When the Holy Spirit reaches the Christian seeker, it is always in this infantilizing context. Indeed, the infantilizing context is *there* in the first place to facilitate the Holy Spirit's transformational workings in the one who craves a "salvation" that turns out to be nothing other than *union with the Parent-God*, existing in the gravitational orbit of the Big One, following after the sacred Shepherd, depending entirely on the protection and love of the Lord—in short, rediscovering an idealized version of exactly the kind of symbiotic relationship one enjoyed during the early period as a little one, a "little child" in the care of a loving parent. Accordingly, the Holy Spirit is a "mystery" only to those who fail to discern how the human mind-brain works in specific ideational contexts. When the accent of consciousness is on a wishful reversion to childhood, the whole mind-brain will follow that accent.

I'm not suggesting, of course, that the whole of Christianity as it manifests itself within a given social order boils down to the process of infantilization that I'm after here. As a full-fledged socioreligious institution, Christianity is busily involved in education, child care, medical services, charity, counseling, camping, and a dozen other worthwhile pursuits that engage people at every level and at every age. One has merely to look around to discern this. I'm suggesting only that Christianity in its theological, doctrinal, ritualistic hearts of hearts—Christianity as we discover it in the New Testament, on the devotional Christian television channels, and in the theological writings and pronouncements of it sources and purveyors from the *Catechism of the Catholic Church* to the myriad inspirational books and pamphlets on the shelf in libraries, bookshops, and in places of worship—Christianity as *religion*, in short, is dedicated overwhelmingly, one might even say entirely, to the intellectual, emotional, and psychological infantilization of all those who turn to it, follow it, subscribe to it for what we commonly think of as "spiritual" reasons.

The reader may well be thinking in the face of that last sentence, hold it! You're reducing complex, variegated theological rites and teachings to a monolithic psychological/neurological analysis, a theoretical view that picks and chooses in a manner that supports its own predetermined conclusions. What fits your notion you seize upon. What doesn't fit, however significant it may ultimately be, you simply ignore. My full response to such objections will be the substance of this book as a whole, of course. But I will say here, very briefly, that the charge of reductionism in the specific context of Christianity as an infantilizing process will not hold and should be dropped. There is just too much supportive material in the major presentational sources of the religion, in the New Testament, in the popular media, and in the enormous, even endless Christian literature that we find everywhere around us, to miss the overwhelming emphasis upon infantilizing the worshiper, upon transforming him or her into an utterly dependent, utterly submissive, utterly obedient "little child" following after the explicitly parental figures of the Almighty Lord and His pastoral Son from Whom he or she continuously seeks provision and protection through prayer. As I just suggested, the reader will have to wait for the book's central chapter to appreciate all this thoroughly, but I want the reader to know right now that I've not only considered the issue of reductionism every step of the way but found myself amazed again and again at the extent to which the Christian religion is dedicated to infantilization as the main component of its transformational, salvational scheme.

## Cultic Christianity

The presentation of Jesus in the New Testament is, of course, multidimensional. We find acts of kindness, of mercy, of concern; we find firmness and authority; we find humility and self-effacement; and we find the ability to suspend the laws of nature, to perform miracles, to walk on water, to heal the sick, to rise up from the grave. Finally, we find the willingness for supreme self-sacrifice, limitless service unto others, even to the Cross itself. It is an arresting, unforgettable portraiture, and its influence upon the development of Western culture is immeasurable.[12] However, from the standpoint of strictly naturalistic, psychological investigation, the standpoint to which I've committed myself unreservedly here, we also find in the depiction of Jesus the familiar outlines of the cult leader, the self-absorbed, narcissistic personality with the charismatic, problematical power to work His will upon the gullible, malleable followers who find their lives turned upside down as they fall under His influence, His spell. Karen Armstrong, writing on the origins of Christianity in her recent volume *The Great Transformation*, bluntly describes Jesus for her readership as "a Galilean faith-healer."[13] While Armstrong's words take us in the right direction, they ultimately fall short of the mark. We have in Jesus an individual whose assumptive healing capacities are only a tiny segment of the extraordinary, astonishing nature He claims for Himself.

Jesus goes about in the belief that He's divine, a kind of god, the promised Messiah of Jewish Scriptural tradition, in direct, immediate contact with mighty supernatural powers. As the be-all and end-all of the world, which revolves around Him, He lays down the law, or perhaps I should say gives marching orders, to the mere mortals with whom He interacts. They are to do whatever He says and to center their lives on His purposes:

> And Jesus came and spoke unto them saying, All power is given unto me in heaven and in earth. Go ye therefore, and teach all nations, baptizing them in the name of the Father, and of the Son, and of the Holy Ghost: Teaching them to observe all things whatsoever I have commanded you: and, lo, I am with you always, even unto the end of the world. Amen.
>
> (Matt. 28:18–20)

Seldom does the word Amen so transparently mean what it means in the Hebrew and Greek: so be it. Clearly, Jesus seeks total control not only over the gathering band of "worshipers" who are already hugging his "feet" (Matt. 28:9); He seeks total control over the whole world, "all nations" as He puts it. Everyone, period, will do "whatsoever" He "commands." Everyone will be "baptized." Everyone will "observe" all the "things" He wishes them to "observe." The very meaning of life, even life itself, will come to be equated with Him. His ideal disciple will have no other focus in his earthly existence besides Jesus. It will be Jesus coming, Jesus going, Jesus all the time. As His chief orthodox proselytizer, Paul, puts it in his Epistle to the Philippians (1:21), "For to me [,] to live *is* Christ." This, then, is what Jesus covets: the utter absorption of others (everyone) in His grand, global design.

As for followers, Jesus has a gift for recruiting them, lots of them, in fact, as all successful cult leaders do. Here are the relevant passages from the New Testament:

> And Jesus, walking by the sea of Galilee, saw two brethren, Simon called Peter, and Andrew his brother, casting a net into the sea: for they were fishers. And he saith unto them, Follow me, and I will make you fishers of men. And they straightway left their nets, and followed him. And going on from thence, he saw two other brethren, James the son of Zeb´-e-dee, and John his brother, in a ship with Zeb´-e-dee their father, mending their nets; and he called them.

> And they immediately left the ship and their father, and followed him. And
> Jesus went about all Galilee ... And his fame went throughout all Syria ...
> And there followed him great multitudes of people from Galilee, and from
> Decapolis, and from Jerusalem. ...
>
> (Matt. 4:18–25)

Once under his spell, Jesus makes it very clear to His devotees that He is now
the Shepherd and they the sheep: "I am the good shepherd ... My sheep hear
my voice, and I know them, and they follow me" (John 10:11,27). But the
members of the flock do not merely owe Him their absolute allegiance. As I noted on the first page of this book, they must substitute Him for their
own real mothers and fathers. They must "love" Him more than their own
parents, and if they are parents, they must love Him more than their
own children:

> He that loveth father or mother more than me is not worthy of me: and he that
> loveth son or daughter more than me is not worthy of me. And he that taketh
> not his cross and followeth after me is not worthy of me.
>
> (Matt. 10:37–38)

Jesus declares in effect that He's the crucial one, not the parent or the child.
Thus ideally His worshipers, His "sheep," will "follow after" Him at once, at
that very moment, as James and John do earlier. A father such as Zeb´-e-dee
is simply left holding the bag, or, as in this case, his tattered fishing nets.
So much for familial cohesion, familial loyalty, familial order.

Surely at this juncture the reader is beginning to recognize the alarming,
cultic scenario with which he or she is doubtless already familiar in his or
her own troubled, modern society: a grandiose, charismatic individual leads
a band of simple, credulous followers ("fishers") into a religious scheme for
changing the world, a scheme that has at its center, of course, the grandiose,
charismatic individual himself. What the Romans finally did to Jesus was
barbaric and disgusting, but let's face it, they had a very good sense of who
He was and what He was up to. The Roman Empire during this period was rife
with potentially disruptive sects and cults that required constant monitoring
and in certain instances immediate suppression lest Roman rule be compro-
mised. As in our own world today, those who have the power, be they gover-
nors, industrialists, or popes, do not want to see it eroded, even a little bit.
Are we not all sinners?

That Christianity commenced its life as a breakaway Jewish sect with Jesus
as the long-awaited Messiah, then gradually metamorphosed into a sizable
cult as followers from several non-Jewish traditions began to join in, is the

most widely accepted version of its beginnings.[14] Let's take a moment to imagine the faithful gathering for worship down in the catacombs during the time of Roman persecution (late second century). With a couple of flickering torches fighting the eerie darkness, the priestly leader of the rites is pouring water over the head of a recent convert and announcing from an altar of stone that the newcomer is now reborn on the spiritual plane as a "little child" of Jesus Christ. Certain members of the group abruptly cry out that they can feel a Holy Spirit descending upon them in the tombs. "He's here," they shout; "He's moving among us." Several participants start looking over their shoulders with wide eyes. A few moments later, the leader holds up a loaf of bread and a vessel of wine, asserting that the words he is about to utter will transform these common substances into the flesh and blood of a supernatural Deity who once walked the earth as a man. The sacred words having been pronounced, the attendees one and all masticate the body and drink down the blood of their God, declaring their blessedness at having Him inside. For some, the feast is joyously transportive: they exult at being merged with their loving provider. Others weep openly as they contemplate their Redeemer's ultimate sacrifice. Still others drift off into trance states mumbling their favorite prayers of adoration and thanksgiving. When noises are suddenly detected elsewhere in the passageways, everyone falls silent. Roman soldiers may well be about, and that, of course, means trouble. To imagine all this, to see it freshly, unexpectedly, out of the blue as it were, is to be struck at once by its cultic, magic nature. If ever conjurations were enacted on this planet, we have an instance of them here.[15]

Having accomplished the long, historical transition from cult to established religion, Christianity is currently a part of our social fabric, as familiar to most of us as the ball game or the movies. Yet at its liturgical, theological core Christianity today is as cultic, as magical, as counterintuitive and fantastical as it was 2,000 years ago in the catacombs beneath the Appian Way. If the aim of this volume is the naturalistic demystification of the magical process as I've been indicating from the outset, then we must recognize the mystification that inheres automatically in the mere presence of Christianity all around us, all the time. We hear about a child born of a virgin. We hear about a dead man rising up from the grave. We hear about bread and wine turning into flesh and blood, about individuals conversing with supernatural entities, about holy spirits flowing into people's minds and bodies. We hear these things, and many more just like them, on the telly, in the office, on the street—everywhere in short, and we simply continue with our activities as if such goings-on were no more unusual than making the bed. Someone tells us that he's just partaken of a god's flesh and blood, or received a personal message from an invisible, three-sided deity, and we say, oh. Vast numbers of human beings have, of course, been raised with such ideas, and one cannot exaggerate the impact of early educative experience on young, impressionable minds, particularly when the education comes from parents, or other figures of authority who are often distinctively, even sumptuously attired, with special bonnets, and with grave, weighty expressions on their faces.

The point is, to underscore the cultic nature of Christian theology and rite is to facilitate our understanding of Christianity's infantilizing process, for the aim of *all* cultic creeds, by which I mean the aim from the top down, is to establish the cultic leader as the embodiment of all truth and all legitimate authority, the cultic teachings and rituals as the summation of all worldly and otherworldly wisdom back to the very beginnings of time, and the cultic membership as the unquestioning, sheep-like followers of the leader: men, women, and children who center their lives on the leader and the leader alone, who look to the leader and only the leader for guidance and protection—in a word, who become within the constraints of the cultic configuration infantilized human beings upon whom the leader ultimately relies for the dissemination of his egocentric, grandiose, narcissistic views. When all is said and done, there is nothing special or even particularly interesting about cultic Christianity other than the colossal, monumental fact that in the crapshoot of history it managed somehow to catch on and to steadily insert itself into the lives and ultimately the traditions of men and women everywhere. Accordingly, this book on Christianity as infantilization can be regarded equally as a book on the cultic core, the cultic essence, the cultic foundation and final nature of the ubiquitous institution that we presently call the Christian religion.

## Notes

1. All the quoted materials in this paragraph are from Joseph Ratzinger, ed., *Catechism of the Catholic Church* (Liguori, MO: Liguori Publications, 1994), pp. 312, 317.

2. Throughout this book my scriptural citations are from the King James Version of the Bible (Philadelphia: National Publishing Co., 1978).

3. This popular Christian song can be discovered in many Christian songbooks. I found the version I'm using here in Barbara Epp's article, "Walking and Talking with God," http://retirementwithapurpose.com/beprayer1.html (accessed November 2, 2005).

4. Alessandro Scafi, *Mapping Paradise* (Chicago: University of Chicago Press, 2006).

5. See note 1.

6. See Friedrich Heiler, *Prayer: A Study in the History and Psychology of Religion* (Oxford, UK: Oneworld Publications, [1932] 1997), p. 258.

7. Kimberly Winston writes that "since the 1960s" the practice of glossolalia "has leapt from . . . traditionally Pentecostal denominations to mainline Protestant and Catholic congregations. There are tongue-speaking Methodists, Presbyterians, Episcopalians, and Catholics." See "Faith's Language Barrier?" *USA Today*, May 24, 2007, p. 9D.

8. Corliss Lamont, "The Illusion of Immortality," in *Critiques of God*, ed. Peter A. Angeles (Amherst, NY: Prometheus Books, 1997), pp. 261–89. My citation is from p. 272.

9. See Colleen McDannell and Bernhard Lang, *Heaven: A History* (New Haven, CT: Yale University Press, 1988), pp. 267–75.

10. The expression "good enough mothering" may be found in D. W. Winnicott, *Playing and Reality* (New York: Basic Books, 1971). See pp. 12–14.

11. For the Holy Spirit's dual nature as both spirit and person, see Billy Graham, *The Holy Spirit* (New York: Thomas Nelson, Inc., 1978), p. 2. "The Holy Spirit is a Person." writes Graham.

12. That Jesus actually existed, that he was a real person as opposed to a mythical creation, is often debated by scholars and laypersons alike. For a lively recent discussion of the matter, see Patricia Biederman, "Documentary Questions the Existence of Jesus," *Los Angeles Times*, August 20, 2005, p. B2. I personally believe, as do the vast majority of individuals who have looked into the issue, that Jesus did, in fact, exist. As for his exact words and actions, we must rely on the New Testament that was not composed until several decades after His demise. I take the New Testamental account to be reflective of both the behavior of Jesus and the mind-set of those who undertook the composition. Accordingly, the New Testament offers us what we can think of as a *truthful narration* of the ideational elements that shaped the Christian religion.

13. Karen Armstrong, *The Great Transformation: The Beginning of Our Religious Traditions* (Toronto: Vintage Canada, 2007), p. 457.

14. See Everett Ferguson, *Backgrounds of Early Christianity* (Grand Rapids, MI: Wm. B. Eerdmans Publ. Co., 2003), pp. 11–67. See also Paul Johnson, *A History of Christianity* (New York: Simon and Schuster, 1995), pp. 21–48.

15. Baptism and the Eucharist have been an integral part of Christian worship since its earliest days.

CHAPTER **2**

# The Developmental Context: Psychology, Neurology, and Magic

If the doctrinal, ritualistic core of Christianity harbors a magical process of infantilization, as I've just suggested and will continue to suggest for this book's remainder, then we'd better pay some attention to life's opening stages as we've come to perceive them in Western culture during the past few decades, as well as to the underlying nature of magical conduct. More specifically, the reader will find the lengthy, detailed discussion of Christianity that comprises Chapter 3 richer and more comprehensible than he might otherwise find it if he has a solid, introductory notion of the pressing developmental, emotional factors that ultimately catalyze the imaginative creation of a magical, infantilizing religious system through which worshipers may address adaptively, or perhaps soothingly, the imperfect, stressful, "fallen" condition in which they discover themselves upon the planet. The religious world in which Christians participate is, in the last analysis, a wishful, utopian response to the daunting realities of our biosocial existence, namely, separation from the maternal matrix, the narcissistic wound of smallness or vulnerability within both nature and culture, and finally, of course, our demise and permanent disappearance from the universe, dust to dust.

## The Basic Biological Situation

Our human lives are perceptual and emotional continuities. While it is mistaken to reduce the present to the past, it is also mistaken to divorce the past from the present. The soil, the ground, from which Christian experience arises is the early period of our existence in the world, the period during which the child and the parent are locked in elemental care-giving, care-receiving interactions, or in what I choose to call henceforth the basic biological situation. Here are a few specifics. The child is hungry; the child cries out. Then what happens? The caregiver appears to nourish and to soothe. The child is frightened; the child cries out. Then what happens? The caregiver arrives to reassure and to placate. The child is wet and uncomfortable; the child cries out. Then what happens? The caregiver appears with dry garments and ministering hands. The child is injured; the child cries out. What then? The caregiver comes forward to examine, and kiss, and "make better." Over and over again, dozens of times each day, hundreds of times each week, thousands of times each month, for years, the little one asks and the big one, the care-giving, all-powerful parent, sees to it that the little one receives. (The New Testamental formula for the heartfelt prayer that draws down the Holy Spirit is, ask and ye shall receive [Matt. 7:7].)[1] Accordingly, life's early stages are characterized by what we can think of as a continuous biological rhythm of expressive need and timely care, an endless series of crises and rescues, of asking and receiving, and in every instance it is a helpless, dependent little one who expresses the need, who does the asking, and it is a nourishing, succoring, protective big one who performs the requested, required ministrations. One would be hard-pressed to discover within the realm of nature another example of physiological and emotional conditioning to compare with this one in both depth and duration. Let's bear in mind that the basic biological situation is quite literally "a matter of life and death." The child is utterly dependent upon the all-powerful provider for his or her very survival. A newly born zebra is up and running (sometimes for its life) a few minutes after emerging from its mother's womb; by contrast, the human infant has no resource but its cry for many, many months after its appearance on the planet. In this way, what happens early on is destined to "imprint" itself upon the child's developing *brain*, to forge permanent, specialized, synaptic connections at the root of the child's perceptual existence. But more of that in a moment.

The little one's drive, or urge, to attach himself to the parent, indeed to elicit from the parent his life-giving nourishment, is sustained and strengthened by *affect*, a motive to action that is *felt* and not merely apprehended as an end. The basic biological situation is not a mechanical process but a living, emotional symbiosis streaked with powerful, dynamic feelings in both directions, with what we generally and informally call "love," and also with anxiety because caregiving and care receiving are far from perfect and often encounter delay and even some sharp dissatisfaction. As it turns out, anxiety, delay, and dissatisfaction only increase the presence of positive affect as needs are finally met, provided that discomfort does not become severe or unbearable. Thus, the child's instinctual endowment is not simply linked to affect;

it is physiologically dependent upon affect for its successful, efficacious expression. Silvan S. Tomkins puts it this way in his monumental volume, *Affect, Imagery, Consciousness*: "In our view, the primary motivational system is the affective system, and the biological drives have motivational impact only when amplified by the affective system."[2] And again, "The drive system is . . . secondary to the affect system. Much of the motivational power of the drive system is borrowed from the affect system, which is ordinarily activated concurrently as an amplifier for the drive signal" (p. 22). It is affect that "guarantees" the motivational power of drives (p. 24). As human beings, and from the inception of our lives, we are in the world feelingly, perceive the world feelingly, interact with others feelingly, and inhabit our minds and our bodies feelingly. The upshot? There is a tight, dynamic connection between what Tomkins calls the affect system and the appearance of the internalized "presence" or "object"[3] within the individual's psychological reality.

As the parent-child relationship develops over time, it is steadily, unremittingly *internalized* by the growing youngster, not in some vague, metaphorical way, mind you, but emotionally, affectively, organically, even *neurally* until it becomes the foundation of his budding perceptual existence. For a psychological understanding of Christianity, this is of the utmost importance. The caregiver is taken psychically inside and set up as an internalized presence, or object, that is integrally connected to, indeed that is inseparable from, the emerging self. The early interaction becomes imprinted on the brain. What occurs as little one and big one revolve around each other like twin stars results in the establishment of actual neural pathways within the recesses of our chief perceptual organ (Hebb's famous principle: repeated behaviors strengthen synaptic connections). When we look within and discover what we take to be the self, our self, we discover not only a *relationship*, we discover not only a oneness that is ultimately a twoness, but we *respond affectively* to our inward perception in a manner that mnemonically recalls (among other things, of course) our early interaction with our primary provider. This holds for the entire course of our lives. As William Wordsworth poetically renders the matter in a famous line of verse: "the child is the father of the man." Thus, we are physiologically, genetically, normally endowed with both a capacity and a predisposition to process current information along neural pathways that harbor our previous experience, including our experience of the basic biological situation, our experience of being a helpless, dependent little one in the care and protection of an all-powerful parent. "We cannot separate our memories of the ongoing events of our lives from what has happened to us previously," writes Daniel L. Schacter in his celebrated volume *Searching for Memory.*[4] Daniel J. Siegel expresses it this way in his equally celebrated book *The Developing Mind*: "The mind emerges from the substance of the brain as it is shaped by interpersonal relationships."[5] And again, "At birth, the infant's brain is the most undifferentiated organ in the body. Genes and early experience shape the way neurons connect to one another and thus form specialized circuits that give rise to mental processes" (p. 14). And finally, "Experiences early in life have a tremendously important impact on the developing mind" (p. 14). The point is, when the Christian believer suddenly, spontaneously senses the inward or outwardly hovering presence of an empathetic "spiritual" entity, or when he accedes with strong emotion to the idea that a benign divinity resides within or watches over him, he is recontacting, or relocating, the benign internalization, the benign inward *relationship*, upon which his life and well-being have been founded. He makes contact easily with the supernatural domain because in a manner of speaking *he has been there all along*. He has been living with or in the company of powerful, unseen, life-sustaining presences since he commenced the process of mind-body internalization, of interactional, physiological *imprinting*, as it naturally and persistently arose from his *affective interaction* with the all-powerful provider, the big one who appeared over and over again, 10,000 times, to rescue him from hunger and distress, and to respond to his emotional and interpersonal needs, to his deep affective drive for *attachment*. The "mystery" of the indwelling (or suddenly present) Lord has existed for millennia, and still exists, because individuals are unable to see and to analyze their early, internalizing, neural development as human beings, the originative unconscious aspect of themselves that responds affirmatively, or accedes to, the religious narratives they are offered consciously as the early period gives way to the verbal, symbolic stage of their lives. Of course the Deity becomes doctrinally complexified (and moralized) as an individual's existence develops over time, but the Deity's naturalistic origins in human psychobiology are always at the foundation of His living presence in the world. Arising from the peculiarity of our brain, the supernatural divine is our peculiar invention.

## Implicit Memory, State-Dependent Memory, and Priming

Here is another decisive, determining point that arises directly from the context: because we recall unconsciously, or "implicitly" to use the neuropsychological term, the early foundational period as we go forward with our lives, the events of the moment harbor the capacity to arouse early, internalized materials and the powerful affect that is attached to those materials. As Schacter notes, "Brain structures that support implicit memory are in place before the systems needed for explicit memory."[6] Although implicit memory "operates outside our awareness, . . . it is a pervasive influence in all our lives, and . . . it affects everyday situations" (p. 10). Thus, our neuronal, mental, and emotional makeup predisposes us as perceiving creatures to what is called in the neuropsychological literature "mnemonic priming" or the emergence of "state-dependent" memory systems: when temporally disparate experiences are associated by virtue of similarities between key experiential elements, the later occurrence is not merely "colored" by the earlier one; it is *interpreted* through mnemonic "feedback loops" (or "engrams") that forge a perceptual connection between present and past events. The state of hunger in the present triggers unconscious (and perhaps conscious) recollection of such states as we knew them both three months ago and during the early phase of our development. Danger signals in the present "prime" us to be on guard in a manner that reflects the way we reacted to danger in the past, all the way back to the inception of our experience as people. This is what we *mean* by "the unconscious." As I suggested toward the commencement of this chapter, our human lives are perceptual and emotional continuities. "Priming occurs independent of conscious memory," writes Schacter; the "retrieval cue reinstates or matches the original encoding" (pp. 167, 60). Accordingly, as Siegel observes, "Our earliest experiences shape our ways of behaving, including patterns of relating to others, without our ability to recall consciously when these first learning experiences occurred." We "act, feel, and imagine without recognition of the influence of past experience on our present reality." Studies of "children and adults suggest that here-and-now perceptual biases are based on these nonconscious mental models, . . . on what has occurred in the past."[7] Emotional events, states Michael S. Gazzaniga in his recent volume *The Ethical Brain*, frequently turn into recurring memories at both the explicit and implicit levels of mnemonic processing. "Our own unconscious feelings" can "affect how we encode information and what information we retrieve from memory."[8] Gazzaniga declares in a pivotal remark that we must bear in mind henceforth, "Memory is not so much a mechanism for remembering the past as a means to prepare for the future" (p. 141). Now, as we wed the notions of "priming" and "state-dependent memory" to the notions of "internalization" and "neural imprinting," we come to a watershed in this brief summary of the thesis.

Christian experience thrives upon the triggering of state-dependent memory, upon the priming of the individual to associate unconsciously his current experience with the early, life-sustaining, originative experience of parental ministration and care. Erik H. Erikson expresses it this way in *Insight and Responsibility*:

> What begins as hope in the individual infant is in its mature form faith, a sense of superior certainty not essentially dependent upon evidence or reason. . . . Christianity has shrewdly played into man's most child-like needs, not only by offering eternal guarantees for an omniscient power's benevolence (if properly appeased) but also by magic words and significant gestures, soothing sounds and soporific smells—an infant's world.[9]

And again, this time from *Young Man Luther*, Christianity works to gratify "the simple and fervent wish for a *hallucinatory sense of unity with a maternal matrix*" (my emphasis).[10] We can enrich "hallucinatory" with the notion of state-dependent memory. However, an individual does not require a formal religious setting to become "primed" for religious experience. Such priming frequently occurs as the individual merely deals with the vicissitudes of his life. Here is a brief, homely example, the sort that turns up routinely in Christian (and other) bookshops. A young male farmer on foot discovers himself lost in a ferocious blizzard. Darkness has descended, and the temperature is falling fast. After wandering fruitlessly about for nearly an hour, the man panics and then inwardly cries out for divine assistance. A few seconds later, miraculously, he has the powerful, unmistakable sensation of a benign, protective presence appearing at his side. (He later refers to this entity as his guardian angel.) Calmed and reassured, the young farmer trudges on, and within 10 minutes finds himself upon the old footpath that leads directly to his farmhouse and his fireplace. He remains convinced to this day that God, working through the angels, delivered him from a dangerous, perhaps deadly, situation.[11] Surely, the naturalistic explanation of all this is perfectly clear from the context. An immediate crisis (a *state* of danger) triggers the implicit memory of rescue at the hands of a loving provider, perhaps the oldest and most persistent memory grooved into our brains by our experience in the world. Indeed, what occurs here is a virtual metaphor of the basic biological situation itself. The infant is hungry (crisis); the infant cries out (proto-prayer). Then what happens? The caregiver arrives to nourish and to soothe (rescue). Because our young farmer cannot grasp the workings of his mind and emotions, he projectively attributes this simple, natural occurrence to divine or supernatural sources in keeping with the supernatural narratives to which he has been exposed. The affective power of unconscious memory, released by an arresting version of the deep biological past, fosters an unshakable, heartfelt belief in the putative supernatural sphere and the succoring, spiritual denizens thereof.

## Dissociation, Infantile Amnesia, and Christianity

Recent clinical work on the psychological state of dissociation enables us to grasp more fully the distinction between explicit and implicit recollection. In addition, to focus on dissociation will allow us to appreciate in a preliminary way the major significance of the following: as human beings none of us can explicitly recall the crucial, life-shaping events of our preliminary years, or ages 1–3—a mnemonic incapacity that is known in psychological circles as *infantile amnesia.*

Dissociation, observes Gary Whitmer, involves "those states of simultaneous knowing and not knowing" in which perceptions are "accurate and fully conscious" yet "have no credibility to the subject" who not only "constructs [his] self-knowledge in interaction with another" but "relegates to another" the job of "interpreting [his] experience." While the subject "registers" his "sensations," it is the other who "names" and classifies them. In this way, what the dissociative person recognizes as himself is actually "determined" by another human being.[12] Whitmer offers us in illustration a married professional patient dubbed Mrs. F who was raped by her father as a child and who has endeavored to remove herself from the event. During "moments of remembering," writes Whitmer, she "felt herself to be outside her body in time and space, frightened, and scarcely able to move." She experienced "a constant struggle" to talk about past occurrences that she could not name. She even suffered from a "bladder infection" that she appeared not to recognize in spite of the constant, considerable pain. Accordingly, Mrs. F was in a "state of dissociation." She felt "like a stranger to herself" as her life took on a "me-but-not-me quality" (pp. 808–9). The aim of Whitmer's intervention with Mrs. F, needless to say, is to resolve the "dissociation," to foster integration as opposed to inner division, to guide the woman toward a full, honest knowledge of herself, toward an undistorted, unclouded perception of her motives and conduct. Whitmer writes that "dissociation at its core is an impairment in the subject's ability to represent his or her own experience" (p. 812). If personhood is to be achieved, not merely for this patient but for people generally, it is the subject and not the other who must serve as the "interpreter" of his existence. We come now to a watershed: there is one time in our lives when a salubrious self-determination of our experience does not and cannot occur, when our normal, healthy mental structure depends and must depend on our relationship with another, and that time is precisely the early one in which our interactions with the caregiver actually shape, actually determine, the basic nature of our minds. The first "self-structure" turns out to be "interpersonal" (p. 815).

Whitmer notes that during infancy and early childhood, or "before the child understands the representational nature of ideas and feelings," what the mother presents to her offspring comprises his "reality." Because the neonate inhabits what is sometimes called the presubjective realm of psychic equivalency wherein perception and interpretation are "identical processes" and sensorial experience is "unmediated" by cognitional awareness, the parent or the adult who "responds to the child" provides him with a "medium" in which he can perceive his experiential world "in tangible form." Thus it is "the mother's words, gestures, and emotional expression" that guide the newcomer "to his own mind." By "finding an image of himself in his mother's mind," by seeing his idea or fantasy represented in the caregiver's mentality, the child is able to create and to structure his own thought processes, his own selfhood, and to discover his way toward his own unique participation in the world (pp. 819–20). Obviously this is a crucial, even dangerous period for the infant-child, one that can lead to perceptual distortion and affective disturbance. But in the vast majority of instances, where mothering is "good enough" to foster normal development, the early period provides the budding individual with a secure foundation for his emerging identity.[13] What we must bear in mind above all as we approach Christianity is that the representation of self and world that emerges here does not comprise merely "one view among many." Rather, the early foundational experience "has the impact of singular truth" and is adopted by the child as the very core of the self. The caregiver's impact on her offspring actually triggers the sensation of "me." The child cannot at this stage say to the parent, "you misunderstand me" because no "me" exists "apart from the parent's understanding." Thus, the "reality" of the caregiver does not become *a* "reality" for the child; it becomes *the only* "reality," the only "place" in which he has *existence*. As for dissociation, it constitutes, as Whitmer sees it, the "pathological form" of this presubjective mode of relating to another person (p. 820).

We may begin to grasp in earnest, now, the decisive, all-important role of infantile amnesia in the onset and advent of Christian conviction. As the child finds his way toward the supernatural divine, he discovers a sphere that bears a striking, uncanny resemblance to the experiential world in which he has been dwelling right along through his presubjective interactions with the caregiver, the ultimate source of his most persistent and powerful implicit memories, the ultimate source of his perceptual, affective core, his selfhood, his psychological structure, his very "me-ness." To put it another way, the religious realm into which the child gradually enters *mirrors* unconsciously, associatively, perceptually, and affectively, the presubjective "reality" that the child has been internalizing and installing neurally as the basis of his gradually emerging identity. The religious realm, in two words, *corresponds implicitly* to the child's mind. It is a realm that contains at its center an invisible parental presence who supports and sustains the child, *who gives him his existence*, his being (the "Creator"). This is exactly what the child has internalized to this point, as he verges upon his symbolic, verbal representations. *He contains*, as microcosm, an invisible, creative, parental presence, or "object" as the psychological lingo has it, that holds him sustainingly in and through a primal, foundational, structural bond, the rock-like support of the religious literature, dependable, unfailing, always there. It is a realm that contains an invisible parental presence who *loves* the child (the loving Jesus), who grapples him unto Himself in an affective life-giving, life-enhancing symbiosis. This is exactly what the child harbors within: the invisible, loving, care-giving presence of the early period, the one who adored him and whom he adored as only the gushing, spontaneous infant-child can adore. It is a realm that contains a powerful, indeed an omnipotent parental figure devoted in large measure to protecting the child, to shielding him from harm, to "watching over" him. Again, this is exactly what the child harbors within his developing mind: an awareness of the parent's all-powerful, protective presence, the parent's capacity to do everything, and, in particular, to do all those things the relatively helpless child cannot do by himself. Not only has the child internalized such a one, such a "mighty fortress," he has for many early months and years identified with the parent's omnipotent quality. As it turns out, such omnipotence was partially and reluctantly relinquished as the child came to recognize during his third and fourth years the limitations of his capacity to control the world (the primal, narcissistic wound); but now, through religious narrative, such omnipotence can be partially regained, recouped, through a vicarious, fantasy-level participation in the Almighty's mightiness. The child can once more identify himself with a limitless, omnipotent protector. Still again, the religious realm *guides* the child, tells him "yes" in response to certain activities, certain behaviors, and tells him "no" in response to other interests and inclinations, thus echoing the primal "yes" and "no" that found their way interactionally to the child's mind during the phase in which the child's every move was subject to the parent's administration. All of this, divine creation, divine support, divine love, divine omnipotence, divine protection, divine guidance, may be subsumed under the general notion of infantile *attachment* to an internalized, all-powerful parental presence.

Accordingly, what the child is capable of projecting, of externalizing psychically as he enters the representational, verbal, symbolic stage of his development, and what Christianity extends to him through its "reality," its doctrinal narrative at the center of which resides the invisible, supernatural

Trinity—these two perceptual realms, or worlds, now begin to touch and to ignite. The child affirms the religious realm because, like the presubjective realm that he has internalized and transmuted into his self-structure, it has "the impact of singular truth" at the *unconscious* level of implicit recollection. Because the child cannot *see* the naturalistic, psychological, developmental *connection* between his own mind-brain, his own internal world, and the transcendent, supramundane narrative to which he is now increasingly exposed at the conscious level, he is impelled to accept the truth-claims of the Christian institutions that surround him "out there" in the wider world. Implicit memory validates cultural myth. The perceptual, affective nature of the child's inward domain is predisposed unconsciously to affirm the culture's religious stories, to say "yes" to the supernatural landscape that looms. On the inside, the child can *feel* the accuracy of Christianity's macrocosmic depictions. As the old expression has it, he's "been there," and he's "done that" already. To view the matter from the "hard" neuropsychological perspective, we might say that the child's mind-brain, primed and grooved by his presubjective interactions, *maps* his early experience onto the religious narrative he encounters. As Gerald M. Edelman would express it, the child's emerging supernatural world, his newly discovered "present" reality, is not only perceived, it is also "remembered," just as all his subsequent "presents" will be remembered as his mind-brain processes information according to "programs" it already "knows."[14] What we have here is a perfect or nearly perfect neurologic, affective correspondence or fit, one that does not require proof because it has the inward ring of truth, the veracious impact of the child's very selfhood that has been molded by his presubjective, interpersonal dealings with his loving caregiver, the dealings that provide the mnemonic "stuff" of his implicit recollection. And indeed, if those dealings contained maltreatments or even abuses of some sort, the child's reentering process, his remapping of the early "data," is flexible enough to transform imperfection into wished-for ideal, the flawed god of the nursery into the wondrous God of Christian doctrine. When the religious world dawns, it discloses a perfection that anyone of any age might detect and crave immediately. The mighty Lord, the mighty Jesus, the mighty Holy Spirit—all of them will love you, protect you, and guide you: what joyful tidings!

Similar unconscious recognition occurs as the child is introduced gradually to Christian ritual and, in particular, to Christianity's cardinal ritualistic enactment, prayer. With an eye to the individual, subjective variety of prayer, we note the child (and later, of course, the adult) going to his knees, adopting a worshipful, dependent attitude, bowing or perhaps prostrating himself, taking his legs away, manifesting submission and helplessness—the chief prerequisites for successful supplication, as we see in a later section. We note also the prayerful requests for assistance, for succor, for protection and nourishment (one's "daily bread"), as well as the expressions of gratitude and love. To proceed at once to the heart of the matter, we note the supplicator acting out an unerring metaphorical version of the basic biological situation, the primal symbiotic attachment, in which the helpless, dependent little one calls on the omnipotent big one for physical and emotional sustenance, for the continuation and the enhancement of life. Thousands upon thousands of times, for years, the child has experienced and internalized this arrangement, this condition, this *state*, and now as he moves toward the Christian domain, he is instructed to recreate it again and again through prayer. The upshot is clear: Christianity's chief ritual, its essential rite, its *sine qua non*, is designed to foster in the supplicator regardless of his age or circumstance an implicit, state-dependent memory of the parent-child relationship from which his self-structure, his identity, his existence initially arose. Prayer returns the pray-er unconsciously to the internalized root of his being and thus triggers a sense of God's loving presence that has "the impact of singular truth." Just *doing this* is enough to awaken the old feelings of dependency, connection, and care. Just doing this is enough to arouse the oldest and most persistent implicit memory that we retain at the affective, neurological level. One has only to *ask* in order to *receive* (Matt. 7:7). One has only to ask in order to make contact with a loving, supportive presence on the "other side," a loving, supportive being from the putative supernatural sphere. Of course the supplicator knows that his Lord is present: he can *feel* the Lord within by virtue of his having internalized into his mind-brain the daily, hourly, moment-to-moment presence of his loving, all-powerful, caregiving provider during the weeks, months, and years of the early period. What we can term only a massive affective and neuronic conditioning has prepared him psychically for the uncanny sensation of the Almighty's engendering closeness. It is in this naturalistic, psychological way, and in this way alone, that prayer is able to "prove" the presence of God, the "miracle" of His caring, responsive existence. Thus, Christianity turns out once again to comprise a fresh neural "mapping" onto a well-established neural and affective "reality." It derives its attractive power, its validity as a "supernatural" enterprise, from precisely the realm of implicit, state-dependent memory, from precisely the condition of infantile amnesia that loads the potential practitioner up with proto-religious beliefs and sentiments that he cannot cognitionally locate, let alone fathom. The way is open for the projection of purely inward materials (one's religious "convictions") onto the external world, as well as for the establishment of Christianity's timeless, official "mysteries": it is the "innocent" who "see." It is the "child" who apprehends the deepest religious truths and who possesses thereby the key to the kingdom of heaven (Matt. 18:3). It hardly needs to be added that billions of "innocent children" currently inhabit the Earth.

The external, explicit supports for religious belief, the aspects of Christianity with which we are all thoroughly familiar, are tied integrally to the unconscious, implicit foundation and make the religion's doctrinal, supernatural claims overwhelmingly persuasive. Obviously such claims take on a life of their own, but their lifeblood flows afresh as each generation internalizes and subsequently projects its primal interactions with the care-giving parent. Christian doctrine would be empty of meaning were it not unconsciously grounded in the basic biological situation of dependency, succor, and love. Indeed, as we have just seen, the presubjective period primes the young believer affectively and neurologically for the transcendent rituals and narratives to which he is now regularly exposed. Religious attachment is reattachment. Religious presentations re-present the past through the workings of implicit, state-dependent memory. The child listened to the parent's verbalizations and took his direction and comfort therefrom. Now he listens to the Omnipotent's "word," directly as it is proffered in His Book or indirectly as it is explained by His official, authoritative interpreters—the priest or the pastor, each in his distinctive and sometimes splendid trappings. The young worshiper is told to sit still and pay attention. He sees his parents doing exactly what he is told to do. He sees hundreds, perhaps thousands of others similarly busying themselves with holy books and supplications, reading, pondering, mumbling, discussing, standing up and sitting down on command, crossing themselves. In the company of his parents, who also instruct him, he gazes at churches, cathedrals, stained glass, gigantic columns, and domes. He hears chanted prayers, harmonic, mesmeric hymns, sonorous sermons, and pronouncements. He is swept along in processions, swept up in festivals, kissed, and congratulated for his loyal participation. What child could resist, particularly as ritual and narrative, including, above all, the rite of supplication and the story of the loving Parent-God, continually echo, or mirror, the unconscious shape of his own experience as it transpired during the years that precede the advent of symbolic enactments and expressions? The variations from culture to culture and from child to child are, of course, notable; yet the underlying neural, affective, causative factors apply generally, worldwide, across the centuries, down to the present day.

The point arises: is not the "map" of the early period only the first in a series of "spiritual" maps, a series that is characterized by increasing moral and theological complexity that mirrors our development over the years, indeed over an entire life span? I reply as follows: assuredly this is so.

However, all the spiritual maps that are devised and entered with time's passage are based upon the first one, which reflects the early period. The initial, unconscious, internalized experience with the loving, care-giving provider holds the primal, "eternal" source of Christianity's affective power, the primal, foundational source of its compelling, persistent appeal, its mystery, its resistance to logic and reason. The initial map in the depths of the mind is the powerhouse. To dislodge it, deconstruct it, destroy it in one way or another is quite simply to lose the living power of one's faith, to dry up religiously, to abandon the holy, life-giving waters in which the "children" and the "innocent" bathe their minds and spirits. Christianity thrives when its adherents remain in close touch with the infantile level of their development, preserving their early, projective realities, their implicit memories of primal symbiosis, of magical asking and magical receiving from the omnipotent parental creator and provider. Although one can grow "spiritually," there is no growing out of the infantile stage. Bear in mind, I am not writing about theism here, or rational arguments concerning the ultimate origin of the universe. I am writing about emotional, heartfelt belief in an anthropomorphic, tripartite God Who is concerned with and responsive to the idiosyncratic wishes and needs of individual worshipers. Precisely this kind of belief is a natural, projective outgrowth of implicitly recollected parental ministrations in infancy. Were we loved parentally in the beginning? Well, we still are. The beginning is now. It is always now in *that* sense where Christianity is concerned. We are never without a parent unless we choose to be by rejecting the existence of a loving, supernatural Provider. If we are "theological animals," as some maintain,[15] then we are such because our "theology" fits in smoothly with our "adult" perception of the universe around us. What after all can interfere with the belief in a supernatural system that does not require a single empirical fact to substantiate its claims and that is felt to be true at the deepest inward level by those who fervently wish it to be so? For secularists, of course, the Christian "program" is irrelevant, or perhaps unengaging, because it has been replaced by other "programs," by other neural, perceptual connections, by other narratives, by other theoretical outlooks and conclusions. To put the matter crudely, Christians continue to be emotionally and intellectually susceptible to facets of the mind-brain to which secularists are susceptible no longer.

## The Early Period

That the issues surrounding Christianity engage deeply rooted, perhaps antithetical, and probably evolutionary tendencies within us should be clear at this juncture. On the one hand, we want to feel safe in the world, connected to the matrix, attached to a meaningful, even loving universe; we want as much security and as little anxiety as possible. On the other hand, we want to *see*, to perceive things as accurately as we can, to clear away the mist of wishful, illusory ideas no matter what the price we have to pay in emotional discomfort, including the discomfort that may arise from an awareness of our mortality. Is there another aspect of our fundamental humanity that goes off like this in two opposing yet perfectly natural directions? However, we can't simply plunge into these issues armed only with a preliminary understanding of our theoretical position as presented in the context. We must sharpen and deepen the particulars of our approach, grow them as it were, in preparation for the conclusions that will eventually emerge. Let's look, first, at the all-important emotional events that rest upon the axis of separation and attachment.

Regardless of the geographical location and the nature of familial organization, the conflict between separation and merger not only dominates the life of the infant but extends itself far beyond infancy and childhood into the life of the adolescent and adult. It revolves around the struggle to become an autonomous, separate person, differentiated and distinct, and at the same time, to retain one's connection to significant others—either the actual parents or their later substitutes in a protean variety of shapes and forms. For the human creature (as I indicated in the previous paragraph), two of life's most powerful needs are, paradoxically, to be joined and to be separate, to be related and to be independent, to be autonomous and to be connected; and it is precisely this paradoxical and in some sense contradictory thrust in human growth and development, this antithetical, two-sided inclination of people, that makes human behavior so problematical, so maddeningly difficult to see and to fathom, and that brings so much confusion to the lives of individuals and societies. Ethel S. Person, in her wonderful book *Dreams of Love and Fateful Encounters*, renders the matter this way: "Without self-will there can be no psychological separation. But neither is there any highly individuated self. The self is delineated only through separation, but the sense of being separated proves impossible to bear. The solitary self feels cut off, alone, without resources. The solitary self feels impelled to merge with a new object."[16] What Dr. Person has captured, if I may be permitted to indicate the issue still again, is that the two needs, to be separate and joined, independent and connected, are from a deep psychological angle one need neither side of which finds expression without engaging the other, like a crab going backward and forward at the same time. When the desire for merger is felt, it typically engages the need to be separate, and the need to be separate engages the wish to be connected, joined. While it is easy to write about the matter, to employ such terms as alogical, paradoxical, and antithetical, it can be most unpleasant to experience the actual conflict when it occurs, along with the inner confusion that it often engenders. I would suggest, in fact, that we have here a major source of human stress.

Because the world of infancy and childhood is not an easy one to capture discursively, because as adults we run the risk of ascribing to the very young aims and motives at work in *us* rather than in them, I would prefer to explore the Christian realm psychologically without also exploring life's early period, but alas, there is just no hope of getting at the truth that way. Christian behavior is an outgrowth, a development, in a special sense an expression of this period with its symbiotic attachments, its blissful transformations, its powerful, persistent anxieties, attunements, frustrations, and fears. Indeed, if the science of psychology has made a lasting and valuable contribution to the understanding of "spiritual" conduct, it is in precisely this area. From the many psychological accounts of infancy and childhood, I choose what is generally regarded as the most methodologically sophisticated, accurate, and helpful, namely, Margaret S. Mahler, Fred Pine, and Anni Bergman's *Psychological Birth of the Human Infant*.[17] A child psychiatrist and pediatrician working with normal children in a specially constructed facility in New York City during the 1950s and 1960s, Mahler (and her associates) places the accent immediately on the struggle between separation and union.

We take for granted, she reminds us, our experience of ourselves as both fully "in" and fully separate from the "world out there" (p. 3). Our consciousness of ourselves as distinct, differentiated entities and our concomitant absorption into the external environment, without an awareness of self, are the polarities between which we move with varying ease, and with varying degrees of alternation or simultaneity. Yet the establishment of such consciousness, such ordinary, taken-for-granted awareness, is a slowly unfolding process that is not coincident in time with our biological emergence from the womb. It is tied closely and developmentally to our dawning experience of our bodies as separate in space and belonging only to us, and to our dawning experience of the primary love object as also separate in space, as having an existence of his or her own. Moreover, the struggle to achieve this "individuation" reverberates throughout the course of our lives: "It is never finished; it remains always active; new phases of the life cycle find new derivatives of the earliest processes still at work" (p. 3). What must be stressed, in particular, here is the strength of both sides of the polarity. Children, with every move toward maturation, are confronted with the threat of "object loss," with traumatic situations involving separation from the caregiver. Thus they are constantly tempted to draw back, to regress, to move toward the caregiver and the old relation as opposed to *away* from the caregiver and the anticipated future, the new reality. At the same time, the normally endowed child strives mightily to emerge from his early fusion (we could say confusion) with the mother, to escape and to grow. His individuation consists precisely of those developmental achievements, those increasing motor and mental accomplishments, that begin to mark his separate existence, his separate identity as a separate being. The ambivalent impulses toward and away, the great urge to differentiate and at the same time stay connected, are in Mahler's words, forever intertwined (p. 4), although they may proceed divergently, one or the other lagging behind or leaping ahead during a given period.

Mahler makes plain that this process is not merely one of many equally important processes that transpire during the early time. On the contrary, the achievement of separation constitutes the very core of the self, the foundation of one's identity and being as a person. Yet this foundation can be gained (and here is the echo of a paradox again) only if the parent gives to the child a persistent, uninterrupted feeling of connection, of union—a tie that encourages the very breaking of it. This delicate balancing act is never perfect, and Mahler emphasizes throughout the course of her study that old conflicts over separation, old, unresolved issues of identity and bodily boundaries, can be reawakened or even remain active throughout the course of one's existence, at any or all stages of the life cycle. What appears to be a struggle for connection or distinctness in the now of one's experience can be the flare-up of the ancient struggle in which one's self began to emerge from the orbit of the *magna mater*. We will shortly be exploring the degree to which this last observation sheds light upon one facet of Christianity in which the practitioner longs to be absorbed into the supernatural body of the Deity. By separation, then, Mahler does not mean primarily the physical separation of the baby in space or the distance from the caregiver, the kind of separation we associate, for example, with the work of John Bowlby. What Mahler has in mind is an inward or intrapsychic separation from both the mother and her extension, the world. The gradual development of this subjective awareness, this inward perception of the self and the other, leads eventually to clear, distinct inner representations of a "self" that is distinguished from "external objects." It is precisely this sense of being a separate individual that psychotic children are unable to achieve. Similarly, when Mahler uses the term "symbiosis," the accent is not upon a behavioral state but an inward condition, a feature of primitive emotional life wherein the differentiation between the self and the mother has not occurred, or where a regression to an undifferentiated state has occurred. This does not necessarily require the presence of the mother; it can be based on primitive images of oneness, or on a denial of perceptions that postulate separation. Thus for Mahler, identity during the early period does not refer to the child having a sense of who he is; it refers to the child having a sense that he is (p. 8). Indeed, the sense that he is can be regarded as the first step in the process of an unfolding individuality. The achievement of separation-individuation is a kind of "second birth," a "hatching" from the symbiotic mother-infant "membrane" in which the child is originally contained (p. 9).

Mahler calls the earliest stage of development "autistic." The infant "spends most of his day in a half-sleeping, half-waking state" (p. 41). He awakens mainly to feed and falls to sleep again when he is satisfied, or relieved of tensions. There is nothing abnormal about this "autism," as Mahler employs the term. The baby simply lacks awareness of the mother as a ministering agent and of himself as the object of her ministrations. From the second month on, however, the baby increasingly feels the presence of the mother, and it is just this sense of the caretaker being there that marks the inception of the normal symbiotic phase, which reaches a peak of intensity at about six to nine months. The most remarkable feature of this phase is contained in Mahler's point that the infant "behaves and functions as though he and his mother were an omnipotent system—a dual-unity with one common boundary" (p. 44). The symbiotic infant participates emotionally and perceptually in a kind of delusional fusion with the omnipotent mothering figure. Later in infancy and childhood, and indeed later in life at all stages when we experience severe stress, "this is the mechanism to which the ego regresses" (p. 44).

In this way, when the autistic phase subsides, or, to use the metaphors characteristic of Mahler's treatise, when the "autistic shell" has "cracked" and the child can no longer "keep out external stimuli," a "second protective, yet selective and receptive shield" begins to develop in the form of the "symbiotic orbit," the mother and the child's dual-unity. While the normal autistic phase serves postnatal physiological growth and homeostasis, the normal symbiotic phase marks the all-important human capacity to bring the mother into a psychic fusion that comprises "the primal soil from which all subsequent relationships form" (p. 48). We commence our existence as people in the illusion that the other (who appears to be omnipotent) is a part of the self. Although the mother is actually out there, ministering to the child, she is perceived by the latter to be a facet of his own organism, his own primitive ego. What the mother "magically" accomplishes in the way of care—the production of milk, the provision of warmth, the sensation of security—the baby omnipotently attributes to the mother and to himself. At the emotional, preverbal level, he declares, in effect, "I am not separate from my symbiotic partner; my partner and I are one. Whatever my partner appears to possess and to do, I possess and do as well. Whatever power my partner has, I also have. We are one, one omnipotent indestructible unit, twin stars revolving around each other in a single orbit of emotion and will." As D. W. Winnicott unforgettably expresses it, the feeling of omnipotence is so strong in the infant (and so persistently clung to in the growing child when the dual-unity of the symbiotic stage begins to break down) that it is "nearly a fact."[18]

What this means, of course, is that the decline of symbiosis, or the increasing awareness of separation on the part of the child, will be experienced as a loss of self. If union with mother means wholeness, then disunion will mean less than wholeness. Let us examine Mahler's account of this original human trauma (the expulsion from paradise), and let us bear in mind as we proceed, first, that the transition from symbiosis to individuation is a multifaceted, complex process that consumes the first three years of life, and second, that for many, many people the loss of omnipotent merger and the narcissistic gratification that goes with it is never entirely accepted at the deep, unconscious level. I am not suggesting that the infant's growing abilities and independence fail to provide him with satisfaction; to be sure, they do, and Mahler is careful to emphasize both sides of the equation—the drive to remain with and to relinquish the mother. I am suggesting only that the movement away is attended by powerful anxiety and by the irrational wish to have it both ways: separateness and symbiotic union. Also, as one would suspect, the babies in Mahler's study often differ dramatically in their developmental inclinations and capacities, but more on that later.

What Mahler terms the "first subphase" of "differentiation" occurs "at the peak of symbiosis" when the infant is about six months old. During his more frequent periods of wakefulness, the field of his attention gradually expands "through the coming into being of outwardly directed perceptual activity" (p. 53). No longer is the "symbiotic orbit" the exclusive focus of his limited, yet evolving "sensorium." As the seventh month approaches, "there are definite signs that the baby is beginning to differentiate his own body" from that of his mother. "Tentative experimentation at individuation" can be observed in such behavior as "pulling at the mother's hair, ears, or nose, putting food into the mother's mouth, and straining his body away from mother in order to have a better look at her, to scan her and the environment. This is in contrast to simply moulding into mother when held." The infant's growing visual and motor powers help him to "draw his body together" and to commence the construction of his own, separate ego on the basis of this bodily awareness and sensation. At times, the baby even begins to move away from the mother's enveloping arms, to resist the passive "lap babyhood" that marks the earliest months of life. As he does this, however, he constantly "checks back" to mother with his eyes. He is becoming interested in mother as "mother" and compares her with "other" people and things. He discovers what belongs and what does not belong to the mother's body—a brooch, eyeglasses, a comb. He is starting to discriminate, in short, between the mother and all that which is different from or similar to her (pp. 54–55).

This incipient individuation on the baby's part is accompanied by considerable anxiety, the most striking manifestation of which occurs in the presence of strangers. Like so much else in the area of separation-union, "stranger anxiety" evinces two distinct yet interrelated aspects. On the one hand, strangers fascinate the infant, who, in Mahler's words, shows great "eagerness to find out about them." On the other hand, strangers terrify the infant by reminding him of the other-than-mother world, the world of separation, the world that appears as symbiosis and dual-unity fade. After pointing out that babies vary in their susceptibility to stranger anxiety (and other anxiety as well), Mahler offers us the example of Peter, who at eight months reacts initially with wonder and curiosity to a stranger's mild overtures for his attention. Yet, two minutes later, although he is close to his mother, even leaning against her leg, Peter bursts into tears as the stranger touches his hair (p. 57). Such is the emotional turbulence that accompanies the onset of individuation during the first subphase (pp. 56–57).

Mahler divides the second subphase into the early practicing period and the practicing subphase proper. During the former, the 10- to 11-month infant becomes more and more deeply absorbed in his expanding mental and physical universe. He begins rapidly to distinguish his own body from his mother's, to actively establish a specific (as opposed to symbiotic) bond with her, and to indulge his autonomous, independent interests while in close proximity to her. In a word, he begins to transfer his absorption in mother to the world around him. He explores the objects in his vicinity—toys, bottles, blankets—with his eyes, hands, and mouth; his growing locomotor capacity widens his environment (p. 66). Yet in all of this, Mahler is careful to point out, the mother is "still the center of the child's universe." His experience of his "new world" is subtly "related" to her, and his excursions into the other-than-mother realm are often followed by periods of intense clinging and a refusal to separate. For an interval, the baby is absorbed in some external object and seems oblivious to mother's presence; a moment later he jumps up and rushes to her side expressing his need for physical proximity (pp. 66–67). Again and again he displays a desire for "emotional refueling," that is to say, for a dose of maternal supplies—hugging, stroking, chatting—after a period of independent activity (p. 69). What Mahler's children (and all children) want—and we come here to a crucial utterance—is to "move away independently" from the mother and, at the same time, to "remain connected to her" (p. 70).

The practicing subphase proper (11–15 months) marks the high point of the child's move toward a separate existence. Not only does he experience a dramatic spurt in cognitive development, he also achieves what Mahler calls "the greatest step in human individuation," his upright locomotion. These "precious months" of increasing powers and skills comprise "the child's love affair with the world": the "plane of his vision changes; . . . he finds unexpected and changing perspectives. . . . The world is the junior toddler's oyster. . . . Narcissism is at its peak. . . . The chief characteristic of this period is the child's great narcissistic investment in his own functions, his own body, and the objectives of his expanding reality" (p. 71). Adding to the exhilaration, notes Mahler, is the child's "elated escape from fusion with, from engulfment by, mother." Here is the movement away in its most striking biological and psychological expression (p. 71). Yet even here, in the midst of this great expansion, this "love affair with the world," the paradoxical, ambivalent aspect of human development rears its head as mightily as ever in the form of deep-seated, pervasive anxiety. "The course of true love never did run smooth," observes Shakespeare, and the words would seem to apply to our earliest developmental experiences. The child's rapidly expanding ego functions bring with them both the threat of "object loss" and the fear of being "reengulfed" by the mother. One minute he expresses a need for "checking back," for "emotional refueling," for knowing exactly the mother's whereabouts; the next minute he forcibly removes himself from mother's caressing arms in an effort to assert his capacity for active, independent functioning. Sometimes the baby runs away to make sure mother wants to catch him up, yet when she does, he shows resentment at being held and stroked (p. 73). Even the enormous step of upright locomotion and the increase in perception that it brings to the child holds both sides of the dual-unity equation. It is the need for mother's emotional support at the instant he learns to walk that Mahler captures unforgettably: "The child walks alone with his eyes fixed on his mother's face, not on the difficulties in his way. . . . In the very same moment that he is emphasizing his need for her, he is proving that he can do without her." In this way, the toddler "feels the pull of separation from his mother at the same time he asserts his individuation. It is a mixed experience, the child demonstrating that he can and cannot do without, his mother." As for the mother's physical absence during this period (she may be working, ill, etc.), it typically sparks sadness, or even depression in the infant.

The "symbiotic mothering half" of the "self" is "missed" during the very subphase that is most obviously filled with the joys of separation (pp. 73–74).

The entire separation-individuation process culminates at approximately 30 months in what Mahler terms "the rapprochement subphase," the period during which the infant perceives with growing clarity and certainty that he and mother are separate beings, that the old symbiosis and the narcissistic gratifications (including omnipotence) that go with it are illusory, that he is physically and psychically alone. Here is Mahler's powerful description of this watershed in a person's life:

> With the acquisition of primitive skills and perceptual cognitive faculties there has been an increasingly clear differentiation, a separation, between the intra-psychic representation of the object and the self-representation. At the very height of mastery, toward the end of the practicing period, it had already begun to dawn on the junior toddler that the world is not his oyster, that he must cope with it more or less on his own, very often as a relatively helpless, small, and separate individual, unable to command relief or assistance merely by feeling the need for it or by giving voice to that need (omnipotence).
>
> (p. 78)

We may note parenthetically at this juncture that the core of Christian doctrine and rite is designed to deny precisely this momentous event, and not only deny it but bring about its reversal through just those mechanisms that Mahler mentions here, namely, "mere feeling" (wishing) and "giving voice" (prayers and invocations). Needless to say, we will soon explore these denials and reversals in great depth.

With the erosion of symbiosis, the "fear of losing the love of the object," as opposed to losing the object, makes itself felt increasingly in the child (pp. 78–79). Up to this point (the rapprochement subphase), the object and the self have been more or less psychically indistinguishable. Now, as differentiation occurs in earnest, the object's love becomes the focus of the child's attention. This does not mean that the original anxiety over loss of the object as a part of the self disappears. It means only that an additional, more conscious or even cognitive anxiety has been superimposed upon the original, primal dread. Accordingly, the toddler begins to demand the mother's constant attention. He is deeply preoccupied with her whereabouts. He expresses enormous anger and anxiety at her leave-taking, and anguish at being left behind. He clings to mother, seeks her lap, and may begin to show a dependent interest in maternal substitutes. In a thousand ways he attempts to coerce the mother into fulfilling his wishes. He tries at times to be magnificently separate, omnipotent, rejecting: he will gain the mother's love and attention by showing her the proverbial "cold shoulder." At other times he plays the helpless baby. For weeks on end his wooing of mother alternates sharply with his expressions of resentment and outrage (p. 97). How do the mothers react to all this? "Some cannot accept the child's demandingness; others are unable to face the child's gradual separation, the fact that the child can no longer be regarded as part of her." Yet, whatever the relational dynamics happen to be, they cannot stop the process: "no matter how insistently the toddler tries to coerce the mother, she and he can no longer function effectively as a dual unit—that is to say, the child can no longer maintain his delusion of parental omnipotence, which he still at times expects will restore the symbiotic status quo." The child must "gradually and painfully give up the delusion of his own grandeur, often by way of dramatic fights with mother—less so, it seemed to us, with father. This is the crossroads of what we term the rapprochement crisis" (pp. 78–79). Mahler observes in a sentence at which we prick up our ears as we ponder the nature of supernatural Christianity that "many uniquely human problems and dilemmas" that are "sometimes never completely resolved during the entire life cycle" have their origin here, during the end of symbiosis and the onset of separation (p. 100).

The resolution of the rapprochement crisis comes about in a variety of ways, the description of which concludes the first half of Mahler's study. As the child experiences a growing capacity to be alone, his clamoring for omnipotent control starts to diminish. He shows less separation anxiety, fewer alternating demands for closeness and autonomy. Not only does he begin to understand empathetically what his mother is going through, but he begins to identify with the problems and struggles of the youngsters around him (p. 110). In this way, he begins to turn to other people, and in many instances to his own father, in his effort to satisfy his needs. And with the wholesale emergence of gender differences, he starts to participate in those activities that are peculiar to his or her sex. Equally important, the child's capacity for verbalization and symbolization begins to lead him toward the cultural realm, toward an endless variety of substitutive objects that characteristically take the form of "blankies," storybooks, toys, pets, and so on. We might say that the child's growing ability to incorporate the world into his burgeoning ego leads him to a series of new internalizations, new inward presences, that are appropriate to his age and to the problems he confronts. He is beginning to live with his own thoughts and with the companions of his inner world. This is what we usually mean by "being alone." In the majority of cases and generally for all normal children, such developments culminate in the establishment of what Mahler calls "object constancy," and with it, the inception of an individuated life. By *object constancy* Mahler has in mind "the presence of a reliable internal image that remains relatively stable irrespective of the state of instinctual need or inner discomfort. On the basis of this achievement, temporary separation can be lengthened and better tolerated" (p. 110). This is the necessary step, the vital inward accomplishment, that permits further growth, further individuation, and further ego strength in the preschooler and eventually in the school child.

Mahler devotes the second half of her treatise to several lengthy case histories in which we see children struggling from normal autism and symbiosis to separation and individuation. She strives in these sections to illustrate her theoretical position at the clinical level, the level from which the theoretical materials originally arose, of course. As she does this, Mahler makes clear something that she stresses in many places in Chapter 3, Part One, namely, that it is the combination of a particular caretaker interacting with a particular child that ultimately shapes the child's emerging character in terms of both conscious and unconscious processes. Projections pass not only from the baby to the mother, but from the mother to the baby as well. "It seemed that the ability to cope with separateness, as well as with actual physical separation," declares Mahler,

> was dependent in each case on the history of the mother-child relationship, as well as on its present state. We found it hard to pinpoint just what it was in the individual cases that produced more anxiety in some and an ability to cope in others. Each child had established by this time his own characteristic ways of coping.
>
> (p. 103)

Thus, when we look at the whole picture, we spy an element of mystery, a unique, intangible quality that pertains to each mother-infant bond and that can never be fully explained by observers, or indeed by the mother and infant who are involved in the relationship. What occurs early on is not strictly an enigma but it has its enigmatic aspect, and we must always bear this in mind. Human behavior finally escapes whatever logical space we try to fit it into. Reality happens, from the inside, and can never be perfectly reconstructed.

As I suggested on several occasions in the context, the struggle for and against separation extends itself powerfully not only into the ritualistic behaviors of Christianity but into the nature and development of our perceptual lives generally, including the whole of culture. Although it may appear a bit strange to express the matter thus, our ordinary consciousness in the widest, most all-inclusive sense is inextricably bound up with the early struggle over separation and cannot be grasped apart from it. We must remember as we proceed that what Mahler describes in the final paragraphs of her theoretical section is the passing of the rapprochement crises, not the passing of the separation-union conflict. Indeed, it is the position of this book, and has been from the outset, that this conflict never ceases, that it so forcefully shapes and directs our conduct as to gain a place among the central conflicts of our experience as a form of life. As Mahler herself observes, a "sound image" of the maternal figure does not mean that the old longing for merger stops, that the fear of reengulfment goes away, that anxiety, ambivalence, and splitting suddenly vanish, along with feelings of omnipotence and narcissistic grandiosity; it does not mean that the primal terrors of rejection and loss miraculously disappear forever. The establishment of a sound maternal image simply means that the little person can stumble ahead still loaded with the great, absorbing issues of the early time, still loaded with the stress that attends the erosion of symbiosis, still wishing contradictorily for both merger and differentiation, and still smarting from the collapse of dual-unity (p. 115). What occurs as the infant undergoes separation has been described by Ana-Maria Rizzuto as a "life-long mourning process that triggers an endless search for replacement."[19] To express the matter from a different yet crucially related angle, the passing of the rapprochement crisis simply means that one is now in a position to act out among others this basic human dilemma, this rooted, unconscious issue as it manifests itself projectively at the levels of both individual and group conduct. It means that one can now seek for omnipotence, fusion, and narcissistic gratification in the wider world. In a manner of speaking, one is loose. The old cliché that we are all more or less neurotic hopefully emerges with fresh clarity at this juncture.

The dynamic, shaping influence of implicit memory on the Christian religion may also emerge with fresh clarity here. As we peruse Mahler's work and come to appreciate the intensity and the complexity of the neonate's initial encounter with the world, we have the impression that the little one is passing through a veritable lifetime of emotional and physical experience, a lifetime of potent, interpersonal events. Yet the whole extended episode, incredibly, is destined to go mnemonically underground, to discover a brain-based pathway to the land of "infantile amnesia"! Make no mistake, this is not because babies can't remember things. On the contrary, they have strong memorial capacities almost from the outset. It is because ongoing mnemonic, neural developments (mainly language), along with a host of emerging tasks and requirements, come sharply to the fore as infancy gives way to childhood and gradually relinquishes its hold upon the mind. As I have been suggesting all along, we have in this remarkable situation the living seed of faith, of the believer's heartfelt conviction that his invisible, mysterious Parent-God is *there*. Not only does the will to believe, to accept the veracity of Christian narrative, push upward ineluctably toward consciousness from an inward source one affectively recognizes yet cannot directly detect, but the narrative's wishful, alluring core holds the promise of *attachment* to a loving provider, to a Spirit through Whom one may lessen the pain of precisely the *separation* just described by Mahler. For human beings the combination is irresistible, and its effects persist with varying degrees of intensity throughout the course of the life cycle.

## The Mirror

The genesis and the formation of the self derive from the baby's initial mirroring experience with the mother. For the past half-century this remarkable aspect of our origins has been studied intensively and has come to be regarded as a central feature of our development. The investigations of René Spitz and his associates during the 1950s and 1960s established at the clinical level the baby's inclination to concentrate on the mother's face—and in particular on her eyes—during periods of feeding. For three, or perhaps four, months the nursing infant does not look at the mother's breast (or at the bottle held close to her breast) but at her face. "From the moment the mother comes into the room to the end of nursing he stares at her face."[20] What is especially interesting in this regard is the connection between such primal gazing and the mouth, or "oral cavity." While the child takes into his mouth and body his physical nourishment, he takes into his dawning awareness or his "visceral brain" the emotional, psychological materials that he discovers in the face, eyes, and bodily attitude of the mother. It is often remarked that the first self is a bodily self and that our later life is influenced at the perceptual level by the foundational experiences our bodies undergo as consciousness awakens. We have here a compelling instance of how this works. When Spitz calls the oral cavity in its conjunction with the mother's body "the cradle of human perception," he reminds us that sucking in and spitting out are the first, the most basic, and the most persistent perceptual behaviors among humans. They underlie at the bodily level our subsequent rejections and acceptances, our subsequent negations and celebrations, of experience.

Although Spitz established the baby's inclination to stare at the mother's face, notes H. M. Southwood,[21] whose discussion I follow closely here, he did not state that mother and infant spend considerable time looking at each other, nor did he contend that such looking, along with the mother initiating the infant's facial expressions and sounds, provided the means for the baby to regard the mother's face and sounds as his own. An inborn tendency on the part of the infant prompts him to seek out his mother's gaze and to do so regularly and for extended periods. The mother, because of tendencies developed during the course of her relationship with her own mother, sets about exploiting this mutual face-gazing activity. As the eye-to-eye contact becomes frequent, and easily observed by the investigator, the mother's inclination to continually change her facial expression, as well as the quality of her vocalizing, emerges with striking clarity. Usually she smiles and nods and coos; sometimes in response to an infant frown she frowns. In virtually every instance, the mother's facial and vocal behavior comprises an imitation of the baby's. Thus, as the mother descends to the infant's level, she provides him with a particular kind of human reflection. She does not simply give the baby back his own self; she reinforces a portion of the baby's behavior in comparison with another portion. She gives the baby back not merely a part of what he is doing but something of her own in addition. In individual development, "the precursor of the mirror is the mother's face."[22] The upshot may be stated as follows: the kind of behavior we connect with our perceptual nature derives in large measure from the behavior of the mother. Not only does she trigger the perceiving self's formation, she determines the kind of stimuli to which the child will attend, including the stimuli that will eventually come through language.

Our mental makeup, then, is shaped by those we internalize during the early phases of our development. Our earliest interactional perceptions become dynamic parts of our personality structure and continue to influence us in all that we do long after the specific individuals who were the aim of our internalizing tendency have ceased to be. By the time we have reached adulthood there exists within us an inner world, a kind of psychic universe that is inhabited by the people that have entered us, or more properly, that we have taken into ourselves along our maturational way. We live in two worlds, from the beginning, and our perceptual life must be regarded as a function of the interaction of these worlds that continually impinge upon one another.

I want to reemphasize here that the parent-child interactions of the early period must not be viewed as primarily cognitive events. In the words of Daniel N. Stern to whose *The Interpersonal World of the Infant* I now turn, "They mainly involve affect and excitement" and become part of the infant's effort "to order the world by seeking invariants." When the preverbal, inward Representation of such Interaction becomes Generalized into what Stern calls a RIG, the infant's "sense of a core self" is well upon its developmental way. "Affects," writes Stern, "are excellent self-variants because of their relative fixity," which means, of course, that affects are a central part of mirroring. By creating a "continuity of experience," and in particular a "continuity of affective experience," the RIG provides the baby with the psychic, emotional foundation of his subsequent perceptual interactions with the world.[23]

As I earlier noted, we see the world "feelingly." Thus, mirroring in its early stages (we'll come to the later stages very soon) comprises for Stern a "mediation" in which the caregiver "greatly influences the infant's sense of wonder and avidity for exploration." It is "only the feeling state" that belongs to the nascent self, that is a "self-invariant," and "merger experiences" become simply "a way of being with someone." The infant lays down over and over again the memory of specific affective episodes; he or she develops RIGs; and he or she becomes susceptible to subsequent experiences (the "spiritual" plane) that recall the foundational ones. Later affective exchanges reactivate the original exchanges; they "pack the wallop of the original lived experience in the form of an active memory." This is the essence of the infant's affective world (pp. 103, 109–10).

Employing terminology that will help us enormously in understanding Christian experience, Stern calls these active memories "evoked companions" and suggests that they constitute what psychology usually refers to as internalized relationships. "For instance," Stern writes in an effort to let us know exactly what he has in mind,

> if a six-month-old, when alone, encounters a rattle and manages to grasp it and shake it so that it makes a sound, the initial pleasure may quickly become extreme delight and exuberance, expressed in smiling, vocalizing, and general body wriggling. The extreme delight and exuberance is not the only result of successful mastery, but also the historical result of similar past moments in the presence of a delight-and-exuberance-enhancing (regulating) other.

It is partly a "social response," but in this instance it takes place in a "nonsocial situation." At such times, the original pleasure born of mastery acts as a "retrieval cue" and activates the RIG, resulting in an "imagined interaction with an evoked companion" that includes, of course, the "shared and mutually induced delight" about the mastery (pp. 113, 116). Equally crucial is Stern's observation that evoked companions "never disappear." They "lie dormant throughout life," and while they are always retrievable, "their degree of activation is variable." He writes, "Various evoked companions will be almost constant companions in everyday life. Is it not so for adults when they are not occupied with tasks? How much time each day do we spend in imagined interactions that are either memories, or the fantasied practice of upcoming events, or daydreams?" (pp. 116–18). Robert Rogers comments on these materials, "The seemingly unaccountable experience by an adult of strong emotion, such as love or anger, as a response to a relatively trivial situation involving a comparative stranger might be accounted for by assuming that an 'evoked companion' has suddenly been mobilized, however unconsciously.

Where else could all that affect come from?" Thus "attachment is the internalized representation of repetitive interactions with caregivers." What is internalized in the earliest representations "is not simply the infant's own action, nor the environments' response, but the dynamic interplay between the two."[24] Can anyone fail to spy here the manner in which these citations touch upon, indeed mesh with, our earlier discussion of separation anxiety as presented in Mahler?

Many individual and group behaviors and beliefs, including those that occur in the realm of Christianity, are designed unconsciously to address the problem of separation (and/or other psychological problems) by offering practitioners experiences that evoke companions. Such experiences grant the solace of companionship to those who are struggling in the after-separation world, those whose aloneness, self-alienation, or persistent separation anxiety prime them to respond to an unseen universe of powerful forces and beings to which they are ostensibly connected. Indeed, many of the figures at the heart of Christian ritual (God the Father, the Son, Mary, and the Holy Spirit) may be regarded as projective, psychological expressions, or complex, multilayered symbolifications, of those longed-for inward companions associated originally with the dynamic affects included in the dual-unity situation, the baby's delicious, regulating, invariant, and internalized encounters with the caregiving figures of the early period.

## The Word

Eighty years ago, the pioneering investigations of the Russian linguist Lev Vygotsky[25] made clear that the development of language was not primarily a cognitive process (the orthodox view) but an interactive, social process loaded with emotional, bodily components from the preverbal period. Because thought and speech develop in a parallel and reciprocal fashion, we must ultimately think of language as a dynamic system of meaning in which the emotional and the intellectual unite. The egocentric speech of the three-year-old does not disappear when the child reaches seven or eight. Instead of atrophying, such egocentric speech goes underground; that is, it turns into inner speech and forms the foundation of that inward babble that, joined to higher cognitive components, comes eventually to comprise a sizable portion of our ordinary consciousness. In this way, the development of thinking is not from the individual to the social but from the social to the individual. The child starts conversing with himself as he has been doing with others.

As for the spoken word, it is initially a substitute for the gesture, for the bodily attitude and bodily expression that precede the verbalized sound.

When the child says "mama," it is not merely the word that means, say, put me in the chair, but the child's whole behavior at that moment, his reaching out for the chair, trying to hold it, etc. In contrast to the egocentric speech that goes inward, verbalized speech goes outward; the child uses it as a method of pointing. It is the fusion of this inward speech and developing outward speech that finally comprises human thought in its ordinary, basic expression. We appreciate from this viewpoint the growing psychological realization, based explicitly on Vygotsky's work, that thinking is an unconscious process in the first instance.[26] Even our conscious speech, the psychological community has come to recognize, is pervaded by unconscious mechanisms to the degree that it is tied to our thinking.

With regard to the role of separation in all of this, we must note that symbol formation (or word formation) arises from the infant's shared experience with the mother. The common act of "referential pointing" starts with the mother's invitation but soon leads to the child inviting the mother to join in the contemplation of some object. This marks the beginning of what psychologists call "intellectual stereoscopy" in which the objectification of the world is dependent on social interaction. The child names things to someone, and the loving feedback he receives becomes the incentive for naming further things. The whole idea of twoness and separateness arises from this mutuality. Thus, the presence and absence of the mother and of important physical objects in the child's world play motivational roles in the development of representational thought. In fact, the ability to recognize mother, to conceptualize her as mother, is goaded into existence by the need to cope with her absence, or loss. The feeling of loss becomes the motive for "acquiring the capacity to represent absent objects or to represent objects regardless of their presence or absence." When the baby names the absent object, he predicates it on the basis of its former presence: thus, mommy gone. The same act can predicate a future presence on a current absence. The ideas of *gone* and *mommy* are linked and placed in relation to one another. The whole business of linguistic predication is thus associated with the problem of separation from the caretaker. Again, as the child links up *mommy* and *gone*, he creates a dependent relationship between two ideas that substitutes for each idea's dependency on actual experience. This gives the child the power to recall the mother at will. Symbolic representation (as in play) comes to comprise a way back to the missing object of one's emotions.[27]

Because the verbal representation of the thing is the culmination of the symbolic process, the word is the magical tie that reunites us with the all-important figure(s) of infancy and childhood. It is not merely that maternal stimulation during the time of language development is necessary for the fulfillment of the child's potential; our symbolic seeing is charged with the emotional energy that went into our life and death struggle to maintain our connection to the caregiver at the same time we were giving her up. Through the early imperfections of mothering we learn to grip the world with our bodies, with our tense anticipation (the time sense). Through the crises of separation, which continue to transpire after the early period, we learn to grip the world with our minds, with our symbols, with our words. The mirror phase of infancy eventually gives way to the presentational mirror of a mind that has separation on its mind. The very running on of our thoughts in ordinary consciousness becomes a link to the figures of the past. To express the matter in terms that recall the context of our discussion explicitly, because the word becomes the child's chief tool for "matching mental states,"[28] the word also becomes the child's chief tool for preserving the "companionship" from which his very selfhood arises. Thus, language as the means of approaching God harbors perforce the unconscious aims and wishes of the early period as they inform the supplications of the adult. In the universe of religious behavior, the word always reaches back to its primitive communicative origins.

## Brain, Mind, and Religion

Of overriding significance here is the extent to which the psychosocial picture presented contextually has come to be supported in recent years by neurobiological investigations of the developing mind-brain. What occurs early on as the infant-child interacts with the parental provider is not registered, or internalized, in some vague, "psychological" way that may or may not be "there" depending upon how one chooses to "view" the matter. On the contrary, what we are calling "the basic biological situation" is registered physiologically, at the synaptic level itself, to become the neurobiological foundation of human perception in general and the essential inspiration of the religious realm in particular. Religious narrative and ritual, the human creature's distinctive planetary signature, spring directly from the interactive nurturing that dominates the early stages of our existence. "Human connections shape the neural connections from which the mind emerges," writes Siegel in *The Developing Mind*. While the "structure" and the "function" of the "brain" are "directly shaped" by "interpersonal experience throughout life," such "shaping" is "most crucial during the early years of childhood." Different "patterns" of "child-parent attachment" are "associated" with differing "physiological responses" and with "ways of seeing the world." It is the "communication of emotion" that serves as the "primary means" by which such experiences of "attachment" mold "the developing mind." In this way, the "repeated patterns of children's interactions with their caregivers" (the basic biological situation of asking and receiving) become "remembered" in the "various modalities of memory" and "directly shape not just what children recall," but "how the representational processes develop. Behavior, emotion, perceptions, sensations, and models of others," Siegel notes, "are engrained by experiences that occur before children have autobiographical memorial processes available to them. These implicit elements of memory also later influence the structure of autobiographical narratives." For countless millions of human beings, needless to say, one's "autobiographical narrative" becomes interwoven inextricably with one's "religious narrative," the timeless, traditional, cross-cultural "myth" that captures the manner in which individuals "see the world" in the widest, most encompassing sense.[29]

At the center of the spiritual "narrative" to which we are devoting ourselves here resides the image of a loving, care-giving Parent-God Who devotes Himself, among other things, to watching over his vulnerable, dependent children, the human flock he has engendered and for which he is ultimately responsible. A genuine understanding of Christianity resides in the conscious comprehension of the manner in which its "core narrative" or "core myth" is "wired" directly into and emanates directly from the human mind-brain as it unconsciously and wishfully projects the implicit memory of one's early "attachment experience" into the "present" reality in which one discovers himself. The narrative with the loving Parent-God at its center is the mnemonic *retrieval* of the early biological pattern of attachment through which one found or tried to find his emotional security and his physical safety in the world. The upshot? Christianity becomes an ongoing attachment narrative designed to enhance one's inward stability, one's calmness, one's happiness, one's vitality, in one's always dangerous and always unpredictable surroundings. It serves the straightforward evolutionary purpose of ensuring and increasing the effectiveness of one's interactions with the environment by ensuring and increasing one's inward psychological equilibrium, in reference particularly to the abhorrence of feeling isolated and alone, "separate" in the psychical sense we discovered in Mahler and others a few pages earlier. "God is love" means God inherits mnemonically, as a synaptically rooted projective entity, the primal love of the early time; He preserves one's attachment to the parental figure as one goes off, inevitably, "on his own." The attachment pattern of the early period is "mapped" onto the religious narrative of an ever-receding future—the unknown. Thus, the God the Christian ostensibly "discovers" at the cultural level turns out to be the "God" he unconsciously *remembers* at the level of his internalizing brain.

To express the whole business a tad more technically, "experience early in life," asserts Siegel, is "especially crucial in organizing the way the basic structures of the brain develop." The "brain's development" is an "experience-dependent process" in which "experience activates certain pathways in the brain, strengthening existing connections and creating new ones."[30] As Donald O. Hebb has axiomatically and famously expressed the matter, "neurons that fire together wire together."[31] What are "stored," observes Siegel, "are the probabilities of neurons' firing in a specific pattern—not actual things." Thus, the "neural net" *remembers* even though the memory itself may not be consciously and explicitly brought to the illuminated center of the subject's focused attention (p. 27). As for the neural "mechanisms" involved in our characteristic way of "encoding" our significant experiences into retrievable "packets" or "engrams," the "amygdala" is believed "to be involved with imparting the emotional significance" to objects and "linking" them to "other memory systems" initially "imparted by the hippocampus" but then "subserved by other complex cerebral pathways potentially involving many hundreds of thousands if not millions of synapses." Just as the "properties of objects" are "synthesized convergently by different pathways," we can "surmise that the historical and emotional significance of objects are likewise synthesized," yet also "edited, updated, and revised" based upon "new experiences." The more complex "associative experiential properties and cues" may be "attached to critical objects in the environment, such as parents, siblings, and even the concept of oneself." Our lives, then, are "filled with implicit influences, the origins and impacts of which we may or may not be aware" (p. 49). Affectively charged, "value-laden" memories are "made more likely to be reactivated" among the "myriad of infinite engrams laid down" as we move ahead. The early period is "encoded" in the brain, and our existence is "shaped" by the "reactivations of implicit memory, which lack a sense that something is being recalled. We simply enter these engrained states" and undergo them as "the reality of our present experience" (pp. 32–33). What William James calls "the varieties of religious experience" offer us the most familiar, striking exemplifications of such neurally rooted "entrances" and such engrained, concealed "presences." Through an endless variety of retrieval cues, from supplications to oratorios, from stained-glass windows to sacred robes, from the interpersonal crises of divorce or illness or death, to the physical dangers lurking in proverbial foxholes, and on and on forever, we "enter" unconsciously the putative spiritual domain and experience the vital, sustaining, soothing attachment of our parental internalizations, as they were originally taken in and as they are modified and complexified by our continuous, wishful enhancements over time. The interpersonal origins of our mind-brain trigger the primal inclination to make the universe in which we abide interpersonal, too.

## Attractions and Addictions

The neurobiological approach to an "attractor state" helps us along nicely as we strive to disclose further the unconscious origin of the Christian's inclination to "people" the world with spirits, and, in particular, with a supernatural Parent-God. "Reinforced patterns" of "activation," writes Siegel, "are called 'attractor states.' " They consist in the "activity" of each "component" of a "system" at a "given point in time." As experience unfolds in the light of a person's "values," specific "brain states" become "more probable," and eventually more "engrained" within the activity of the "system" as a whole. It is "emotional response," observes Siegel, that serves as the system's building block and that ensures the "neural firing," or the "activation," of the concerted "state." As states become engrained through repeated expression and emotional intensity, they become "more likely to be activated." And when a "state of mind" is continually and powerfully aroused, it is prone to configure into "a deeply engrained attractor state." Finally, declares Siegel, in the crucial words upon which our line of reasoning rests, "repeated states of activation at the critical early period of development shape the structure of neural circuits which then form the functional basis for enduring states of mind within the individual."[32] Accordingly, what transpires between offspring and caregiver during the early period comes gradually to comprise not merely one neurobiological "state" among many, but the central, enduring "attractor state" of our ongoing lives. The basic biological situation gives rise at the implicit, unconscious level to the perceptual, emotional "scheme" from which emanate our deepest emotional longings and perceptual inclinations. How could it be otherwise? For many crucial months and years our physical and mental survival depend entirely on the caregiver; thus the affective intensity of this "critical" early stage is colossal; we attach ourselves to our provider with utterly spontaneous, unabated ardor; nothing is held back; our needs for nourishment, for care, for love, are "activated" continuously, over and over again, thousands upon thousands of times, to become rooted synaptically in our brains; our emotional "values" are established in an indelible, permanent manner that seeks fulfillment forever after along lines that affectively recall the initial, primal interaction. In short, we internalize into our developing minds early on the instinct-driven, affective "pattern" that will govern our behavior as we relinquish the immediate familial unit and move into the wider world of culture, including, of course, culture's religious dimension.

The "truth" of the Christian narrative with the loving Parent-God at the center is confirmed implicitly, unconsciously through a primed, fully readied "attractor state" that resides at the foundation of the believer's interpersonally sculpted, interpersonally wired brain. He is not simply attracted *to* the religious narrative to which he is eventually exposed; the system is completely dynamic: it is *he who also attracts the narrative to himself,* yanking it in, absorbing it, mapping it onto the model, the scheme, upon which he's been relying all along. The attractor state within him is as eager for confirmation of its core perception as those who offer the narrative to him are eager for his acceptance of it and his entry into the flock.

It is not only Christianity, needless to say, but a wide variety of human participations that are linked firmly to the basic biological situation: our ongoing interpersonal relationships at both the individual and group level (spouse and family); our national loyalty and identification with "motherland" and "fatherland," including the "leader" or "chief"; our absorption in music, art, literature; and, of course, our inclination to make gods out of other institutions such as science or philosophy. However, because the Christian domain is imponderable, invisible, entirely unsupported by what we term empirical criteria, because for millions of people everywhere mental and emotional stability depend significantly on their Christian ties, and finally because Christianity must compete with other emergent systems and brain states that come into play as an individual develops over time, Christianity's humble, worldly task is to reinforce, to strengthen, to deepen the participant's original, brain-based convictions through steady, even continuous exposure to ritual and to word from early childhood onward. The neurons that fired together and wired together to create the primal attractor state during the early period must be regularly activated in the proper devotional context to ensure the continuation of the supernatural attachment that emerged on initial exposure to official, sacred narrative. To put it another way, the worldly task of institutional Christianity is to provide the flock with the inspiration to continue its mapping of the primal, core experience of attachment to the parental figure onto the orthodox version of the substitute Parent-God. Unless this happens, both flock and earthly shepherds are apt to disappear. Accordingly, to employ a familiar example in illustration, when we hear the gospel choir on TV singing, "Jesus came and found me/And put His arms around me," we detect the primal attractor state of union with the biological caregiver humming along quietly beneath the mapped-on surface expression of the core fantasy. Surely we begin to spy, now, the full emotive source of Winifred Gallagher's observation that "mother and offspring live in a biological state that has much in common with addiction. When they are parted, the infant does not just miss its mother; it experiences a physical and psychological withdrawal from a host of her sensory stimuli, not unlike the plight of a heroin addict who goes cold turkey."[33] The building block of the attractor state, as I've suggested in passing on a couple of occasions, is *affect*, or emotions, feelings of attachment and love that reach all the way down to the core of the developing self, or alternatively, to the neurobiological foundations of the developing mind-brain. As the Christian enters the putative supernatural realm and spontaneously shifts toward the basic biological situation, now outwardly projected in the "sacred" image of Parent-God and filial worshiper, he does so ardently, passionately, reverently, needfully, in search of his primal, foundational connection, his felicity, his security, his stability—in a word, his affective "fix." The gravitational power of Christianity emanates from precisely this psychological direction.

## More on Infantile Amnesia

That the decisive, determining source of our most powerful, compelling emotions as people should be inaccessible to our direct apprehension during the entire course of our lives can be described only as one of the most extraordinary and defining aspects of our fundamental humanity. For years as little ones we passionately and unceasingly interact with our caregivers; for years we depend on them for everything, including our very survival. Yet we cannot explicitly recall these events; we cannot "find" them mnemonically, no matter how long and how hard we try. As far as conscious perception of our emotional roots is concerned, the early period has simply vanished from view. This is not because infants and young children can't remember things. On the contrary, from nearly the beginning, and equally for both sexes, infantile memory is robust. "Studies on infant memory carried out at the University of Toronto," writes Richard M. Restak, "suggest that infants may remember more about events than, only a few years ago, the most optimistic researcher would have thought possible."[34] Nor is it solely in a "wide" or "general" sense that memory emerges as an integral feature of our early mental functioning, with past experience exerting an effect on current behavior. As Restak observes, infants remember in a fashion that makes plain their powerful "associative" capacities: mother's "face" goes with mother's "voice"; this particular "object" calls that particular "object" to mind; the baby is "storing information"; the "association tracts" in his developing mind-brain are open for business—toward the inception of his days and, of course, forever after (p. 169).

Let's look further into infantile amnesia now with an eye to distinguishing sharply the quality of early (or implicit) memory and later, autobiographical (or explicit) memory. The distinction will lead us nicely to a number of compelling realizations. "Infantile amnesia," writes Elizabeth Johnston,

> refers to the general inability of people to remember specific events from the early years of their lives. On the basis of both free recall studies (What is your earliest memory?) and studies for memories of notable and datable early events (the birth of a sibling, hospitalization, the Kennedy assassination) psychologists have concluded that there are very few memories from before the age three years. The average age of the earliest memory reported is three-and-a-half, with a small but consistent gender difference indicating that females reported earlier memories.

Johnston goes on,

> If people are asked to recall episodes from the entire life span the number reported before age eight falls off sharply in comparison to other periods. This indicates that it is not the age of the memories per se that accounts for their relative paucity, rather it is the life period that they occur within (the earliest years) that is sparsely represented in long term autobiographical memory.[35]

To apply accurately an understanding of memory to an understanding of religious belief, then, we must employ what investigators currently term a "dual memory system" that characterizes the nature of our memorial capacity from the inception to maturity. On the one hand, we have the "non-verbal, image-based system," with the following characteristics as presented in Johnston: "1) primitive; 2) present from birth; 3) addressable by situational or affective cues; 4) contains fragmentary information; 5) memories expressed through images, behaviors, or emotions; 6) learned routines; 7) generalized past experiences not linked to specific events; and 8) accessed through reinstatement." On the other hand, we have the "socially accessible system" as follows: "1) emerges slowly throughout the preschool years; 2) addressable through intentional retrieval efforts; 3) personally experienced events; 4) encoded in narrative form; 5) actively thought about or processed; 6) can be accessed and recounted in response to social demands; 7) contains information specific to time and place; 8) develops with the acquisition of language" (p. 3). When we put these "systems" together, of course, we begin to perceive the whole mind-brain at work—not merely in some general, theoretical sense that floats about in the realm of pure ideas, but in relation to specifically the substance and the expression of Christian belief. We perceive the image-based nature of the creed, the depictions of sacred materials contained in sacred texts and sacred objects (He walked upon the waters; the Madonna cradles the dying Jesus in her arms). We perceive the endless affective cues in an endless variety of ritual contexts (let us kneel in our helplessness before our Almighty Creator); the memories contained in emotions and behaviors (your Heavenly Father loves you; bow your heads humbly in recognition of His blessings, in gratitude for your daily bread, which He provides); the learned routines that come to comprise a sizable portion of one's Christian religious life (the ceremonies of the service, the holiday celebrations, and the garb); the generalized past experiences not linked to specific events (this accident is tragic, but we cannot fathom fully the ways of our loving God [anymore than we could fathom what our parents were doing early on]); the access through reinstatement (let us open our Bibles once again and read of His wondrous works). One might continue in a similar vein forever. Indeed, even those aspects of Christianity about which we "think" discursively, even those aspects that are intentional, conscious, accessed in response to social demand, are themselves based ultimately upon our early experience, our early, internalized, unconscious associations that give such "higher" aspects their compelling, affective power, their emotional bite as it were. When we "sin," for example, we undergo *separation* from our Lord, Who is unconsciously linked to the caregiver; we experience once more the threat (and the torment) of primal, foundational loss, what Dante calls in *Inferno*, "the eternal isolation of the soul." When we love others as ourselves in response to Christ's directive, we bring to others that primal, foundational love we internalized in response to the timely ministrations of our parental provider. Our "conscience" as we feel it in wrongdoing, and as we express it in our compassionate concern for the welfare of others, is rooted in our deepest affective core, in the part of us that we informally call "the heart," that wordless region from which comes the expression of our basic emotional nature, shaped in the first years of life.

As for the issue of *why* the early period is lost to our explicit recollection, there is no universally accepted, definitive answer because the question (for obvious reasons) does not easily lend itself to empiric, observational investigation. Generally accepted and ubiquitous in the literature, however, is the notion that what we have called the nonverbal, image-based system becomes increasingly unavailable to direct apprehension as it simply gives way to the emergent, brain-based modes of recollection linked to the socially accessible system. As we mature neurologically, the later configuration is the one we are fated to *use* when we employ our will and our capacity to remember. The answer that reigns in the literature, then, is Piagetian: an early "scheme" of cerebral functioning gradually yields to, and is finally absorbed into, a later "scheme." As Johnston expresses the matter, "The inaccessibility of early childhood memories [is] due to a disjunction between the earliest and later modes of processing information. . . . While there is no abrupt neurological watershed corresponding to the offset of infantile amnesia, there is good reason to believe that neurological maturity must be one of the factors that limits early memory" (pp. 1–2). Thus the *way* we remember things changes, leaving the socially accessible system "on top," or "in the light," and the nonverbal, image-based system "below ground," or "in the dark." We have in all this a provocative and relatively straightforward method of talking about a highly disputatious topic in modern (and postmodern) awareness: the unconscious mind, an entity that each person possesses whether or not he's been "repressing" specific and presumably stress-laden aspects of his thought and behavior.[36]

We come now to a major consideration. As the early, nonverbal memorial mode gives way to the later, verbal, socially accessible system, it is "narrative memory" that bears the weight of the past and begins to influence the shape of the future. "Infantile amnesia," states Johnston, "is overcome through the linguistic sharing of memories with other. . . . Various pieces of empirical evidence support the idea of a later onset of narrative memory" (pp. 3–4). By way of illustration, Johnston offers us, among several items, the following representational vignette:

> Tessler studied 3 year olds and their mothers on a visit to a natural history museum. She found that none of the children remembered any of the objects that they viewed in the museum if they had not talked about them with their mothers. Mother's talk alone was not facilitative, nor was a child's mention alone effective in leading to subsequent remembering. Creating a narrative together cemented particular objects in memory.

And then, summarizing the matter for us neatly, Johnston writes, "Through sharing memories with others language becomes available as a means of reinstating memory" (p. 4). Johnston calls this the "Vygotskian model" referring to the famous Russian linguist, Vygotsky, whose work we explored a few pages earlier. The point is, the two major narratives, or stories, that come to comprise the "world" or the "universe" of the developing person, namely, the familial narrative and the religious narrative, are destined to inherit, to contain, to absorb, and to harbor, precisely the early, preverbal experience that resides at the core of that person's mind-brain. The affect, the perception, the attachments and longings of the early period as they are steadily internalized during life's first years, become the human "stuff" out of which the religious realm is fashioned and toward which religious practice is finally directed. "If the infant's environment provides frequent opportunities for reactivation," notes Johnston, "then theoretically an individual's early experiences could be remembered over a lifetime" (p. 3). Memory turns out to be an "emergent property" of the "cue and the engram" (p. 3), and it is precisely the "engram" of the first relationship, or what we have called the attractor state as grounded in the basic biological situation, at which Christianity aims its traditional or sacred "cues," the substance of its doctrinal and ritualistic enactments.

We must ask ourselves, what is *there* in the young person's mind-brain after all to accede with emotion to Christianity's "story," to the narrative with the loving Parent-God at its center, if not the immediate context of the young person's *life*? Clearly, there is *nothing else*. Equally, as the familial narrative takes shape and the young person increasingly apprehends the inevitable psychic (if not physical) *separation* that looms as its culmination, the Christian narrative begins to assume a central, affective position in the psychic economy of the developing individual. While he must relinquish eventually the actual parent, he can retain forever the mysterious Parent-God, the supernatural surrogate whose attractive power emanates unconsciously from that very mnemonic place from which the attachment to the actual parent initially arose. As he becomes a predominantly verbal, narrative creature as opposed to a "primitive," preverbal creature, lo and behold, there is his religious narrative to greet him, to offer him another loving, protective Parent, another Guide, another Nourisher, another Omnipotent Companion and Ally Whose hand he may clutch as he proceeds upon his increasingly separate way. At the affective, perceptual, synaptic level of his existence the Christian narrative presents itself as another version of and the direct successor to exactly what he has just experienced interactionally as a little one; and it derives its compelling power, its compelling timeless appeal, from precisely the direction of his implicit recollection: he can't *see* the realistic, empirical link between the two stages, the two systems; all he can do is *feel* the connection inside; the unconscious associations impel him to judge the religious narrative as "true." In other words, the narrative *implicitly confirms* what he's just experienced as a person; it returns him to his familiar internalized reality at his emergent verbal level of understanding, and this fills him with the irresistible sensation *that he is what he is*, that no break exists in his being, that no separation will snatch him away from his inward emotional reality, or world. In the neurobiological terms that recall the early stages of our discussion, the Christian narrative permits him to *map* his early experience onto his ongoing and increasingly separate life. Reason, needless to say, is not *there* yet to question the assumptions of his supernatural outlook. He simply projects his way happily to the spiritual universe that is offered to him by his directional elders. Where the arms of the actual biological caregiver held him in the beginning, the arms of sweet Jesus hold him now. As the fleshly body of the mother recedes, the spiritual body of the Deity appears mentally to take her place. The believer will not be alone. With the help of society's institutional promptings, and with the assistance of his capacities to imagine, to play, to create substitutes for the treasured caregiver he must gradually relinquish as he grows, his mind-brain will accord him just what his mind-brain requires for his peace of mind.

The religious story to which Christians are introduced as the early, preverbal stage gives way to the narrative style of perception is all-encompassing, all-satisfying, completely reassuring—that is, if they stick to the rules and dutifully propitiate their Parental Provider. They are allied with omnipotence once again; the all-powerful parent returns in the form of the Parent-God. They will live forever, be loved forever, be guided forever, be "housed" forever in the mansions of their benign, supernatural Benefactor, their Shepherd, their Savior and Spiritual Nourisher. All their questions will be answered; all their wonderings about the nature of Nature will be met with some sort of explanation, thus allaying anxiety over the shape of the unknown. Their religious narrative has, like all good dramatic tales, a beginning, a middle, and an end. They discover their provenance, their duties in mortal life, and their destination upon mortal life's conclusion. They can continue to question and to wonder as much as they like, of course, but they don't *have* to wonder and question; they can rest content in the reassurances of doctrine whenever they wish to do so. All who seek shall find. All who submit shall be comforted. All who kneel to their loving Parent-God shall be uplifted, over and over again, each time they supplicate, forever more.

## Magic

Anthropological attempts to fathom magical behavior commenced in earnest during the course of the nineteenth century and culminated in Sir James G. Frazer's monumental study, *The Golden Bough*, originally published in England in 1890. The century as a whole was given to what we may regard as an "us and them" approach to things, an approach that crept unhindered into many fields of intellectual endeavor, including anthropology and comparative religion. Over here were enlightened, contemporary, Christianized Europeans of good social and economic standing, and over there were pagans and primitives past and present, prone to quaint, crude, formulaic attempts at controlling a world they didn't understand scientifically (an exception was sometimes made for the ancient Hebrews, one of whom was, after all, Jesus Christ). Primitive magic was goal directed (or "efficacious") superstition; it was tied to power-charged objects and spells wielded by all manner of purblind necromancers, from exotic tribal chiefs to lowly, credulous villagers mumbling over navel-strings and afterbirths. Frazer's towering book, which still repays investigation, harbored in its core a loyalty to the progressive or perhaps evolutional notions of the day: humankind was culturally, intellectually, spiritually on the move, from the stage of primitive magic to the stage of religion (a refinement of primitive magic), to the stage of rational, scientific understanding that for some of Frazer's contemporaries was compatible with refined religion (the old Baconian ideal of the New Atlantis) and that for others (say, Freud and his circle) was not.

Although Frazer's progressive vision was historically and culturally problematic, to put it mildly, it became (and remains) widely popular in England, on the Continent, and in North America. Yet that vision also nourished fierce controversies over the nature of enlightened religion, controversies that proved useful to those who took up magic and religion during the course of the twentieth century. For example, the famous Scottish historian-anthropologist Robertson Smith (1842–1896), one of Frazer's intellectual mentors, opined that certain denominations, such as Catholicism, were more reluctant than other denominations, such as Protestantism, to jettison their magical baggage and join the parade toward refinement. Further, he was inclined to express this view in his well-attended university lectures. "He could show with unrivalled erudition," writes Mary Douglas, that in the course of history "the ideals of Christianity . . . had moved from Catholic to Protestant forms."[37] Needless to say, such scholarly conclusions might easily lead not only to bitter, partisan debate but to genuine confusion as to what exactly religion is, distinguished from its putative forerunner, primitive magic. As I just suggested, twentieth-century anthropologists took the hint.

Although comparative studies of magic and religion are still disputatious, and will no doubt always be so given the deeply personal nature of religious belief, a general (as opposed to universal) consensus currently exists: religion and magic are closely affined, even connected inextricably, and it is more helpful, more productive of truth, to collapse the old dichotomy (including its "us-them" component) than to shore it up. Writes Mary Douglas in *Natural Symbols*, "Sacraments are one thing, magic another; taboos are one thing, sin another. The first thing is to break through the spiky verbal hedges that arbitrarily insulate one set of human experiences (ours) from another set (theirs)."[38] She continues,

> Sacramental efficacy works internally; magical efficacy works externally. But this difference, even at the theological level, is less great than it seems. For if the theologian remembers to take account of the doctrine of the Incarnation, magical

enough in itself, and the even more magical doctrine of the Resurrection and of how its power is channeled through the sacraments, he cannot make such a tidy distinction between sacramental and magical efficacy. Then there is the popular magicality of Christianity. A candle lit to St. Anthony for finding a lost object is magical, as is also a St. Christopher medal used to prevent accidents . . . Both sacramental and magical behavior are expressions of ritualism.

And finally, "I see no advantage . . . in making any distinction between magical and sacramental" (pp. 8–9).

Douglas renders the matter even more succinctly perhaps in her *Purity and Danger*: "The division between religion and magic" is "ill-considered." Indeed, "the more intractable puzzles in comparative religion arise because human experience has been thus wrongly divided."[39] Such passages not only go to the heart of the matter, they allow us to witness firsthand the kind of professional insight that has prompted *The HarperCollins Dictionary of Religion* to present magic and religion as ultimately "compatible" for "twentieth-century scholars," or the *Penguin Dictionary of Religions* to declare that "magic shades off into religion," or *The Oxford Dictionary of World Religions* to assert that for present-day anthropologists magic is "embedded in religion" where it "acts as an organization of context and meaning," or the *Merriam-Webster's Encyclopedia of World Religions* to view the notion that magic and religion are integrally related as a twentieth-century commonplace.[40] Here are John S. and David Boyer Noss summing things up for us temperately in *A History of the World's Religions*:

> Magic may be loosely defined as an endeavor through utterance of set words, or the performance of set acts, or both, to control or bend the powers of the world's to one's will. *It cannot be wholly divorces from religion,* . . . but it is discernibly present when the emphasis is placed on forcing things to happen rather than asking that they do.[41]

Does this imply that magic may be covertly present in prayer, where the emphasis is placed on asking rather than forcing? I believe that it does, as I will soon try to establish. As for the us-them thinking that characterized Victorian approaches to magic and religion, it has bequeathed to us, once again in Mary Douglas's words, "a false distinction between primitive and modern cultures." It is a "mistake to suppose that there can be religion which is all interior, with no rules, no liturgy, no external signs of inward states. As with society, so with religion, external form is the condition of its existence." The proper model for appreciating "primitive ritual," observes Douglas, is not "the absurd Ali Baba" but the modern psychologist. It is modern psychology precisely that can provide us with "pertinent suggestions" for the understanding of "religious beliefs."[42] Surely the great French anthropologist Marcel Mauss was thinking along similar lines when, several decades before the appearance of Professor Douglas's writings, he declared in *A General Theory of Magic*, "In magic, as in religion, it is the unconscious ideas that are the active ones."[43] Accordingly, the old us-them dichotomy must be retired from active service lest it wreak still more havoc on our comprehension of human behavior. Let's give Susanne K. Langer the last word on the subject: "Once we recognize a truly primitive trait of human experience in a naïve form, we usually end up by finding it still operative in our own subjective experience."[44] We have far too much history behind us as millennial Westerners to doubt the veracity of that sentence.

Frazer provides us with a useful, preliminary framework in *The Golden Bough*: "Magic rests everywhere," he remarks, "on two fundamental principles: first, that *like produces like*, effect resembling cause; second, that *things which have once been in contact continue ever afterwards to act on each other*." The "former principle" is tied to homeopathic or imitative magic, the "latter" to the contagious variety.[45] Let's open with contagion, "the most familiar example" of which is the "magical sympathy" that is "supposed to exist between man and any severed portion of his person, such as his hair or nails; so that whoever gets possession of human hair or nails may work his will, at any distance, upon the person from whom they were cut." Frazer goes on:

> Other parts which are commonly believed to remain in a sympathetic union with the body, after the physical connexion has been severed, are the navel-string and the afterbirth, including the placenta. So intimate, indeed, is the union conceived to be, that the fortunes of the individual for good or evil throughout life are often supposed to be bound up with one or other of these portions of his person, so that if his navel-string or afterbirth is preserved and properly treated, he will be prosperous; whereas if it be injured or lost, he will suffer accordingly.

Again, "magic may be wrought on a man sympathetically not only through his clothes and severed parts of himself, but also through the impressions left by his body in sand and earth. In particular, it is a worldwide superstition that by injuring footprints you injure the feet that made them" (pp. 62–63, 68).

We may think of contagion generally as a transfer of power by contact or by proximity, and as a species of magic that is frequently associated with sacred objects and with pollution.[46] In illustration of homeopathic or imitative magic, the idea that like produces like, Frazer cites "the familiar application" in which an attempt is made to injure or to destroy an enemy "by injuring or destroying an image of him," or, in the "amiable" sphere of "winning love," an arrow is dispatched into "the heart of a clay image," thus "securing a woman's affection" (pp. 35, 40). Here magic rests overwhelmingly on a fallacious understanding of causality: like produces like. If thunder accompanies rain, then to beget rain during a drought, we can beat drums and roll boulders noisily down hills; if fertility produces crops, and an eventual harvest, then we can copulate in the newly sown fields and transfer our sexual energies to the precious, unpredictable seeds; if fish must open their mouths and swallow our hooks or we don't catch them, then we can open our own mouths in imitation of the fish and thus induce the effect we desire: like begets like.

Frazer notes that many examples of homeopathic magic are "supposed to operate at long distance. Whatever doubts science may entertain as to the possibility of action at a distance, magic has none; faith in telepathy is one of its basic principles" (p. 46). We might bear this in mind henceforward as a kind of telepathy is often presupposed in prayer, and in two directions: we can detect or perceive the presence of the ambient Almighty, and the Almighty can read our hearts, indeed can know precisely what is in them before we have uttered our supplication.

Edward Tylor's famous "minimum definition of religion" as a "belief in Spiritual Beings" places the emphasis upon the mind, upon concurrence with an all-determining conception, or idea.[47] For this writer, and for other writers as well,[48] Tylor's definition points us firmly in the right direction. Belief in spiritual beings is the great global agent that distinguishes the religious from the nonreligious, fundamentally and forever. Those who believe in God, to express the matter familiarly, are at least minimally religious; those who do not believe in God are not, even though they may consider themselves religious in some popular, secular sense that generally means "in awe of the galaxies," or "fascinated by the mysteries of nature" of some such. The believers are potentially religious in the full sense, capable of moving utterly into the religious sphere if they are not there already. The nonbelievers, by contrast, must hold back; they just can't commit until a major shift in attitude occurs. So be it. For Émile Durkheim, however, the emphasis on mind, intellect, assent, and concurrence draws the understanding of religion away from the realm in which it properly and supremely belongs, namely, the social realm, society, with its laws, rules, morals, mores, customs, and traditions—its collective, organized institutions. Durkheim did not believe the psychology of the individual could account for the emergence of societal forms.[49] It helps enormously in grasping Durkheim's view to remember that he was not concerned with the ultimate origin of spiritual beings. Who knows where they ultimately come from? Who knows when, or how, or why they ultimately appear in human thought and culture. Who has removed the mists of time, looked into the distant past, and seen? For Durkheim, religion is there; it is a reality one discovers on the planet, either directly as one travels about, or indirectly as one reads and ponders. Having discovered it, what one finds in turn (Durkheim concentrated on primitive cultures) is that religion is made up of rites and observances designed to propitiate the gods and thus gain their support, that specific rites and observances are delegated to specific members of the community, that deities themselves have fixed, explicit functions to perform, and that religion exists primarily for the benefit of the social order and not for addressing the spiritual needs of the individual.

In this way, a society's "spiritual beings" turn out to be an integral facet of the overall system. "The religious," maintains Durkheim, is identical with "the social." For "in a general way . . . a society has all that is necessary to arouse the sensation of the Divine in minds, merely by the power that it has over them; to its members it is what a God is to its worshippers" (p. 206). We immediately appreciate, of course, the accuracy of all this. Anyone who has been raised in a religious home, a religious tradition, or who has simply read and digested feelingly the work of Honoré de Balzac, or James Joyce, or Bernard Malamud knows very well the extent to which religious beliefs and customs can determine a person's existence. The person of religion as a directive, social force is undeniable. Yet surely the psychology of the individual plays a crucial, causal role in the total picture. To make God equal society or society equal God finally raises more questions than it answers. Observes Bronislaw Malinowski: "The social share in religious enactment is a condition necessary but not sufficient . . . Without the analysis of the individual mind, we cannot take one step in the understanding of religion."[50] Thus the problem arises, how do we go about bringing the "individual mind" to Durkheim's social analysis? How are we to understand from an individual perspective that society's "power over its members" is "what a God is to its worshippers?"

The best way is to concentrate not upon society as we usually think of it but upon the first society, the first social order the individual encounters, the first social reality he is obliged to negotiate, the first "fixed relation" he confronts during the course of his days. To express it as unoriginally as possible, we must begin at the beginning—and I don't mean at the beginning of the individual's career as opposed to the individual's societal enactments precisely because the distinction is otiose: we are social to the root; our individual and our social experiences are inextricably connected. The dyadic circularity of the infant-mother bond is the individual-social matrix of our bodily-emotional-psychological lives. Of overriding significance here is the appreciation that we internalize our experience during the early period. We take the parent into our primitive body-self, into our very tissues, our very guts, as well as into our growing minds, our growing brains. We set up the caregiver as the scaffolding of our developing selves, as the mind-body presence on which we rely in utter life-or-death dependency and need. When we begin to separate from the parents, from the life-supporting matrix of our early experience, and move toward the wider social world, we bring our internalizations with us; indeed, we use them to navigate (and to survive) the passage. The internalizing monad becomes the gradually socialized member of the community. Thus, the tie to societal institutions is grounded in the tie to the parent. The power of societal directives derives from the internalized bond to the caregiver. We are more or less hooked. There is a vital, dynamic continuity here that, if we ignore it, obfuscates our grasp of social forces and that, if we apprehend it, allows us to let in some light. Let me render the whole basic business from another, related angle.

Because social institutions (religion, education, occupation, marriage, and family) come to replace the "institution" of the early parent-child interaction, because social institutions assume a parental role, we transfer to society the feelings, the energies, the needs, the wishes, the loyalties, the loves (and frequently the hatreds) that motivate us during the early period. The social realm becomes an extension of the inner realm; it draws us, compels us, holds us through the mind-body attachment that comprises the very core of the first relationship. To a significant, even determining degree, then, our relationship with society is a transferential one. "Culture," writes Géza Róheim in a classic psychological statement of the issue, "leads instinct into acceptable channels by the creation of substitute objects. The most important of these substitutions is a human being, the wife who replaces the mother. The basis of society is formed by these substitutions and therefore the psychology of growing up falls, in many respects, in line with the psychology of culture." And again, "civilization originates in delayed infancy and its function is security. It is a huge network of more or less successful attempts to protect mankind against the danger of object-loss, the colossal efforts made by a baby who is afraid of being left alone in the dark."[51]

Accordingly, if our transferential relations with the social order turn out to be hostile or in some manner unhealthy, the social order does to us (or threatens to do to us) precisely what we dreaded early on as we interacted dependently with the parent: it confronts us with "the dark," with rejection, separation, isolation, even death, the bogeys we discovered as newcomers when parenting was either forestalled or malignant. To lose our place in society can feel like losing our place in the arms of the caregiver, which is why we tend generally to obey the rules, or to rebel in a fashion that will not result in ostracism, in the temporary or permanent loss of everyone and everything. Let's recall now Professor Durkheim's contention: "The power of society over its members" is "what a God is to its worshippers." The social and the religious go together because religious society inherits the first society, or function, as continuation of the initial social bond. The asking and the receiving that we do in Christian prayer is but a small specific instance of the way in which our early biosocial situation moves toward the wide social world, its providential successor.

Winnicott's famous discussion of "transitional objects" (the blankie, the teddy, and the Raggedy Ann) illustrates very well the process of cultural succession. Confronted with the closing stages of symbiosis, the newcomer (20–36 months) gravitates creatively and trustingly toward the "potential space" of the "intermediate area." He lessens his emerging oneness by engaging in illusory twoness. He mitigates the terror of separate, individual existence by constructing an intimate relationship with a symbolic companion, or ally. He plays it both ways. He strikes out on his own, and he returns imaginatively to the kind of psychic fusion to which he's been accustomed. "With human beings," states Winnicott, "there can be no separation, only a threat of separation; and the threat is maximally or minimally traumatic according to the experience of the first separatings." However, "at the same time," Winnicott goes on, one can suggest that "separation is avoided by the filling in of the potential space with creative playing, with the use of symbols, and with all that eventually adds up to cultural life."[52] The upshot is clear.

Transitional objects are magical objects designed to control and to alter reality in keeping with the wishes and needs of their youthful, omnipotent creator. They have a practical magical purpose that is open, transparent. They serve as symbolic substitutes for the relinquished parent, as transferential entities that point motivationally toward the major symbolic, cultural substitute for the receding parental figure, namely, the godhead. When Roheim characterizes "the wife who replaces the mother" as civilizations' chief substitute object, he errs. Not only does he leave one-half of the human species out of the equation, but he fails to appreciate the lengthy period that intervenes between the relinquishment of the caregiver and the begetting of a spouse. Not for everyone, of course, but for millions of Christians, it is the Deity Who takes over the transitional realm; it is the Deity Who instrumentally replaces the early, illusory, magical creations and Who provides the believer with the inward security he craves as he assumes his separate existence in the world. From exactly this angle we begin to appreciate in earnest the extent to which religious conviction, or faith, is a species of the uncanny. God is real, He feels real when we sense His presence, his "face," in unexpected or ritually induced moments of transformation, or grace, or gratitude, or mystical merger, because our primal, loving internalizations are real, are there. To discover the Lord is to discover revelationally the self because the self and the Lord are birthed in the same psychological soil: internalized attachment to the loving biological provider. We create the Almighty projectively out of our powerful transference love, our ever-active, lifelong wish for union, protection, and care.

Concentration on the early period also helps us to focus and put to very good use Malinowski's seminal views on the nature of magical conduct. Malinowski pointed out more than half a century ago that magical acts, one and all, are "expressions of emotion" and, more particularly, emotion bound up with the possession or the lack of power. Engaged in a series of practical actions, an individual often comes to what Malinowski calls "a gap." The hunter loses his quarry, the sailor his breeze, the warrior his spear, or his strength. What does an individual do in such a case, "setting aside all magic and ritual?" Whether he is savage or civilized, in possession of magic or without it, his "nervous system and his whole organism drive him to some substitute activity." He is possessed by the idea of the desired end; he sees it and feels it. Hence, his "organism reproduces the acts suggested by the anticipation of hope." The individual who is swayed by impotent fury clenched his fists or imagines an attack upon his enemy. The lover who aches for the unattainable object sees her in visions or mentally addresses her. The disappointed hunter imagines the prey in his trap. Such behaviors are natural responses to frustrating situations and are based upon "a universal psycho-physiological mechanism." They engender "extended expressions of emotion in act or word" that allow the individual to "forecast the images of wished-for results" and by doing that, to regain equilibrium and "harmony with life." Thus, a "strong emotional experience that spends itself in a . . . subjective flow of images, words, or gestures" leaves a "very deep conviction of its reality." To the "primitive man" or to the "credulous and untutored" of all ages, the "spontaneous spell or rite of belief, with its power, born of mental obsession," must appear as a "direct revelation" from an external, impersonal force.[53]

Now, when one compares this "spontaneous ritual and verbiage of overflowing passion or desire" with "traditionally fixed marginal ritual," one cannot but note a "striking resemblance." The two products are "not independent of each other." Magical rituals "have been revealed to man" in those "passionate experiences which assail him in the impasses of his instinctive life and of his practical pursuits, in those gaps and breaches left in the ever-imperfect wall of culture which he erects between himself and the . . . temptations and dangers of his destiny." We must recognize in this, writes Malinowski, "the very fountainhead of magical belief." Magic does not come "from the air" but from "experiences actually lived through." As for magic's persistence, its ability to survive failure and disappointment, it comes from the fact that positive cases always overshadow negative ones ("one gain easily outweighs several losses"). Also, those who espouse and practice magic, at least in "savage societies," are individuals of "great energy" and "outstanding personality," that is to say, individuals who are capable of swaying others to their view. In every "savage society" stories of a "big magician's wonderful cures or kills" form the "backbone of belief" and contribute to the pool of living myth that gives the authority of tradition to current formulas and rites (pp. 80–81).

To these hugely helpful and insightful remarks I would immediately add the following: the magical behaviors of the early period also derive from "experience actually lived through," also address a "gap," and "crisis," or "impasse of instinctive life." I am referring to the primal, traumatic experience of disruption that attends the passing of the symbiotic stage, that brings with it feelings of separation and smallness, and that reverberates powerfully and painfully in the psyche of many individuals for ever after, as Mahler suggested. The first natural, instinctive response to this crisis is the creative, imaginative turn to transitional objects, to magical, illusory creations that wishfully restore the dyadic circularity of the infant-mother interaction. To be more directly in line with Malinowski's chosen terminology: having felt the gradual diminishment of the life-sustaining symbiosis and the accompanying anxiety of separation, the child's nervous system, the child's organism, drives him to an "obsessive, substitute activity" that permits him to enjoy the images of a "wished-for result" (reunion or remerger) and thereby to regain his equilibrium and "harmony with life." Thus does the child address the initial gap in the "ever-imperfect wall of culture." Subsequently, as a developmental outgrowth of magical successes (or gains experienced early on) we have the customary turn to the socially sanctioned Deity, including, of course, the turn to individual, subjective prayer. Here, the basic biological arrangement of empathetic, symbiotic dependency is imitatively restored as the helpless one, the suppliant, asks the mighty one, the Lord, to be there for him, to guide him morally, to forgive his transgressions, and to manifest His loving, caring presence.

Róheim was among the first investigators to spy the connection between magic and the traumas of the early period, and like Malinowski, he drew upon this anthropological work in making his observations. "Magic must be rooted in the child-mother situation," he writes, "because in the beginning the environment simply means the mother. Therefore, wishing or manifesting the wish is the proper way to deal with the environment."[54] Róheim then goes on to say—and let's keep our eyes open for the gap we found in Malinowski—"the mother is not only known by the fact that she gratifies the wishes of the child. In truth, she would never be discovered were it not for the fact that there is a gap between desire and fulfillment." More specifically,

> Magic originates from the child's crying when he is abandoned and angry; it is not merely the expression of what actually takes places in the dual-unity situation, but is also a withdrawal of attachment from the object to the means by which the object is wooed, that is, from the mother of the word and back again to the mother.
>
> (p. 12)

Thus it is "obvious," asserts Róheim, "that we grow up via magic." We "pass through the pregenital to the genital phases of organization, and concurrently our mastery of our own body and of the environment increases. This is our own 'magic' and it is analogous in some ways to the invocation of his own 'luonto' (or nature) by the Finnish wizard" (p. 44). In a series of key, summarizing sentences, Róheim states that magic is our "great reservoir of strength against frustration and defeat. Our first response to the frustrations of reality is magic, and without this belief in our own specific ability or magic, we cannot hold our own against the environment." The baby "does not know the limits of its power. It learns in time to recognize the parents as those who determine its fate, but in magic it denies this dependency. The ultimate denial of dependency comes from the all-powerful sorcerer who acts out the role which he once attributed to the projected images." While the "magical omnipotence fantasy of the child is a part of growing up, magic in the hands of an adult means a regression to an infantile fantasy" (pp. 45–46). Magic says, in the end, I refuse to give up my desires.

Let's turn now to a detailed examination of Christian rite and doctrine. Let's see the extent, if any, to which Christianity bears out the theoretical picture we've just developed.

## Notes

1. As I have already stated, I will be using the King James Version of the Bible throughout this book.

2. Silvan S. Tomkins, *Affect, Imagery, Consciousness*, vol. I (New York: Springer, 1962), p. 6.

3. The term "object" is used customarily in psychology because the infant has yet to perceive the caregiver, usually the mother, as a separate, full-fledged *person* in the way we normally intend the term. *Object* is an attempt to render the phenomenology of the infant's perception.

4. David L. Schacter, *Searching for Memory: The Brain, the Mind, the Past* (New York: Basic Books, 1996), p. 5.

5. Daniel J. Siegel, *The Developing Mind: Toward a Neurobiology of Interpersonal Experience* (New York: Guilford Press, 1999), p. 1.

6. Schacter. *Searching for Memory,* p. 174.

7. Siegel. *The Developing Mind,* pp. 24, 29, 30.

8. Michael S. Gazzaniga, *The Ethical Brain* (New York: Dana Press, 2005), p. 134.

9. Erik H. Erickson, *Insight and Responsibility* (New York: W. W. Norton, 1964), p. 153.

10. ———. *Young Man Luther* (New York: W. W. Norton, 1958), p. 264.

11. See Joan W. Anderson, *Where Angels Walk* (New York: Ballantine Books, 2003).

12. Gary Whitmer, "On the Nature of Dissociation," *Psychoanalytic Quarterly* 70 (2001): 807.

13. As noted in Chapter 1, "good enough mothering" is D. W. Winnicott's terminology. See D. W. Winnicott, *Playing and Reality* (London: Penguin, 1971), p. 12.

14. Gerald M. Edelman, *The Remembered Present: A Biological Theory of Consciousness* (New York: Basic Books, 1989).

15. See Otto Rank, *Psychology and the Soul,* trans. W. Turner (New York: A. S. Barnes, 1950).

16. Ethel S. Person, *Dreams of Love and Fateful Encounters: The Power of Romantic Passion* (London: Penguin, 1990), p. 132.

17. Margaret S. Mahler, Fred Pine, and Anni Bergman, *The Psychological Birth of the Human Infant* (New York: Basic Books, 1975).

18. Winnicott, *Playing and Reality,* p. 13.

19. Ana-Maria Rizzuto, *The Birth of the Living God* (Chicago: University of Chicago Press, 1979), p. 49.

20. René Spitz, *The First Relationship* (New York: International Universities Press, 1965), p. 81.

21. H. M. Southwood, "The Origin of Self-Awareness," *International Journal of Psychoanalysis* 66 (1973): 235–39.

22. Winnicott, *Playing and Reality,* p. 22.

23. Daniel Stern, *The Interpersonal World of the Infant* (New York: Basic Books, 1985), pp. 74–75, 90–93.

24. Robert Rogers, *Self and Other* (New York: New York University Press, 1991), p. 41.

25. Lev Vygotsky, *Thought and Language,* 1934, trans. E. Hanfman and G. Vakar (Cambridge, MA: MIT Press, 1979).

26. See Michael Basch, "Psychoanalytical Interpretation and Cognitive Transformation," *International Journal of Psychoanalysis* 62 (1981): 151–74.

27. I am indebted in this paragraph to David Bleich's paper, "New Considerations on the Infantile Acquisition of Language." Presented to the Psychological Center for the Study of the Arts, SUNY Buffalo, March 16, 1990, pp. 1–28.

28. Henry Plotkin, *Evolution in Mind: An Introduction to Evolutional Psychology* (London: Penguin, 1997), p. 249.

29. Siegel, *The Developing Mind*, pp. 2–5.

30. Ibid., p. 13.

31. Ibid., p. 26.

32. Ibid., pp. 218–19.

33. Winifred Gallagher, "Motherless Child," *Sciences* 32 (July 1992): 12.

34. Richard M. Restak, *The Infant Mind* (New York: Doubleday, 1986), p. 149.

35. Elizabeth Johnston, *Investigating Minds* (Bronxville, NY: Sarah Lawrence College, 2007), p. 1.

36. For an outstanding discussion of the unconscious mind and its implicit intentional nature, see John R. Searle, *The Rediscovery of the Mind* (Cambridge, MA: MIT Press, 1992).

37. Mary Douglas, *Purity and Danger: An Analysis of Concept of Pollution and Taboo* (New York: Arks Paperbacks, 1984), p. 18.

38. ———. *Natural Symbols: Explorations of Cosmology* (London: Routledge, 1996), p. 7.

39. Douglas, *Purity and Danger*, p. 28.

40. J. Smith, ed., *The HarperCollins Dictionary of Religion* (New York, HarperCollins, 1995), p. 673; J. Hinnels, ed., *The Penguin Dictionary of Religions* (London: Penguin, 1995), p. 282; J. Bowker, ed., *The Oxford Dictionary of World Religions* (New York: Oxford University Press, 1997), p. 598; W. Doniger, ed., *Merriam-Webster's Encyclopedia of World Religions* (Springfield, MA: Merriam-Webster, 1999), p. 678.

41. David S. Noss and John Boyer Noss, *A History of the World's Religions* (New York: Macmillan, 1990), p. 14. Emphasis added.

42. Douglas, *Purity and Danger*, pp. 58, 62, 72.

43. Marcel Mauss, *A General Theory of Magic*, trans. R. Brian (London: Routledge and Kegan Paul, [1902] 1972), p. 116.

44. Suzanne K. Langer, *Mind: An Essay on Human Feeling* (Baltimore, MD: Johns Hopkins University Press, 1988), p. 307.

45. James Frazer, *The Golden Bough* (New York: Mentor Books, [1900] 1959), p. 35.

46. See Smith, *HarperCollins Dictionary of Religion*, p. 287.

47. Edward Tylor, *The Origins of Culture*, vol. 2 (New York: Harper and Brothers, [1871] 1958), p. 8.

48. Weston La Barre, *The Ghost Dance: Origins of Religion* (New York: Doubleday, 1970), p. 15.

49.  Émile Durkheim, *The Elementary Forms of Religious Life*, trans. J. Swain (Boston: Allen and Unwin, [1912] 1976).

50.  Bronislaw Malinowski, *Magic, Science, and Religion* (New York: Anchor Books, 1954), p. 69.

51.  Géza Róheim, *The Origin and Function of Culture* (New York: Doubleday, 1971), pp. 122, 131.

52.  Winnicott, *Playing and Reality*, pp. 108–109.

53.  Malinowski, *Magic, Science, and Religion*, p. 79.

54.  Géza Róheim, *Magic and Schizophrenia* (Bloomington: Indiana University Press, 1955), p. 11.

# PART ONE

# The Infantilizing Process

## Baptism

Baptism is "the basis of the whole Christian life"[1] because baptism restores the worshiper to a version of the early period wherein he or she is once again a "little child" in the care of a loving, omnipotent protector and provider. Within this basic ritualistic framework the whole of Christian doctrine and practice will transpire because Christian doctrine and practice attain their full, magical potential only upon the mnemonic background or "screen" of life's initial stages. For the promise of salvation to ring true and thus arouse the Holy Spirit, the bond with Christ must implicitly recall at the level of state-dependent memory the bond with the biological caregiver, the ultimate, tangible source of the Christian's "spiritual" convictions. "You can be born again," cries the Reverend Robert H. Schuller; you can become "a child of God. . . . Heaven is for real."[2] And then, in another place, mixing the biological with the "spiritual" in an attempt to explain this, Schuller writes, "The old negative blood is drawn out" and "the new spirit of Jesus Christ [the Holy Spirit], like new blood, flows through your entire nervous and emotional system" (p. 156). This is "what God can do inside your mind," asserts Schuller (p. 156), which is to say, this is what worshipers can do inside their own minds when they unite implicit memory with magical belief and practice.

As one receives the Holy Spirit through baptismal rite, declares Neil T. Anderson, "he puts on a whole new nature and gets to go to heaven."[3] He becomes "a child born of God" (p. 9) and also "a saint" (p. 12). His "identity" is no longer determined by his "physical heritage." How he "formerly identified himself no longer applies." For now, "Christ is all" (p. 9). One "learns to walk again not by sight this time but by faith" (p. 145). We "fix our eyes on Jesus" as we "learn to walk," states Anderson, calling vividly to mind the manner in which one learns to walk in the initial biological instance. Before one is baptized, writes Anderson, he is "separate from God" and "spiritually dead." Jesus "came to remove that separation." The "converted" are "in" Him, and He is "in the converted. . . . He is in you" (p. 145). Here is the primal symbiotic union toward which the whole of Christianity directs the believer.

Baptism, declares Tim Stafford, "opens the door for a lifelong love affair with Jesus."[4] One is afforded the "glorious privilege" of becoming "a child of God," but not a child who must eventually confront separation, or loss of the parent's "familiar face" (p. 234). The Holy Spirit, writes Stafford, "would come as something better than Jesus-on-earth; He would be Jesus within" (p. 235), which means, of course, Jesus is always there, is always present, and is always available when the devotee, Christ's "little child," feels the need to cleave unto his loving provider, the Big One upon whom he depends, as in the basic biological arrangement, for everything including life itself. In a word, "Jesus within" magically recreates the organ relationship of the mother-infant dyad. The "little child" becomes a "member" of Christ's body (I Cor. 6:15).[5] Christian unity within God is ultimately morphological.

What matters in all this, obviously, is not the baptismal ceremony in and of itself but the state of mind one achieves through one's participation in the ceremony's goal as announced and underscored in the New Testament by Jesus:

> Verily I say unto you, Except ye be converted, and become as little children, ye shall not enter into the kingdom of heaven.[6]
>
> (Matt. 18:3)

As I noted toward this book's beginning, Jesus is not playing symbolical games; he means business: His followers must love Him *more* than their actual parents, and if they are parents, they must love Him *more* than their own offspring.

> I am come to set a man at variance against his father, and the daughter against her mother. . . . He that loveth father or mother more than me is not worthy of me; and he that loveth son or daughter more than me is not worthy of me.
>
> (Matt. 10:35, 37)

Clearly, Jesus intends to take the parent's place in the worshiper's life, and He intends to transform the worshiper into His own little child and a member of His extended family of followers. For this and only this will trigger the psychology essential to the successful working of the salvational scheme that is Christianity itself. Just as the potential Christian merged with the biological caregivers early on, so will Christ's "convert" merge with the almighty

Parent-God whose loving, salvational presence will reverberate all the way down to the level of implicit, state-dependent memory where the biological caregiver mnemonically resides. The magical "mystery," or "trick," of the religious substitution is facilitated by the convert's infantile amnesia: he can't recall the early period explicitly and thus can't *see* what is actually occurring as he undergoes his "conversion" and apprehends the appearance of the putative Holy Spirit, the enigmatic Spirit-Person whose entrance into the magical procedure ostensibly confirms its veracity. Accordingly, baptism is not a single, solitary ceremony one undergoes along the way, often toward the beginning of his earthly existence. It is an inward, psychological process one is undergoing all the time as one becomes and continues to be the "little child" of the Redeemer. "We are baptized but once," writes G. P. Fisher in his *A History of Christian Doctrine*,

> yet the act is in the fullest sense eschatological: it sets its seal on our whole life, which is "nothing else than a daily baptism, once begun and constantly lived in," nor do we "perfectly fulfill the sign of baptism until the last day." Baptism is indeed for Luther the "outward and visible sign" of his whole doctrine of justification.[7]

Infantile baptism, holds the *Catechism of the Catholic Church*, "is certainly valid and efficacious," but "Christian initiation remains incomplete." It is "confirmation" at "maturity" that leads the Christian "to a more intimate union with Christ," that "imprints on the soul an indelible spiritual mark, the 'character' which is the sign that Jesus Christ has marked a Christian with the seal of His Spirit [the Holy Spirit] by clothing him with power from on high."[8] Thus, confirmation "unites us more firmly with Christ" as our "maturity" goes forward; "increases the gifts of the Holy Spirit in us[;] . . . roots us more deeply in the divine filiation which makes us cry, Abba, Father!" (p. 330). Surely the upshot is perfectly apparent: baptism's aim is to position the Christian in filial union with his Parent-God, his "Abba," his "Father," to make sure this inward conception, this inward apprehension, this "seal," is present to the worshiper on a daily basis, all the time, so that the worshiper might feel all the time the working of the "Spirit" within him, which means from the psychological/neurological angle the persistent implicit recollection of the biological *person* (the Holy Spirit is doctrinally *a person*) who ensured his security as a vulnerable, helpless, biological organism during the course of his early days. Baptism is "the basis of the whole Christian life" because the basic biological situation (which baptism recreates) is the foundation of our natural life from which and only from which the power of Christianity as a religion derives.

## Prayer and Faith

With baptism, then, the homeopathic magical system of Christianity is under way. The worshiper is developing an alternate identity that he will activate alongside his worrisome "physical heritage," as Anderson put it at the beginning of this chapter.[9] No longer separated from his parental provider, his "Abba," no longer on his own, no longer small and insignificant (through baptism he becomes a "chosen" one [John 15:16]), and above all, no longer ultimately mortal, no longer bound ultimately for extinction, the "convert," the newly emergent "little child," is able to stand his biological life upon its proverbial head and to replace it transformationally with the perfections of his newfound "spiritual" existence. To go around this way, to consider himself inwardly to *be* this way, in other words, to *imitate* in mind and emotion the identity suggested in baptismal doctrine comprises, of course, the homeopathic or imitative aspect of his magical conduct. However, it is hardly sufficient in fashioning a magical identity simply to think about or to believe in the "new man" (Col. 3:10). One must also behave accordingly, manifest one's new identity through one's words and deeds, in short *act it out*—which is precisely what Christians do through the chief *expression* of their belief, their *faith*, namely, prayer.

There is no tighter connection in the realm of Christianity, indeed in the religious realm generally, than the connection between prayer and faith. They are spiritual symbionts, inextricably intertwined, breathing the same supersensible air, and destined to flourish, or to perish, together. Granting them each a single clause by way of compact definition, I would suggest the following: faith is the willful assertion that God not only exists but is there for one, available to one, involved caringly in one's life and affairs; prayer is faith in action, faith manifested, expressed, the actual calling upon God in the supernatural world. The mutuality, or perhaps the "system," is ironclad: if one has faith, one prays; if one prays, one demonstrates faith; if one fails to pray, faith slumbers; if one ceases to pray permanently, faith dies. And it goes without saying, of course, that faith's demise is Christianity's demise. Note this passage from Friedrich Heiler's classic study, *Prayer*,[10] to which I introduced the reader early on, and which presents the orthodox position on the matter: "Faith is, in Luther's judgment, 'prayer and nothing but prayer. He who does not pray or call upon God in his hour of need, assuredly does not think of Him as God, nor does he give Him the honor that is his due.'" Heiler continues,

> The great evangelistical mystic, Johann Arndt, constantly emphasized the truth that: "without prayer we cannot find God; prayer is the means by which we seek and find Him." Schleiermacher, the restorer of evangelical theology in the

nineteenth century, observes in one of his sermons: "to be religious and to pray—that is really the same thing." ... The same thought is expressed by the gifted evangelical divine, Richard Rothe, when he says, "the religious impulse is essentially the impulse to pray. It is by prayer, in fact, that the process of individual religious life is governed, the process of the gradual fulfillment of God's indwelling in the individual and his religious life. Therefore, the non-praying man is rightly considered to be religiously dead."

(p. xiii)

The upshot is clear: to get at the essence of Christian prayer is to get at the essence of Christian faith; to get at the essence of Christian faith is to get at the essence of the Christian religion.

Personal, individual, informal prayer, as opposed to codified, congregational prayer, is my main interest. This opposition, as it turns out, has a complex, disputatious history that is not our business here. It is enough to say that the individualism of prayer is usually traced back to Jeremiah and the Psalms of the Old Testament, that Jesus's prayer on the mount is widely regarded as the model prayer for individual Christians ("Not my will but Thine be done");[11] that Paul views personal, intercessory prayer as a cornerstone of spiritual practice; and that by Luther's day subjective, solitary prayer in which the worshiper gives himself over to a fervent, one-to-one relationship with his God is moving steadily toward the heart of Christianity, first for the Protestant, and then, with rather less momentum perhaps, for the Catholic as well. Accordingly, what follows will find us exploring from our particular theoretical angle the motivational dynamics of personal prayer in the Judeo-Christian tradition.

I rely upon a wide variety of sources, but for much of the discussion I utilize three pivotal, relatively recent treatments of the subject, namely, Heiler's *Prayer*, regarded by Hans Küng as the classical work on the topic and perhaps the most scholarly and comprehensive book on prayer ever to appear in the West; Ole Hallesby's *Prayer*, another classic, translated into several languages, reprinted 15 times in English alone, and probably the most widely read and influential Protestant discussion composed during the twentieth century; and Romano Guardini's *Prayer in Practice*, a treasured work among Roman Catholics and penned by one of the Church's most astute and respected thinkers—undoubtedly another classic treatment. Needless to say, for all three of these authors, prayer and faith are integrally connected: faith depends upon prayer for its existence, and prayer is nothing other than faith's signal manifestation. "We must bear in mind," declares Guardini, "that faith itself depends on prayer. ... Prayer is the basic act of faith as breathing is the basic act of life."[12] Until we pray, maintains Hallesby, we have no access to God, and God has no access to us: "He cannot gain admittance. To pray is to believe."[13] Faith is "prayer and nothing but prayer," writes Heiler, echoing Martin Luther, as we've just seen; without prayer, "we cannot find God" (p. xiii). The issue could hardly be plainer.

As we demonstrated at length in Chapter 2, the basic biological situation of parent-child interaction is centrally concerned with asking and receiving. Over and over again, thousands upon thousands of times, for years, the little one calls upon the big one for sustenance and support, and the big one responds. As I've stated, one would be hard-pressed to discover within the realm of nature another example of physiological and emotional conditioning to compare with this one in both depth and duration. As the parent-child relationship deepens and develops, it is steadily, unremittingly internalized by the growing youngster, not in some vague, metaphorical way, mind you, but emotively, affectively, organically, even neurally until it becomes the foundation of his budding perceptual existence. The caregiver is taken psychically inside and set up as an internal presence that is integrally connected to, indeed that is inseparable from, the emerging self. The early interaction is imprinted on the brain.

That the Judeo-Christian tradition of individual subjective prayer is ultimately petitionary in nature, in other words, that *asking* the Parent-God for help and loving support resides at its theological core, is indisputable. "The heart of all prayer is petition," states Heiler in one place (p. 17); and in another, "The free spontaneous petitionary prayer of the natural man exhibits the prototype of all prayer" (p. 1). "Whether we like it or not," declares C. H. Spurgeon, "asking is the rule of the Kingdom."[14] "Petition is the heart of prayer," writes Patrick Cotter.[15] Prayer is a "reverent petition to God," asserts James Pruitt.[16] The Judeo-Christian tradition of prayer, derived from both the Old and New Testaments, has always been "essentially petitionary," observes Walter A. Elwell in the *Evangelical Dictionary of Biblical Theology*.[17] Prayer is a "palpable thirst to ask," maintains Timothy Jones in *The Art of Prayer*.[18] "Prayer" is a "trustful appeal for aid in our necessity," holds the great sixteenth-century theologian Huldrych Zwingli.[19] "Give us this day our daily bread," requests the Lord's Prayer. One could cite a thousand similar passages.

As for asking and *receiving*, we have the following: "One has only to ask the Father in order to receive what is needed," states Elwell, echoing Scripture.[20] "Whatsoever ye shall ask in prayer, believing, ye shall receive," writes Hallesby, quoting Matthew 21:22.[21] "Petition" for "divine grace" is "freely bestowed," observes Heiler (p. 243). "God's power" is "capable of giving everything," maintains Guardini.[22] "Asking is our staple diet," asserts Gordon Lindsay; "the spirit suffers when it is not fed the Bread of Life."[23] "Prayer is the spiritual practice of asking God for what you want and accepting that it has been done once you have made the request," suggests Joshua David Stone in *Soul Psychology*; "God hears and answers all prayers."[24] "Do you know why the mighty God of the universe chooses to answer prayers?" inquires Richard S. Foster. "It is because His children ask."[25] "Everything will be given to you," declares Cotter in *How to Pray*; you are merely claiming "what is already yours."[26] Our asking is itself "God's answering," holds Jones.[27] The classical expression on the asking side has already been given, of course: "Give us this day our daily bread." On the receiving side we have, from Psalm 23, "The Lord is my shepherd; I shall not want" (vv. 1–2). Taken together, these two lines contain the pith of the petitionary mind-set.

My aim here, needless to say, is to establish a clear motivational link between the immediate context of supplicatory ritual and the basic biological situation of asking and receiving as earlier described. With such an aim in view, we must inquire, first, how does one go about this individual subjective praying, this asking the Parent-God for succor and support? Second, do the instructions for prayer proffered by the authoritative theologians call to mind *explicitly* the early parent-child interaction, the interaction in which the helpless, dependent little one calls upon the all-powerful provider for nourishment, attention, love, and care?

To pray successfully, one must adopt a certain attitude, a certain psychological posture, or stance. One does not come to God in just any way but in a very specific way indeed. I'm referring to an attitude of utter dependency, utter helplessness, utter submission, a willful attempt to get rid of one's will entirely. "Helplessness," writes Hallesby, "is unquestionably the first and surest indication of a praying heart. As far as I can see, prayer has been ordained only for the helpless" (p. 13). Hallesby goes on in the personal style that has made his book so influential:

> Listen, my friend! Your helplessness is your best prayer. It calls from your heart to the heart of God with greater effect than all your uttered pleas. He hears it from the very moment that you are seized with helplessness, and He becomes actively engaged at once in hearing and answering the prayer of your helplessness.

Thus "helplessness is the real secret and impelling power of prayer," the "very essence of prayer," the "decisive factor" that makes us "attached to God" and "more strongly dependent on Him" (pp. 14, 17, 16, 21). At the heart of successful prayer, states Heiler, dwells the "expression" of one's "weakness and dependency." One "submits" entirely to "God's will" and strives to make such "submission" a "permanent attitude" (p. 268). In fact, the "feeling of dependence" is the "universal feeling" that "animates" the whole of humanity's relation with the Deity; "no where . . . is it revealed so clearly as in prayer" (p. 77). "Man is ever conscious of his want and helplessness," maintains Guardini; "it is only right, therefore, that he should turn to the bountiful and almighty God, who is not only ready to give and to help, but greatly rejoices in it." Unless we "surrender without reservation" to the Creator, Guardini continues, unless we realize that "our very existence depends on God and His grace, our praying will be futile" (pp. 78, 64). Whereas our powers are limited, even puny, God's are infinite. He allows us "to breathe, to be, and above all, to approach him with our needs" (p. 134). Identical views may be instantly discovered in a thousand places. "Thy will be done," writes Cotter in *How to Pray* (p. 28). The "value of surrender" in prayer is "extraordinary," declares Larry Dossey in *Healing Words*.[28] "God's plan involves daily dependence on Him," asserts Lindsay in *Prayer That Moves Mountains*; "without Him we can do nothing" (p. 37). Nor is it only one's inward attitude, or stance, that determines the emotional, psychological quality of one's praying. One's bodily conduct may also enter integrally into the homeopathic picture. One can, of course, worship in any manner one chooses, at any time, in any place, in any posture. Yet for millions of Christians everywhere, inward dependency, helplessness, and submission are outwardly expressed, or mirrored, by prayer's traditional, ritualistic behaviors: suppliants kneel, bow down, close their eyes, fold their hands, even prostrate themselves entirely. Stephen F. Winward, in *Teach Yourself to Pray*, cites Psalm 95 as follows: "O come, let us worship and bow down, let us kneel before the Lord." In these "familiar words of the Venite," he observes, "the Psalmist invites us to let our bodies also participate in the worship of God."[29] Let's take a moment now to see how this theme of dependency, of helplessness, of submission is developed in the literature we are employing. Remember, we are looking for open, explicit, indubitable references to the basic biological situation of asking and receiving, in which the helpless little one petitions the caregiver for loving ministration and support.

"If you are a mother," asserts Hallesby,

> you will understand very readily this aspect of prayer. Your infant child cannot formulate in words a single petition to you. Yet the little one prays the best way he knows how. All he can do is cry, but you understand very well his pleading cry. All you need to do is see him in all his helpless dependence upon you, and a prayer touches your mother-heart, a prayer which is stronger than the loudest cry. He who is Father of all that is called mother and all that is called child in heaven and on earth deals with us in the same way.
>
> (p. 14)

Thus, we leave everything "in His hands." We cling in our helplessness to the "spirit of prayer" whenever we pray. We know "the Lord is at our side," and therefore we no longer feel frightened (pp. 105, 102, 119). Indeed, we know He is there constantly, and so we may tell Him "throughout the day," and during the nighttime, too, "how dependent we are upon Him." When his own "little boy" comes to him with "round baby eyes" and asks for his assistance, Hallesby writes, he sees at once the manner in which everyone should approach the "heavenly Father" (p. 121). We must "let our holy and almighty God care for us just as an infant surrenders himself to his mother's care" (p. 20).

And by the way, Hallesby is perfectly aware of the psychological dimension of the discussion; he is not using the theme of dependency in some metaphorical fashion: "Psychologically," he states, "helplessness is the sustaining and impelling power of prayer" (p. 25). Heiler agrees (p. 32) and also turns to childhood in illustration. The feeling of "dependence and impotence" is the key to successful praying, for we have no genuine power of our own; we are like "children who can do nothing" (p. 36). It is precisely this child-like mind-set, this child-like "trust and surrender," holds Heiler (pp. 130–31), that marks all the "eminent men" with a "genius for prayer," all the "great men of religion" (p. 253). We turn to God "in prayer," writes Guardini, "as the child in distress turns to his mother." Jesus taught us, Guardini goes on, "that we should turn to the Father and ask Him for our daily bread," for the "necessities" of our "daily life" (p. 77). This is because the Almighty knows best what is "needful" for us. He knows how to love us truly, how to look after us in our "helplessness" and "want" (p. 78). "God will be found in supplication," claims George Arthur Buttrick, "not by our seeking" but "by a response . . . to One of whom we are dimly aware—as a child, half waking, responds to the mother who bends over him."[30] When we pray, maintains Jones, "we take hold of His willingness to listen and move; we exercise our right as children to influence a loving parent" (p. 107). Cries Horatius Bonar in *The New Book of Christian Prayers*: "Lead me by Thine own hand, choose out the path for me."[31] Once again, a thousand similar quotations may be instantly found in the literature. The dependent child relying on the loving Parent-God is probably Christianity's most common depiction of the supplicatory relationship. Thus a culminating question arises: why does successful prayer hinge so decisively upon the assumption of an infantile, child-like state, a state of helplessness, dependence, and submission that is persistently rendered in terms that recall the early parent-child interaction?

The ritual is designed to trigger the attractor state, to "prime" the worshiper for the reawakening of the core relationship with the biological caregiver. One's praying becomes the "cue" for the emergence of implicit, state-dependent memory, for the inward perception and feeling that one is still united with the parental object, now transmuted through religious narrative into the invisible, compassionate Deity of the putative supernatural realm. This is why the worshiper "turns to God as the child in distress turns to his mother"; why he "lets God care for him as an infant surrenders himself to his mother's care"; why he adopts an attitude of "child-like trust," of utter "dependency" and "helplessness," frequently upon his knees (preambulation). In the performance of this infantilizing enactment or "play," the very heart of Christian faith, the worshiper seeks unconsciously to undo the past, to reverse the flow of time, to restore the enormous adaptational advantages he possessed as a symbiotic partner or "organ" of an omnipotent, loving protector and provider. The rite of prayer attests, on the one hand, to the preciousness and power of the first relationship, to the severity of our early needs, to the depth of our conditioning as little ones when asking and receiving were the order of the day, to the persistence of our longing for unconditional love and care—in a word, to the urgency of our unconscious requirements as they arise from the foundational years. On the other hand, and just as significantly, the rite of supplication reflects the anxieties and the exigencies of the moment, the problematical now of the prayer's existence, his present concerns, his present wishes (including those for the future), his present need for reassurance and support. Writes Walter Burkert, "Rituals are complicated, ambivalent, and not seldom opaque even to those who practice them. . . . It makes more sense to see them as cultural attempts to make the 'facts of life' manageable and predictable; to perform an act of artificial social creation, as if to veil biology."[32] We don't have to puzzle very long to espy the biology that is veiled by supplication: separation from the matrix; the loss of infantile omnipotence; dealing with a dangerous, unpredictable world; the inescapable facts of accident, illness, aging, and death. The point is, Christianity is not merely based imagistically on an infantile model through baptismal doctrine; it actually recreates one in prayer. Suppliants, spurred on by their synaptic structure, by the very neurological makeup of their mind-brains, *act out* their infantile wishes. The biological foundation of infantile life is ritualistically transformed through homeopathic magic into the cornerstone of Christian practice.

## Toward the Nature of the Holy Spirit (Prayer and Faith Continued)

The appetite for symbiotic merger, the longing to undo the past, to dissolve ego boundaries and reunite with a succoring, all-powerful provider appears with striking, unmistakable clarity everywhere in the Christian literature of supplication. How could it not? The passion for symbiotic union is but a variation on prayer's central figure, namely, that of the helpless child crying out to the mighty Parent-God. In this way, the most primitive, elemental asking and receiving that one enacts in prayer stems from the most primitive, elemental experience one undergoes early on, namely, that of existing as an "organ" of the parent, that of being oneself and the caregiver, too. The "yearning for union," maintains Guardini, is the "first motive of prayer." Our "soul longs for union with God." We "cannot be without Him." When we pray, "our prayer becomes love, for love means seeking to be completely at one with another autonomous being" (pp. 55–58). Yet, Guardini goes on, "only God can create that nearness that fulfills our yearning." Because desire for the Almighty is "inborn in human nature," we "cry" for Him "again and again." Guardini sums everything up with the assertion that *the yearning for God, for union, is also prayer*" (pp. 56–58, my emphasis). Let's look further.

Prayer's "deepest motive," observes Heiler, "is the burning desire of the heart which finds rest in blissful union with God" (p. 104). The "yearning for blessed union," Heiler continues, is capable of "overbearing" all the other "themes" that often find their way into supplication, namely, "guilt, grace, and sin" (p. 127). In fully successful prayer, states Heiler, "God and soul are bound together in indissoluble unity." The "contrast of subject and object which rules the soul's normal life is dissolved." One "fuses with Him in deepest unity." One encounters Him "face to face" (pp. 141–42, 160). "God is in me and I am in Him," cries Elsa of Neustadt (cited in Heiler, p. 142). "I sink myself in Thee; I in Thee, Thou in me," exclaims Gerhard Tersteegen (cited in Heiler, p. 190). "Thou alone art my food and drink," pronounces Thomas à Kempis (cited in Heiler, p. 209). "If I am not united with Thee I shall be forever unhappy," insists Gertrude of Hefta (cited in Heiler, p. 209). "I am Thou and Thou art I," declare ecstatic, mystical prayers worldwide (see Heiler, p. 190). The famous historian Arnold Toynbee expresses it this way:

> When prayer—the communion between human person and divine person—has been raised to its highest degree of spiritual intensity, it is transmuted into another kind of experience. At this higher spiritual level, personality is transcended, and, with it, the separateness that is personality's limitation. At this supra-personal spiritual height, the experience is unitive. At this height, God and man do not communicate with each other because, at this height, they are identical.[33]

Of special fascination is the extent to which the urge for prayerful union with God reflects, or better, picks up, the phenomenology of the early parent-child interaction. To adopt the infantile model is to reexperience psychologically key relational features of the intimate primal bond. "As a true mother dedicates her life to the care of her children," writes Hallesby, "so the eternal God in His infinite mercy has dedicated Himself externally to the care of his frail and erring children" (p. 15). Specific, clinical details on the biological side of this simile actually present themselves as wondrous, "spiritual" attributes on the religious, supplicatory side. Needless to say, if prayer recreates through imitative magic the asking and receiving of life's initial stages, as it surely does, then the appearance of those clinical traces in supplication is exactly what we should expect. We note in Christopher Bollas's study, *The Shadow of the Object*, for example, the manner in which the caregiver transforms the infant's world. "It is undeniable," Bollas declares, "that as the infant's other self, the mother transforms the baby's internal and external environment." If the infant is distressed, Bollas continues, the "resolution of discomfort is achieved by the apparition-like presence of the mother" who arrives in a timely manner to remove the distress. Bollas calls this a "primary transformation": emptiness, agony, and anger become fullness and contentment.[34]

Over and over again during life's opening stages—thousands upon thousands of times—the parent and the child are joined in such ministering, transformational encounters. When we discover the Lord through our supplication, Heiler informs us, "a wonderful metamorphosis takes place." No longer do we feel uncertain about things; no longer do we have sensations of doubt and dread. Rather, we undergo "the blissful consciousness of *being cared for*" by a "protecting higher Power" (pp. 259–60, my emphasis). "Confidence, peace, hope, and trust" suffuse us, "often quite suddenly," and always, Heiler notes, involuntarily and unconsciously (p. 259). Surely the reader will recognize at once what is going on here. The adoption of the supplicatory, infantile model (as a response to some sort of crisis or stress) triggers the old transformational feelings that reside at the core of maternal ministration, maternal care. We undergo again the elemental transformational experience that we underwent thousands of times during the early period when our call to the succoring figure brought about a change in our internal and external environment. To pray is to reactivate both wishfully and adaptively a basic, primitive, biological conditioning that simply went too deep into our neural structure ever to be forgotten or relinquished. What served us well at the start will, through imitative or homeopathic magic, continue to serve us along the way. We will ask, receive, and feel transformed—which is to say, better—by the time the process concludes.

Everywhere in the literature of supplication we come upon this theme. "God was present, though invisible," declares one of William James's praying subjects; "He fell under no one of my senses, yet my consciousness perceived Him." And then, "It was . . . as if my personality had been transformed by the presence of a *spiritual spirit*."[35] We might note here Bollas's point that the mother's appearance in response to the little one's summons has an "apparition-like quality."[36] "Prayer has true transformative power," states Terry Lynn Taylor in *The Alchemy of Prayer*. Not only is God always there but just by connecting to Him through supplication we are altered alchemically, our leaden existence turning suddenly to gold.[37] To pray, observes Guardini, is to shed our old being and enter into a nascent state of spiritual communion at the heart of which resides "the seed of a new life." This seed, this new life, says Guardini—and here is the early biological arrangement itself—"is given to us to tend as the new born child is given to the mother" (p. 8). "Change me into Thyself," cries David of Augsburg (cited in Heiler, p. 183). "Take me up and transform me," cries Peter of Alcantara (cited in Heiler, p. 183). Clearly then, to supplicate along Christian lines, to indulge the infantile, baptismal model of asking and receiving, is to engage in what Bollas calls "the wide-ranging collective search for an object that is identified with the metamorphosis of the self." The suppliant "sustains the terms of the earliest objective tie within a mythic structure" (the overall religious creed). The object (God) is sought for its "function as a signifier of transformation." The quest is "to surrender to it as a medium that alters the self" (Christianity's "new man" as in Col. 3:10).[38] In many instances, of course, a specific crisis sparks the longing for the transformational presence, as was exactly the case early on. Yet a basic, underlying motivation of Christian prayer as a whole is to experience the hit of *transformational union* over and over again, in one's daily existence, just as one experiences it regularly during the addictive, crisis-laden phase of the initial parent-child interaction. To paraphrase Jesus, Christians enter a heavenly place when they become as little children (Matt. 18:3), and there is no better way to become as little children than to act the role out through the imitative magic of prayer.

With the context firmly in mind, let's examine a specific, high-quality guide to successful supplication for Christians. How are they to go about their praying? What should they expect along the way and at the moment of truth when the Holy Spirit (or Ghost)[39] joins them? Let's get down to the nitty-gritty of this magical business. If prayer "does not well up from our innermost being," writes Guardini, "we had better not pray at all" (p. 1). Forced prayer is inadvisable. At the same time, successful prayer depends upon the "right attitude" (p. 3), upon a firm decision to work at it, frequently and methodically. After all, we are attempting to plant the seed of a "new life" (p. 8), and unless we plant that seed carefully our spiritual project will fail. We must always bear in mind, contends Guardini, that our new life, in contrast with our old, natural one of thoughts and feelings, is essentially hidden; in fact, "it rarely penetrates the threshold of cognition" (p. 8). Thus, the danger ceaselessly lurks that one may "neglect it and allow it to be smothered." How can this be? That is, how can our new life be so precious to us, so crucial, so all-determining, and at the same time so indistinct, so elusive, so fragile? The answer lies in the fact that this life emanates from a spirit, from the "Holy Ghost" (p. 8). It is given to us by God through the "Holy Ghost," and we must tend to it as the "mother" tends to her "new-born child" (p. 8).

As Guardini develops this theme over several pages, a number of key ideas and images emerge. Although we need God and God knows we need Him, "we cannot perceive" Him "in the manner in which we perceive objects and people" (p. 9). God is "more real than anything else," and yet He is also hidden. He can be seen only by "the inner eye of faith," by an "inner vision" that is "often clouded" (p. 9). In this way, *we have no immediate experience of God* (p. 9, my emphasis). Only through "faith" may we find him in *"the emptiness and darkness of the unknown"* (p. 9, my emphasis). It is, notes Guardini, "a great mystery" (p. 9).[40] To prepare ourselves for supplication, then, we must concentrate; we must "exclude everything else" from our perception; we must "recall ourselves from everyone and everywhere." God alone "matters now" (pp. 13–14). We must go inward until we can say with Moses, "Here am I" (Exod. 3:4) (p. 15). Additionally, we must "awaken our inner intention" so that it may "focus itself on its object." We must "clear the inner eye" so that it sees true (p. 16). We must step into that *"mysterious place"* of supplication, into that "centre of power" where the self resides, where the self can "take root" and "be present" (p. 18, my emphasis). What is this mysterious place? It is "the realm of the spirit," states Guardini (p. 19), a realm where we may realize, in the midst of our concentration, that "God is here," the "Living," the "Holy," is here, and "here also am I" (p. 21). Accomplishing this supplicatory task, observes our theological instructor, means drawing upon sources that lie deeper in our being, deeper than our "conscious faculties" (p. 21). We have to find the depth of our "essential being" and dwell therein. Although God is in the world, He is not of the world. When we say He is present, He "remains hidden," even as we say it (p. 22). Only our "faith" can sustain us as we *journey out into this silent darkness* (p. 22, my emphasis), for God is "as nobody and nothing is. He is from Himself and by reason of Himself" (p. 24). His attributes, His vibration, His breath alone are in this world (p. 25). He is that which can't be named, the "all-embracing ineffable," the "mystery of existence." He has "no face as we understand it."

He is indeed "beyond all human concept" (pp. 25–26). These are the strange, even astonishing truths that we must digest before we can successfully make the journey. Guardini then moves closer to the thing itself, recapitulating key notions in the context as he goes.

With the reader's permission, I will also head directly toward the goal in a series of brief, bold strokes. We withdraw to a secluded, silent place; there, we find "the sanctuary of our innermost heart" in which He is "always present" (p. 35). We try to visualize his reality with our "inner eye." Alone, concentrated, reverent, and kneeling, we achieve what Guardini terms "the invisible attitude" (p. 39). The experience of prayer now commences: we enter a void that is "vibrant with being." We have the feeling He may be present in a "special, intimate way," close to us, abiding, even though "we cannot see Him" (p. 43). Then comes the climax: "into this void of not-seeing, not-hearing, and not-experiencing, there may at times enter something, something inexpressible, yet significant—a hint of meaning amidst apparent nothingness which prevails over the nothingness" (p. 44). What is this something that enters? What is it that is here, that is present with us? What is it that "our spiritual organs of perception" are detecting (p. 45)? It is, declares Guardini, a "breath," a "vibration," both "faint and intangible" (p. 44). And he continues, with great conviction,

> This breath, this vibration, is the manifestation of God; faint and intangible though it is, it can support our faith, so that we may persevere. If faith perseveres the void may suddenly be filled, for God is not a mere fantasy or idea, or feeling, but the all-pervading reality. He does not dwell above us indifferent in the blissful remoteness of celestial spheres, but with us.
>
> (p. 44)

If we want Him, if we wish to have Him in our lives, then we must ask for Him, seek for Him, cry out for Him in prayer (p. 45). There is no other way. Prayer alone opens the door to the "reality of God" (p. 45).

What we have here are vividly descriptive, detailed instructions for reaching, not the realm of the Spirit, but the realm of implicit recollection, the unconscious, the uncanny. We withdraw from everyday reality; we choose some isolated, solitary spot; there, we turn our attention inward toward the sphere of our subjectivity; we concentrate intensively as we enter the void, the mysterious darkness, the deep psychic strata well below the threshold of our consciousness. What are we looking for in our "invisible attitude"? What is it that we are seeking in our withdrawn, concentrated condition, upon our knees, reverently, as "little children"? We are seeking a hidden spirit with a nonordinary face and body, a concealed "centre of power," where the self, our self, not only takes root but enjoys its essential being. The loving God we struggle to detect is inextricably connected to us. Then what happens, if all goes well? We sense that we are not alone; the "void" is filled; something else is with us; something else is "present." We detect, perhaps, a breath, or perhaps a vibration, and as Guardini says, it is enough to convince us that we've made contact. The elusive, hidden, mysterious spirit (Holy Spirit or Holy Ghost) is *there*. Intimate union prevails over "nothingness." As it turns out, of course, that "spirit" has always been there in a perfectly natural, nonspiritual way. What we've contacted through our supplicatory action is the deeply internalized, synaptic trace of a relationship, not an object or a thing, but a relationship. More specifically, we've rediscovered the origins of our selfhood in loving, affective attunement, the intimate, awakening interaction from which our awareness of and participation in the world arose—a breath, a vibration, a hidden, mysterious, foundational presence, namely, ourselves and the ministering other in face-to-face, life-sustaining symbiosis. Guardini's "void" is the great space of *memory*, the yawning past, the yawning implicit, unconscious region, the darkness from which we emerge through the succoring attentions of the apparition-like parental figure who hovers over us in the beginning. Once again from Buttrick, "God will be found by a response [in prayer] to One of whom we are dimly aware—as a child, half-waking, responds to the mother who bends over him."[41] Remember, the caregiver is attuned to our needs. When she responds empathetically to our requirements, we are filled with wonderful, addictive sensations, vibrations, energies, with our feeling response to her powerful transformational capacities. Indeed, the caregiver's loving, feeling ministrations may be said to awaken us to life, to "switch us on," to make us "hum" with the feeling of existence itself. We are alive, we are vibrating, not simply because she was, but because she communicated her aliveness to us and through us, or conversely, because her rays, her energies, protected us from the deadness that the lack of mothering invariably engenders. Our genetic vitality must be nurtured into life. It is not the Holy Spirit who does this but another human being. A person, not a spirit, has this power, which explains why Christianity paradoxically and passionately and intuitively insists that the Holy Spirit is both a spirit and a *person*: the worshiper must be reminded of this personhood doctrinally so that he may bring to supplication, as well as to various other rites and beliefs that foster sacred union, an implicit or feeling recollection of his own biological life, for it is precisely such recollection that will trigger the attractor state of parent-child bonding and hence, the worshiper's theological, emotional assent to the particulars of the creed, its spiritual entities and supernatural claims. We pray for many reasons, of course, and among them is the longing to get back to the source of our aliveness, to feel still again the indelible, primal "hit" we felt over and over again during the early time as the caregiver focused her loving energies, her loving rays, upon us. We eagerly adopt the infantile model of supplication because we would have that, again and again, just as we had it early on—world without end.

Guardini's guide to supplication returns us to the period of one common breathing, one common heartbeat, the period of not only face-to-face but breast-to-breast contact, of exquisitely sensitive empathetic bonding, of keen, almost subliminal registration of the smallest bodily sign, the tiniest shift of mood, of atmosphere, the tiniest stirring of infantile life, the breath, the vibration of our inchoate existence as it was neurally mapped onto our emergent mind-brain. This is what we are listening for in Guardini's "void." This is what we may detect within our inward organs of perception. Let's bear firmly in mind that Guardini asks us (p. 77), as do other doctors of prayer, to approach the Lord as the child in distress approaches his mother. We are instructed to return psychologically, attitudinally, perceptually, emotionally to specifically *the first relationship* from which our awareness of things arises. Clearly then, the principles of imitative magic lurk between the lines of Guardini's *Prayer in Practice*. His discussion comprises a kind of magical sequence directed at the self, a kind of self-magic, a kind of self-induced magical trance that entirely depends upon our empathy toward ourselves, upon our own keen listening, upon our own keen attention, upon our own keen ability to detect our essential, originative being, our own relational roots in the mysterious interactional past of intimate vibrations and breathings. The face of God is unique, mysterious, and nonordinary because it is both a face and a mirror; it contains the unconscious lineaments of the relationship in which the self was born; the body of God is unique, mysterious, nonordinary because it reflects both a oneness and a twoness, a process of symbiotic joining, or *union*, from which a single, living creature emerges into personhood. "We have no immediate experience of God" (p. 9) because our experience is embedded in the mnemonic recesses of our early existence (the realm of infantile amnesia), the strong time of life-giving nurturance and vitality when the parental "centre of power" was our center, our universe, our all. Accordingly, we are able to discover the supernatural realm because we've been there all along; we've always existed in a realm of hidden, unseen presences. Guardini is merely guiding us to our own inner world, to the traces of elemental, affective "vibrations" that resonate at our deepest psychological levels, and when we find that place we are persuaded and call it "God" or "Holy Spirit" because we have no other perceptual way of explaining it to ourselves. We can't *see* our implicit recollections, of which the Holy Spirit is ultimately one. There is a mystery here, to be sure, but it is the mystery of the unconscious, not of the supernatural. Everything involved in the Holy Spirit's arrival, everything without exception, has been in our minds and only in our minds all along; or, to turn the coin over, there is nothing involved here outside of ourselves.

We continually hear from the religious experts that prayer is rooted in the unconscious, reaches into the unconscious, arises from the unconscious, engages the unconscious regions, and so forth, but we are never offered anything specific on this score, never told how the process works, and never made aware of the connections. "Religious emotions in the pious man," states Heiler, "force their way unconsciously and unexpectedly, from evident and inner necessity, to expression in prayer. Prayer wells up from the subconscious life of the soul" (p. 233). And again, "Men take over faith in God from the community in which they were born; but how it first arose cannot here be discussed; doubtless it flowed from a whole series of psychological forces" (p. 3). Prayer, asserts Dossey, is grounded in "the power of the unconscious instead of the conscious mind"; it "need not always be 'thought.' . . . 'Unconscious prayer' is possible" (p. 18). When we pray successfully, holds James, "subconscious forces take the lead" (p. 195). One's "whole subconscious life," one's "impulses, . . . faiths, . . . needs, . . . divinations," has "prepared the premises of which [one's] consciousness now feels the weight of the result" (p. 73). As for those premises themselves, as for the "divine personages" that determine the attitudes and practices of the believer, including his supplication, they are "exerted by the instrumentality of pure ideas, of which nothing in the individual's past experience directly serves as a model" (p. 55). We may now appreciate, however, that something *is* there in the "individual's past experience" that *does* "directly serve as a model." I am referring, of course, to the basic biological situation, internalized deeply into the worshiper's mind-brain and explicitly extended in Christian theological handbooks as the chief imitative prerequisite to successful supplication. No one invented prayer. It arose from the unconscious strata through the irresistible interaction of neurological structure and wishful affect. It was and still is dedicated to the emotionally attractive, soothing proposition that we are not separate, and alone, and impotent, and mortal, in an enigmatic, indifferent universe. Surely from this perspective we may now grasp why the doctors of prayer inform us that we *receive* simply by *asking*, indeed, that our asking *is* our receiving. It goes like this: when we *ask* we restore the early period; we trigger in the unconscious the symbiotic union we enjoyed in the beginning; we jog through our prayerful *state* the state-dependent memory of our attachment to the loving provider. Merely to pray, then, is to gain what we are seeking.

## The Eucharist

Baptism creates the broad psychological framework within which the practice of Christianity will move forward, namely, the framework of the parent-child relationship with Jesus as "Abba" and the practitioner as "little child" following after his parental guide. Prayer, as we've just seen, encourages the worshiper to act out this relationship on a regular basis by adopting an attitude of helplessness and dependency, by asking the Big One for assistance, love, and support. When the Christian turns to his Lord as an infant in distress turns to his mother, to echo the theological experts, he manifests his faith, which is to say, he establishes himself as a genuine believer in the Christian plan for achieving "salvation." With the Eucharist we come to what we may regard as the third pillar of the ritualistic structure on which the Christian religion is founded, to what the *Catechism of the Catholic Church* calls "the source and summit of the Christian life."[42] Here, through a ceremony in which the body and the blood of a god are actually or symbolically consumed, the magical nature of the believer's participation, the believer's construction of his alternate, magical identity, becomes so palpable, so striking, may I say so transparent, that it has for 2,000 years elicited the critical attention of a wide variety of observers including ardent, devout Christians themselves. Writes Stafford in *Knowing the Face of God*, "In a sacrificial meal an ox never became other than an ox. The sacrificial meals were certainly not considered divine flesh. They were mere dead animals augmented by cereal or oil. Nor is there a precedent in our own experience. No host has ever asked me if I would like to nibble on him. How, then, can we understand what Jesus meant?" Stafford then declares, "It was not entirely unjust that the early Christians were accused of cannibalism. Any religion that has a meal for its sacramental centerpiece and that speaks of eating the flesh and the blood of its God is asking for misunderstanding."[43] With an eye focused sharply on the potential for "misunderstanding," then, let's begin to examine *both* what Jesus may have "meant" by all this and what all this means to us from the naturalistic, analytical angle we're developing here.

John Wesley's famous devotional poem takes us straight to the essence of the matter.

> Ah, show me that happiest place,
> The place of Thy people's abode,
> Where saints in an ecstasy gaze,
> And hang on a crucified God.
>
> 'Tis there I would always abide
> And never a moment depart,

Concealed in the cleft of Thy side,
Eternally held in Thy heart.[44]

Here is the core magical wish of the Christian religion as a whole: to enter (or better, reenter) the body of the Parent-God and to remain in that body forever, "eternally" as Wesley renders it. Christianity seeks to transform, to metamorphose, to turn inside out or upside down nothing less than the chief biological facts of our earthly existence, namely, the cessation of infantile symbiosis, our separation from the original matrix of parental care; our smallness, our vulnerability to the forces of nature, to the implacable material world of accident and illness; and last, of course, our mortality, the final, inevitable manifestation of the biological circumstance in which we discover ourselves. All of this is simply erased as we crawl into the crucified Jesus, using the wound in His side as our entrance way, and take up our permanent residence there as "members" or "organs" of His sacred body. Suddenly, magically, we are eternally secure, united with an all-powerful protector and provider whose chief preoccupation and purpose in the world is (like mother's) neither more nor less than watching over *us*.

The biological facts of separation, smallness, and death are biblically presented in the Book of Genesis where the writer endeavors to explain why an omnipotent, loving God would fashion such harsh realities for his specially created offspring, His children. Adam and Eve, god-like, immortal, and enjoying regular, consistent contact with their beneficent, all-powerful Creator, succumb to the wiles of Satan (originally a diabolic figure in dualistic Zoroastrianism appropriated by the ancient Hebrews) and immediately lose their utopian advantages: they are separated from the paradisal garden and its parental Designer; they are vulnerable to the adversarial forces of their new, fallen surroundings against which they must now struggle mightily and continuously; and finally, they must die and disappear from the world forever—the most chilling result of their disobedience to God's injunctions. As for the advent of Jesus Christ in relation to the Old Testamental depiction of our fallen, tragic nature, He arrives upon the earth to put everything right again, to achieve, or better, reachieve, the beginning, the strong time of loving union, empowered security, and immortality as expressed in both baptismal rite and in the verses of John Wesley, to which the reader's attention was directed a few sentences earlier. In a word, the advent of Jesus creates for the Christian a way *to get back in* the paradisal garden his forebears lost, to regain the salvational arrangement the Bible depicts in its opening passages. In the naturalistic terms I am employing here, the Christian now possesses a magical, ritualistic method to cancel out, to erase, to remove from the landscape the biological facts of separation, smallness, and death that comprise the sorrowful conditions of his "fallen" planetary journey.

What interests us here above all is the way in which the mythical materials in the Book of Genesis simultaneously *echo and veil* the biological realities upon which our lives are based. We *are* separated (or expelled) from the garden of infantile, child-like innocence, as we develop toward adolescence and maturity; we *are* deprived of our initial grandeur, our narcissistic omnipotence, as our global identification with the parental big one gradually fades off; our symbiotic, dependent relationship with our provider, our feeder, *does* ultimately terminate as we begin to make our own way in a challenging and frequently difficult environment; we *do* confront eventually our own personal mortality, our own personal demise and disappearance from the world: one day, as everyone else preceding us and following us, we will be bodily, sensorially *gone*. All of this reverberates beneath the mythical surface of Genesis which, as I've suggested already, was fashioned by Hebrew scribes with a very good sense of the human condition and a very strong urge to indicate *how* that condition arose in a Creation molded by a loving Parent-God upon Whose mercies they relied and to Whom they addressed their prayers.

The connection between "sin" and separation is a key item, of course, and reflects in itself the biological reality of the first society, or the personal, private Eden in which each of us discovers himself early on. When the child is "bad," he or she experiences the diminishment of his or her affective affiliation with or closeness to the governing parental presence; such looming separation serves as a powerful incentive for the child to "behave." Yet no matter how "good" the child is, no matter how carefully he or she follows the rules, he or she must still one day undergo separation from the initial symbiotic interaction. Accordingly, the Edenic materials in the Book of Genesis trigger in the believer foundational, implicit recollection of his actual, developmental experience as he moves from primal union, from primal symbiotic bonding with the big one, toward his present, grown-up condition of separation, smallness, and mortality. *At the same time*, the magical, supernatural *reversal* of that "fallen" condition, its veiling, its erasure, its cancellation, is also linked to biological facts, is also connected integrally to biological conditions that are deeply grooved into our neurological makeup at the level of implicit or unconscious memory. I mean, the supernatural reversal, the veiling, the solution in short, also carries within itself the first Edenic conditions of symbiotic union and narcissistic perfection that the believer actually experienced at the biological level during the opening months and years of his earthly existence. They too reside in the realm of implicit memory; they too are rooted firmly, neurologically, and synaptically in the unconscious realm of infantile amnesia and can thus be utilized on the plane of magic. When the good news comes to supplant the bad news, it finds its origins in the same biological place from which the bad news emanated. The believer *was* at one time *in*, not out; the believer *did know* at one time that someone was always *there*, watching over him. When Jesus enters with his "comedic" resolution of life's "tragedy" (restoration of Edenic perfection, the cleansing of "sin," and the saintly transcendence and immortality of each and every sheep-like follower), He relies as do all talented healers and gurus upon the biological realities the believers once experienced for themselves during the course of their own lives. Salvation cannot be based on air, on "spirits," on words alone; it must also be based on flesh, for it is flesh ultimately that prompts accession, that arouses the "yes, I believe" in the candidate, in the prospective convert. The Savior's invitation back into the Garden feels *real* because the Garden is *still there* at the level of implicit, biological, affective or fleshly memory.

To put the whole matter somewhat differently and in the process to recall our earlier discussion of prayer's nature and efficacy, when Jesus offers to His followers His Edenic salvational scheme of divine union ("we ... are one body in Christ" [Rom. 12:5]), saintly cleansing ("called to be saints" [I Cor. 1:2]), and immortality ("O death, where is thy sting?" [I Cor. 15:55]), when He invites His devotees to *go back in*, to enter His body, which is the Church itself in its pure, Edenic, sinless condition, He awakens the Holy Spirit in the worshiper, which means, He jogs the early, implicit recollection of actual, biological experience, of infantile, childhood security, protection, provision, and love that resides neurologically, mnemonically, at the foundation of the worshiper's mental apparatus. The early period of symbiotic, biologic interaction is mythically *reentered* or *resubmitted* into the mind-brain such that it calls forth the implicit, unconscious, feeling recollection of the desired salvational condition. In the simplest possible terms, to be "saved" Christian style, one must be "innocent" *as a baby is innocent*; and one must be *attached to* or *contained in* the body of a Parent-God, or a God/Church that *is* the body of a Parent-God (Jesus's body [I Cor. 12:27]). One must be *in* an organ relationship. Salvation is finally *morphological* and entails the interfusion of *bodies*, which is the vital, primal essence of neotenous, human, biological infancy and childhood. When this essence is reexperienced mnemonically, when it is reentered into the perceptual apparatus disguisedly yet recognizably through sacred myth and magical rite—in short, when this essence is experienced again through state-dependent memory it precipitates the emergence of associative affect known doctrinally as "the Holy Spirit."[45] One can *feel* his own salvation, and the truth of Christian doctrine, because one harbors a premanufactured version of both in his own neurologic, memorial makeup. "Yes," says the convert, in the grip of his wishful emotions; "I *can* be saved; I can unite with Christ; I can be pure and innocent; I can escape extinction; the Edenic message is true; Paradise *can* be regained. Hallelulia!" In this way, the entire magical, mythical structure of Christianity, as founded on the Old and New Testaments, and especially on the New Testamental notion of the Holy Spirit, is rooted in the biological experience of the worshiper and in nothing else. Paradoxically revealed and veiled in the same mythic, magical, religious moment, Christian theology provides the believer with an alternate "spiritual" self in which he can defensively or adaptively indulge himself while the biological facts and destiny of his actual bodily life simply go forward on the earth. No wonder the Holy Spirit is regarded by the Christian faith as "the Comforter."[46] It, the Holy Spirit, provides the religious seeker with the implicit memorial materials that goad him or in a very real sense "spook" him into accepting the reality of supernatural entities with the capacity to alter, metamorphose, and transform the ineluctable biological facts of separation, smallness, and death to which his earthly existence is and always will be irreversibly linked.

The Eucharist's significance from this analytic angle comes clearly into view: it, the Eucharist, provides the believer with a magic, ritualistic way to get into the body of Jesus, and to get Jesus's body into his own. It is psychologically morphological, devoted to the interfusion of bodies. Let's remember, the rite of baptism from which the believer emerges newborn as the "little child" of the Parent-God is officially, theologically, doctrinally *completed* in and through the Eucharist wherein the worshiper becomes "a living member of," indeed "ingrafted to," the "body" of Jesus Christ, either symbolically as in various Protestant enactments, or "transubstantially" as in Catholic and High Protestant practices.[47] Accordingly, the Eucharist allows the worshiper to reinstate mnemonically the organ relationship, the morphological interfusion, that distinguishes his initial biological condition, the opening circumstance of his existence on the planet. His baptismal, Eucharistic *state* achieves as its implicit, dynamic underpinning the neurological, *state-dependent memory* of what he actually *knew* and *relied upon* during the months and years in which his neotenous, helpless condition made him utterly dependent on the big one for his survival and well-being. He *fed* upon the caregiver physically and emotionally in order to *have life*, and now he does so again. Here, precisely here, is the origin of the magical, homeopathic, alternate identity with which Christianity provides its followers to ensure not only their sense of security as they go about their lives but also their passionate attachment to the creed, their wish, their longing to cleave unto the Church, a Church that offers itself to the worshiper as literally *the body of Christ*.[48] Separation, smallness, mortality; our biological heritage; the consequence of our putative lapse in the Garden of Eden—all of that vanishes miraculously when we eat the Lord's flesh and drink the Lord's blood, thus getting Him inside of us and us inside of Him. The worshiper gets "hooked" on his religion, or alternatively, surrenders to the Holy Spirit working within him, when the implicit recollection of his original biological dependency (the "opiate") bites mythically into his emotive memorial structure. It helps markedly, of course, that such magical goings-on transpire within cathedrals and churches, otherworldly, mysterious, cultic habitations in which priestly, "spiritual" emissaries from the beyond, attired in special, distinguishing garb, administer the miraculous bread and wine. Kneeling with open mouths, the bedazzled "little children," the religious seekers, take in their transformational materials like little birds, trusting in the all-powerful Big One to give them union, protection, and everlasting life: "Rock of Ages, cleft for me,/let me hide myself in thee," or as Wesley put it in the verses at which we earlier glanced, "concealed in the cleft of Thy side,/Eternally held in Thy heart."

Let's recall Jesus's New Testamental pronouncements on the ingestion of His flesh and blood:

> Verily, verily I say unto you, Except ye eat the flesh of the Son of Man, and drink his blood, ye have no life in you. Whoso eateth my flesh, and drinketh my blood, hath eternal life; and I will raise him up at the last day. For my flesh is meat indeed, and my blood is drink indeed. He that eateth my flesh, and drinketh my blood, dwelleth in me, and I in him. As the living Father sent me, and I live by the Father: so he that eateth me, even he shall live by me.
>
> (John 6:53–57)

Thus are we returned to the Beginning, to the strong time of our inception: the flesh and blood of Jesus, who has taken the place of the biological parent (Matt. 10:35–38) and become the Parent-God of His newly baptized "little children" (Matt. 18:3), give "life" *explicitly* to His followers, His offspring, creating them afresh and altered along magical, ritualistic lines. When His devotees, His communicants, eat His flesh and drink His blood, they abolish ego boundaries; they restore the stage of symbiotic oneness, the initial biological condition that precedes the passage to the separation stage of development. The partakers "dwell" in their Parent-God, and their Parent-God dwells in them, with no separation stage in view. The organic interfusion, the morphological mixing of bodies, goes on forever, "eternally" as John Wesley wished it to do in the devotional poem with which I opened this section. Separation, smallness, and mortality simply *vanish* from the individual Christian's brand-new salvational existence on the planet. The perfections of Eden are regained, once and for all. How does the magician express it as he pulls the curtain away from his ingenious, unfathomable contraption? "Presto chango!" In reality, of course, the Christian's new, infantilized nature (or the restoration of his prelapsarian self) derives entirely from his own implicit recollection of dyadic parent-child unity during the primal portion of his own biological life. The magical Eucharistic *state* triggers the *state-dependent memory*, designated by Christians themselves as the elusive, airborne, transcendental Holy Spirit. "We are members of his body, of his flesh, and of his bones," declare the Scriptures (Eph. 5:30). We are "sealed" in Christ forever through the working of the "Holy Spirit" (Eph. 4:30).

Note the way in which recent Christian literature corroborates the gist of the previous paragraph. The Lord's Supper, writes Gerhard O. Forde, following Luther closely, "gives us life—actually and literally."[49] Jesus comes "into" our "human flesh," our "mouths," our "hearts" in what is ultimately an "invasion of our isolation" (p. 87). The old, lonely, tragic "Adam" is "put to death" as a "new man" arises through the working of "the Spirit" (p. 86). Once we've partaken of the miraculous "body and blood," Christ "is never absent" from our lives (p. 82).

Through our participation in the sacraments of Christianity, holds H. Richard Niebuhr, through our "faith" in baptismal and Eucharistic rites as they are mediated by the "Holy Spirit," we gain not simply a "historic" individual named Jesus but an "inner personal companion," a divine, beneficent "person" who dwells permanently in our "memory" and "expectation."[50] We "cannot and do not live except in this companionship," declares Niebuhr. "He does not let me go and I cannot let him go." Indeed, "Christ is the personal companion who has been engrafted into my personal existence" (p. 105). Could it be put more emphatically than that?

Asserts Stafford, "I cannot think of any aspect of Christianity that the Lord's Supper does not touch."[51] As Christians "we draw our life" from Jesus's blood and body. The transformational bread "gets inside you. It becomes part of you. . . . He Himself comes to us and gets inside of us," just as we, by eating, "participate in Jesus Himself, in His life and His power" (pp. 93–94). Nor does it finally matter, says Stafford, whether we take the Eucharist transubstantially or symbolically: "a symbol in the best sense is the kernel of reality." Jesus "becomes part of us. God offers us a meal not symbolically but really. Those who say that the bread and wine are symbols and those who say they are the real substance of Christ are not as far apart as they sometimes think" (p. 96). The sacrifice of Jesus and our partaking of the Holy Supper are a "living reality" (p. 97). What Stafford intuits here is the extent to which the Eucharist, accomplished along both Catholic and Protestant lines, has the associative power to penetrate the communicant all the way down to the foundational levels of his mind wherein reside the "most intimate" affective wishes of his human life.

Clearly then, Eucharistic magic as it follows upon baptismal regeneration from which the Christian emerges as a "little child" of the explicitly parental Deity provides the worshiper with exactly what he craves in his "fallen," biological condition of smallness, separation, and mortality: an "inner personal companion" who is always there, even in the hour of death. "He will not let me go." The practicing follower of Christ will never be alone again, will never be separated from his loving Protector and Provider, will never be *out* as opposed to *in*, will never be at the mercy of the biological forces to which raw nature exposes him. The curses of "life" as we know them ordinarily are lifted. Interfused with, ingrafted to, sealed into, contained within and also containing Christ's body, Christ's person (remember, the Holy Spirit is a person), the Christian only *seems* to be walking around on his own, a small, separate, vulnerable mortal man or woman. In the alternate, magical "reality" of his baptismal, Eucharistic state, with Jesus in his belly, the Big One in his prayers, and the Holy Spirit suffusing his existence from within, he is just the opposite: "perfectly united" (Fisher, p. 406) with his Parent-God in whose "power" (Stafford, p. 94) he participates, and headed toward heavenly, everlasting bliss rather than a dreary grave. Here is the substitutional, homeopathic identity the Christian seeks at the deep, primal levels of his anxious, mortal frame. Here is the world of the "Holy Spirit" in which he may feelingly luxuriate forevermore, "saved" as he is from what the poor, tragical rest of us must undergo and endure.

Note the dynamic, unforgettable expression of all this transformational magic in *Great Christian Prayers*.[52] Read the following lines with the theoretical context of this section sharply in focus.

I know that the Immovable comes down;
I know that the invisible appears to me;
I know that He who is far outside the whole creation
Takes me within Himself and hides me in His arms,
And then I find myself outside the whole world.
I, a frail, small mortal in the world,
Behold the Creator of the world, all of Him, within myself;
And I know that I shall not die, for I am within the Life,
I have the whole of life springing up as a fountain within me.

He is in my heart, He is in heaven:
Both there and here He shows Himself to me with equal glory.

                   (Saint Symeon, p. 70)

Saint Symeon's words literally *sum up* the naturalistic, psychological approach to Christianity that we've offered in this book to this point. The original symbiosis is magically restored. The little one is again within the big one, safely "hidden" in the parental "arms" of the "Creator." The "frail, small mortal" discovers the omnipotent God "within" himself. He is now immortal, with the "whole of life" miraculously "springing up" within him. The bugbears of separation, smallness, and death are simply banished.

Note these famous, supplicatory verses attributed to Saint Patrick:

I bind unto myself today
The power of God to hold and lead;
His eye to watch, His might to stay,
His ear to harken to my need. . . .
Christ be with me, Christ within me,
Christ behind me, Christ before me,
Christ beside me, Christ to win me,
Christ to comfort and restore me,
Christ beneath me, Christ above me,
Christ in quiet, Christ in danger,
Christ in hearts of all that love me,
Christ in mouth of friend and stranger.
I bind unto myself today
The strong name of the Trinity.

                   (Saint Patrick, p. 77)

Could there be a more vivid expression of proceeding through life with an alternate, invisible companion or presence created through homeopathic or imitative magic ("I bind unto myself today," etc.)? Christ is everywhere, in every nook and cranny of the writer's existence. These verses come across, ultimately, as obsessional, even possessed. They speak for the total absorption of the writer into the fantastic, supernatural Redeemer.

Here is another prayerful example, attributed this time to Saint Bernardine:

We rejoice, O Lord our God, in Thy almighty power and glory. Raise Thou us up with Thee, O Blessed Savior, above all earthly desires. Inspire us with thoughts of joy, of hope and love. Enter Thou within the chamber of our hearts, and say unto us, Peace be unto you. Give us the grace to see Thee, blessed Saviour, the eyes of our understanding being enlightened, that we may know Thee walking by our side, in this our earthly pilgrimage. Come unto us, O our Lord, and dwell within us.

(Saint Bernardine, p. 86)

Here is the image of the companion Himself "walking by the side" of the Christian believer, indeed "dwelling" within the believer's "heart" as ego boundaries dissolve. How does that famous old Christian tune go? "And He walks with me,/And He talks with me,/And He tells me I am His own." Have we hallucination in all this? Mildly, we do. But in the main, we have the powerful sensation of the *person* (the Holy Spirit) *being there* as that sensation arises from the realm of implicit recollection, or state-dependent memory. When the religious magic bites, it creates in the worshiper an inward state that affectively recalls the symbiotic arrangement of the early time that was taken indelibly into the memorial apparatus.

Finally we have, from our own era,

O Lord God, I thank Thee that Thou leadest me by a way which I know not, which is above the level of my poor understanding. I thank Thee that Thou are not repelled by my bitterness, that Thou are not turned aside by the heat of my spirit. There is no force in this universe so glorious as the force of Thy love; it compels me to come in. O divine servitude, O slavery that makes me free, O love that imprisons me only to set my feet in a larger room, enclose me more and more within Thy folds. Protect me from the impetuous desires of my nature—desires as short-lived as they are impetuous. Ask me not where I would like to go; tell me where to go; lead me in Thine own way; hold me in Thine own light. Amen.

(George Matheson, p. 181)

Here is the wishful, appetitive "surrender" to the implicitly recollected big one who "led the way" early on, who offered protection, love, and infallible guidance, who told the little child (Matt. 18:3) what was good for him in a relational pattern of dependency designed to assure the survival of an utterly helpless biological specimen who would take the pattern in so deeply and firmly that it would never be forgotten or relinquished but become the inspiration of a magical, alternate, religious identity later on.

Accordingly, if we had to boil Christianity down to a single psychological longing on the part of the worshiper, it would be the longing to contain and be contained in the Big One, just as one was contained early on, before the stern biological facts of one's planetary journey emerged fully into one's awareness. When the *Catechism of the Catholic Church* describes the Eucharist in one place as the "heart and summit of the Church's life" and contends in another place that the Church's "message is in harmony with the most secret desires of the human heart,"[53] it forges for us a connection the ultimate significance of which we can now fully see and understand. It is the primary psychological meaning of the Eucharist that comprises not only the "heart" of the Church but "the most secret desires of the human heart," namely, the intertwining desires to be inside the Big One and to have the Big One inside oneself. The worshiper, the churchgoer, does not want to confront the universe alone; he wants to confront it as he did during the opening stages of his existence when someone was *there*. We are not in the realm of the miraculous divine here, the realm of "ultimately inexpressible mystery," as Maurice Wiles puts it in *The Oxford Illustrated History of Christianity*.[54] Indeed, the so-called mystery arises *only* from the difficulties attendant upon psychologically deciphering the magical system conjured up by Christian thought and practice. From where, after all, could the powerful emotions and devotions of Christ's followers come if not from the flesh and blood experiences of their own actual lives? The Holy Spirit is a *person*, an *actual person*, because persons and *only* persons make up the foundational core of our earthly being. We're the only ones home.

## Moment-to-Moment Christianity

Reborn as God's "little child" through one's ongoing baptismal frame of mind, persistently "asking and receiving" (Mark 11:24) as the Lord's helpless, needy, prayerful petitioner, ingesting and mixing bodily with the Almighty on a regular basis through Eucharistic rite—here is the central outline of the Christian's alternate, magical identity, the homeopathic other self that transcends one's stark biological condition, the imperfect handiwork of postlapsarian nature. Yet all this is not enough—far from it! To make the transformation more thorough, to approximate the goal of escaping the small, separate, mortal state in which one discovers himself on earth, to accomplish the Beginning all over again by resurrecting the symbiotic union of loving caregiver and sheltered offspring, the Christian must go about his daily life, his routines, his normal activities and commissions, in a mental and emotional attitude of total, unremitting, moment-to-moment dependency on the supernatural Big One. His frame of mind, his mode of being, his entire existence in every aspect of it, must *imitate*, act out, magically recreate the relationship of the impotent, powerless, vulnerable child in the care of the protective, succoring parent (the inner companion). Everywhere in the literature of Christianity this theme is ceaselessly, ardently trumpeted forth in a stream of remarkable, unforgettable passages that demand psychological explanation and that are inspired directly by Jesus's New Testamental pronouncement, "without me ye can do nothing" (John 15:5), a pronouncement the *Catechism of the Catholic Church* dutifully echoes as follows: "without Him we can do nothing."[55]

State Henry T. Blackaby and Claude V. King in their reverential *Experiencing God*,

> He alone has the right to initiate what you are to be involved in. . . . As you respond to Him in simple, childlike trust, you will find a whole new way of looking at life to begin for you. Your life will be fulfilling. You will never have to sense an emptiness or lack of purpose. He always fills your life with Himself.[56]

They continue,

> He calls you to a relationship where He is Lord—where you are willing to do anything He chooses. . . . God's assignments come to you on a daily basis. . . . A yoke is an instrument built for two oxen to work together. Jesus' invitation is for you to get into His yoke with Him. . . . God is crying out to us, don't just stand there! Enter into a love relationship with Me.
>
> (pp. 30–31)

And then, in a decisive utterance that repeats the words of Christ and the *Catechism* just cited: "without Him you can do nothing" (p. 31). Allow me to offer a few more lines from Blackaby and King so as to capture the full flavor of their thinking. "Lord, just tell me what to do one step at a time and I will do it. . . . Just tell me where I am heading, then I will be able to set my course and go. . . . Wherever you want me to be, I'll go. Whatever the circumstances, I'm willing to follow" (pp. 32–33). And again, "if I do everything He says, I will be in the center of His will. . . . God is absolutely trustworthy. You can trust Him to guide you and provide for you" (pp. 34–36). In this way, you can be "dependent on God above" (p. 42). He will "do through you whatever He chooses, anything He pleases" (p. 46). And finally, in a heartfelt supplication Blackaby and King declare, "God, I know I can do nothing on my own. I know You can do anything You choose to do. I give myself completely to You. Work through me any way You want to work" (p. 48). At only one stage of our lives does a single, all-powerful provider and protector *fill* our entire universe. At only one stage are we *yoked* to another in an organic, dyadic relationship of absolute trust, absolute love, upon which our survival and well-being entirely *depend*. At only one stage does our whole existence consist in *following after* a big one from whom

The Infantilizing Process **103**

we fully and absolutely derive our *guidance*. At only one stage do we give ourselves over completely to the *will* of a monumental controller. What we have here are instructions for reawakening the early period, for reexperiencing the movement of the caregiver within the realm of our implicit recollection. And sure enough, as Blackaby and King make clear, if we *do* all this, if we actually *imitate* (homeopathic magic) the behavior of a "simple child" to employ their terminology, we "square ourselves up" with the "Holy Spirit" (p. 114) who begins to stir powerfully within us—which is to say, we begin actually to rekindle the sensations of the initial symbiosis as they reside in the mnemonic attractor state toward which we dutifully gravitate as we obey Christianity's instructions for our supernatural transformation. The magical system, in the last analysis, is quite simple and straightforward: imitate the early stages of your life (act like a child) within this lofty, mystifying, religious context and you'll arouse a variety of powerful, soothing, delicious sensations that seem to come miraculously from within and that may be easily attached to putative spiritual entities that your cognitive apparatus ultimately accepts as "there," particularly when such entities are theologically urged upon you by authoritative figures such as parents, priests, and pastors.

The Holy Spirit, assert Henry Cloud and John Townsend, is "not a thing" but a "person."[57] If we "yield" to the Almighty, if we "follow" Him, if we "cry to Him" for succor and support, "He will come," and not only come but, through the Holy Spirit, "abide"—which is to say "live in us" (the inner companion) (p. 99). When that occurs, we "don't have to live alone" ever again (separation reversed), and we don't have to exist "in our own power" ever again (relinquishment of autonomy). He will be "there" for us always (pp. 98, 104). Accordingly, we must conceive of our relationship to the Almighty, to Christ, and to the Holy Spirit—and here are the crucial words—as a "moment-to-moment relationship of dependency" in which we "yield and follow," in which we surrender all "control," in which we fully "submit" (the dyadic essence of the early period) (p. 99). This, hold Cloud and Townsend, is the "formula" for eternal salvation, the formula that "woos us to Jesus," that transforms and transfigures us (pp. 94, 99). "Remember," they write, "He will come to live inside you" (again, the inner companion); indeed, He will "invade" you if you "ask and then follow" (p. 99). What we have in this, needless to say, is a striking, vivid *counterpart* to what we've just discovered in Blackaby and King. Let's sample a few more counterparts.

"I need help! I can't do it alone," explains Rev. Schuller, indicating for his readers the proper Christian posture in the presence of the all-powerful Deity.[58] "Cry out, surrender, ask for help," Schuller admonishes, and do it *all the time* as you adopt a "Be-Happy Attitude" toward your Savior, through the Holy Spirit (p. 21). In other words, pray continuously, "face up to your emotional lack, admit your weakness, stop trying to do it all by yourself" (p. 28). Query your Heavenly Father as follows, Schuller persists: "Can you help me? Can you direct me?" (p. 31). Confess to Him, "I'm helpless! I'm ready to let go and let God take over" (p. 33). "Are you there, Jesus?" Schuller urges us to ask. "Do You love me as much as I love you?" (p. 30). Could there be a more compelling example of the Christian's struggle to refind, recontact, and reactualize the relationship of "moment-to-moment dependency" that he enjoyed during life's opening stages as he cleaved unto the Big One in whose elemental, life-sustaining care he discovered himself? For the Christian, simply to mature biologically is to *lose* inward security, a life-defining loss that drives him to indulge in magical behaviors through which (he believes) he may *regain* security: "Christ, come to live in me. . . . Oh, God, I turn my life over to You" (Schuller, p. 41). Now I am "a child of God" (p. 115). Here is the "formula" indeed. Here is the naturalistic, psychological system of inward reattachment to the original caregiver that dwells at the heart of Christianity under the designation of "Holy Spirit."

"We were never designed by God to function independently," asserts Anderson indelibly in his volume *Who I Am in Christ*,[59] with the *in* recalling our analysis of Eucharistic "function," namely, to place the believer back *into* the body of the big one, back into the symbiotic, organ relationship of the early period, a "function" that applies to Christianity across the broad range of its teachings and rituals. Whatever leads us to "function" on our own, autonomously, as independent organisms on the earth, is rejected, repudiated, and through homeopathic magic (rebirth and reattachment to the supernatural Parent-God) inverted, or turned upside down. "Without Christ," claims Anderson, "we are incomplete." With Christ, which is to say *in* Christ, "we are made complete and fulfilled" (p. 98). God says to us, "You don't need other people to make you happy; you need only Me. . . . No other person can fill the vacuum. You were created to relate to God in soul-union, and you can only find rest and purpose in your life"—and here are the vital words—"when you put your total dependence on Him," which is but another way of describing, holds Anderson, a worshiper who is "filled with the Spirit" (p. 99). Anderson declares in a powerful concluding statement that calls to mind again both John 15:5 and the *Catechism of the Catholic Church*, "If I am not operating by the power of the Holy Spirit, I can accomplish nothing. I am complete *only* in Christ" (p. 99, my emphasis). From our analytic, psychological perspective we may understand Anderson's final remarks this way: only when I recapture through the homeopathic magic of Christian rite and doctrine the symbiotic union of the early period and actually *feel* myself *in* that original, life-sustaining, one-to-one dyadic unity ("soul-union with God") can I experience in my separate condition as a grown-up human being the perfect security and emotional fulfillment I hungrily, even desperately seek. As a typical Christian, I can be happy *only* in a state of emotional, psychological *merger* with a parental big one. For me, functioning independently is a distress.

According to Stafford, "God does not relate to us only from the outside, as our friends do. Through the Holy Spirit, God gets inside us and forms a unity with us. He is there as an active and personal influence."[60] Stafford continues,

> The Spirit teaches us about God and also creates in us the faith that makes us love that knowledge. Theologians have been driven to despair by this fact: We cannot speak objectively about God; only through the eyes of faith may we speak truly of Him. . . . His own Spirit is the light in which we see Him.
>
> (p. 32)

And finally,

> I want to reclaim the sense that God's personality fills the earth. He is every-where we turn, holding Himself out to us, asking to be known. . . . Jesus is all around you. . . . His personality is spilling out on every side. . . . If you can begin to see His personality as Himself, I think you will pursue the means of grace with clearer eyes and greater excitement.
>
> (p. 33)

Alright then, we may ask, how does one accomplish this? How does one discover the Holy Spirit, and through the Holy Spirit his "faith" in God? How does one manage to live in a world in which a personal, loving, unifying presence "fills" one's reality, is "everywhere," "all around" one, "spilling out on every side," as *was* the case *exactly* during the early period when the biological parent entirely filled, entirely sustained one's universe?

Stafford wastes no time in informing us. To "know God" through the "Spirit," he declares—and here are the crucial words, "we must be dependent on Him" (p. 32). We must be born again as His "small children" (p. 40). We must address Him with the "babyish terms" *Abba* or "Daddy" (pp. 40, 45). We must follow the direction of the New Testament and put Him in the parent's place, telling Him, "I love you" (p. 45). We must recognize through the Holy Spirit, "Who plants this seed of love in us," that God gives us "everything we need for life" (pp. 28, 45). And finally, we must accept our "dependence" upon Him as never-ending, as "eternal" (p. 148). God "loves us as His little children," as a "parent" who is willing to "sacrifice his life" for his offspring, asserts Stafford, and we must never fail to "remember our utter dependence upon His care" (pp. 56, 143). Can anyone fail to see what we have here? We have the same magical system of thought and conduct that we found in this section's contextual authors. When the worshiper thinks like a child, acts like a child, approaches his explicitly parental Deity as a small, needy, dependent child approaches the parental big one who watches over him—in short, when the worshiper refashions imitatively the primal childhood mentation and behavior upon which his actual biological existence is founded, he triggers the implicit, feeling recollection of both his original, vulnerable self and the loving, provisional caregiver who nurtured him toward his maturity, who mitigated his discomforts and anxieties, who simply kept him alive in his helpless, defenseless, condition as a neotenous newcomer. Thus, the worshiper "knows God" through a "Holy Spirit" that *is* those early, precious, powerful recollections and longings as they are repositioned outwardly (or projectively) into the putative supernatural sphere and then loved all over again in the exuberance of passionate rediscovery and theological idealization: God's love for us is perfect, unconditional, and everlasting. The worshiper resides *in* Christ and Christ *in* the worshiper, forevermore.

Here is a final example, one that takes us to what we might think of as the outer limits of this particular aspect of magical Christian behavior. Having seen Jesus in her mind as "God wrapped in human flesh," having told Him, "I love You," having cried out to Him "I open my heart and invite You to come live within me," and "I surrender all that I am to Your authority," Anne Graham Lotz feels herself totally "filled with the Spirit." She then asks the reader, in reference to this last item, "what does that mean?" This is her answer: "To be filled with His Spirit is to be moment-to-moment surrendered to His moment-to-moment control in my life." The result, Lotz goes on in a remarkable, pivotal utterance, "is that I am increasingly His look-alike and His act-alike and His live-alike. . . . My body is His dwelling place, . . . twenty-four hours a day, seven days a week."[61] Thus does the magical *imitative* return to the symbiotic arrangement of the early time, to the period of "moment-to-moment control" by the all-powerful, all-absorbing parental presence, harbor the potential simply to blur ego-boundaries *away* and to leave the worshiper *fading off* into the mentalistic Big One of the putative supernatural sphere. When Lotz declares, "I am increasingly His look-alike and His act-alike and His live-alike," we recognize immediately that her autonomous existence as a grown-up increasingly *disappears* as she blends herself perceptually and emotionally into the idealized parental Deity toward Whom she gravitates through her longing to collapse her separate status in the world. Lotz doesn't want to be *out there* on her own. She wants to be *in* the Big One or to have the Big One *in* her (it amounts to the same thing). She wants to "surrender," as she puts it, to His "moment-to-moment control" of her "life." It is as if Lotz is saying just beneath the surface of her homeopathic conduct, Rescue me, Jesus, from the burden of my biological being, from the burden of my separation, my smallness, my mortality. Take me inside You as Your special child. I can't make it on my own.

The question arises, as individuals such as Blackaby, and King, and Stafford, and Lotz, and presumably millions of other Christians go about their business in a "moment-to-moment relationship of dependency" with Jesus Who, for every second of the day and night, is in "control" of their lives, what are they actually doing? How does the Lord's "control" express itself? Is the believer reflecting his "dependency" when, for instance, he checks the air pressure in his tires, or pays the utility bill, or opens his umbrella in the rain, or passes the salt at the dinner table? When Blackaby and King offer us examples of those who let God run the show by mentioning, on the one hand, Biblical figures such as Moses and Joshua and, on the other hand, dedicated ministers serving their congregations, we understand at once (pp. 206, 208). But what about the vast majority of "ordinary" Christian people who are simply attending to their mundane affairs? How do they fit in? How do they manifest Christ's "moment-to-moment control"? A valuable hint resides in Darcey Steinke's review of Heather King's autobiographical volume, *Redeemed: A Spiritual Misfit Stumbles toward God.*[62]

A hard-drinking Los Angeles lawyer given to casual love affairs, King toughs it out for 20 years until one fine day, she discovers herself filled to the brim with disappointment and disgust. Embarking upon her "spiritual journey," she visits numerous places of worship but nothing clicks until she attends a noonday Mass at St. Basil's Catholic Church and is, all of a sudden, "stopped cold." With the light shining "like honey" on the "teakwood pews," she gazes up at Jesus and feels everything within her striving to "move toward Him." King writes, "I saw that like us, He was in pain and He wasn't sure why, whether it would ever end, or what it was for. I saw He'd come to address the deepest mystery of humankind—the mystery of suffering" (p. R2). In one sense her journey is completed, and in another sense it is just beginning.

Jesus becomes the "core" of King's existence, the ground of her being; she feels herself transformed, healed, redeemed through the miracle of His Spirit, body, and blood. Darcey Steinke declares in a crucial sentence of the review that takes us to the heart of the naturalistic, psychological analysis we are fashioning here, "On the outside, her life doesn't look very different from anyone else's, but on the inside King's flesh 'faints for Christ'" (p. R2). The point is, the "moment-to-moment relationship of dependency" on Jesus, the "moment-to-moment control" of one's life through Christ, has very little to do in the vast majority of cases with anything other than the way the Christian *feels* during his ordinary day-to-day activities. In contrast to Moses leading the Jews out of Egypt, or the dedicated pastor preaching to his flock, the ordinary Christian actualizes God's "control" merely by *sensing that God is there, on the inside*, as his daily life goes forward. What one "faints" for as he cleaves unto the Savior is nothing other than the "inner companion," as theologian Niebuhr expresses it,[63] Who is with one or *in* one benignly, caringly, lovingly as one checks his tire pressure, or pays his bills, or passes the salt at dinner. One's "dependency" is the sense of being *held*.

To put it somewhat differently, what Christianity offers its followers, and what King discovers in the Church of St. Basil, is precisely what one *had* early on as one luxuriated securely and endlessly within the original symbiotic union of the early period when the big one *was* always there, and the little one functioned morphologically as a kind of organ of the big one, psychologically *in* the big one's body and emotions, the big One's "flesh." As I've suggested, one cannot explicitly remember that arrangement but one can feel its life-altering power when it is cued through Christian thought and practice, as it is cued one magical day for King when she gazes up at her crucified God. Where else, after all, might her primal, all-conquering religious devotion come from, where else but from her own actual experience in the world, her own life history, her own deep "core"? King calls her change a "divine intervention" (p. R2) because like all Christians she can't *see* the psychological/neurological processes behind the event. Jesus opens for King the way of her return to the Beginning, to the early life of security and loving union that she knew and internalized into her own mind-brain as a little one, as a "little child." Indeed, the whole aim of Christianity is to position the believer back there again so that the believer might, like King, attach herself to the orthodox Parent-God with an enthusiasm and tenacity sufficient to endure for the duration of her earthly existence. All who ask as the helpless "little children" of the *Abba* shall receive; all who seek as His "moment-to-moment dependents" shall find. King's life "looks just like anyone else's" on the outside but on the inside she is "hooked" on her companion (she "faints" for Him); on the inside she enjoys a perpetual "fix" of "spiritual" attachment to an idealized recollection of her own biological being. It is world without end, companionship without end: the Beginning (Edenic perfection) *becomes the end*, and *stays the end*. The time of separation and searching is over. Is there regression in all this? Of course there is. Without regression, and lots of it, Christianity doesn't work. But the regression to which I am referring at this particular juncture is *not* regression for regression's sake, regression that enables the Christian simply to float around in the delicious recollection of the early period. It is, rather, regression in the service of the ego, to employ a famous psychological phrase; it is regression designed to sooth life's wounded traveler, to restore the broken heart and the broken spirit, to *address* in short, the *current* difficulties that confront the believer as he goes about his day-to-day affairs. When King cleaves unto Jesus she feels *better* than she did before she found Him. Her drinking and her sleeping around come to an end. Her newly discovered faith has a positive *adaptational* effect upon her. But more of that particular topic in subsequent sections.

Surely the reader will appreciate, now, the psychological significance of the metaphors through which the New Testament expresses its contention that the individual who chooses to pursue his or her existence without depending upon Jesus every step of the way "can do nothing." Here are the relevant lines uttered by the Savior Himself:

> Abide in me, as I in you. As the branch cannot bear fruit of itself except it abide in the vine, no more can ye, except ye abide in me.
>
> I am the vine, ye are the branches; He that abideth in me, and I in him, the same bringeth forth much fruit: for without me ye can do nothing.
>
> If a man abideth not in me, he is cast forth as a branch, and is withered; and men gather them, and cast them into the fire, and they are burned.
>
> (John 15:4–6)

Thus does Jesus offer Himself to his followers, to the members of his flock, to His newly baptized "little children" as a kind of *psychic umbilicus*, the originative *root* not only of their spiritual fecundity but of their very lives ("I am the way, the truth, and the life" [John 14:6]): those who fail to "abide in" Him, to *attach* themselves to Him as the branch attaches itself to the vine, shall wither up and disappear forever. The newly born "child" of baptismal rite shall become a dead child, a lifeless heap of ashes, dust to dust. Again and again in this brief passage Jesus stresses what we have chosen to term the core magical wish of the Christian religion as a whole, namely, the wish to be *in* the Big One and to have the Big One *in* oneself, as expressed most vividly in the Eucharist. "Abide *in* me," declares Jesus; "I am the vine . . . ; he that abideth *in* me, and I *in* him, the same bringeth forth much fruit: for without me ye can do nothing" (my emphasis)—nothing, that is, except wither up and perish, as the dependent infant does in the absence of his indispensible nourishment. Christianity derives its persuasive power from the natural *root* of the worshiper's biological existence, as that existence extends itself through implicit recollection into the now of the individual's "spiritual" seeking. Is it any wonder after all that the Church routinely presents itself to the devotee as explicitly his "mother," and the See of Peter as the "womb and the root" of his faith?[64] "He who does not have the Church as Mother cannot have God as Father."[65] Such language goes straight to the heart of Christianity's homeopathic magical procedures. The worshiper must be mnemonically *infantilized* to ensure both his initial commitment and his continued participation. He must *depend* upon his Parent-God every second of his life; he must *attach* himself to the Big One and *stay* attached, if he wishes to flourish, indeed to *continue* in the world.

Pastor Anderson pins the matter down nicely for us in his volume *Who I Am in Christ* (once more, note the *in* in the title): "Spiritually, Jesus is the true vine, the trunk that connects it to the roots. He is the source from which all growth begins. No vine, no branches. The branches cannot exist without being grafted to the vine" (p. 200). Anderson goes on,

> We have to realize that apart from the vine (Christ), we can do nothing. We are in Christ—we have been grafted in—but if we attempt to operate independent of Him, we will not bear fruit. We can't! . . . Our light will not shine unless we are plugged in to the energy source [attached].
>
> (pp. 200–201)

Anderson then turns to his own exemplary life in an effort to guide the reader: "I try to maintain," he writes,

> a constant awareness that God is always present in my life. I begin my day and start every ministry by declaring my dependency upon the Lord. . . . We must stay plugged in to the source of our life and make it our ambition to live in such a way as to please Him.
>
> (pp. 201–2)

The "nutrients" of the "vine," concludes Anderson, "must go to the grapes" (p. 202). Here again is the pivotal notion of the dependent Christian, the "little child," *feeding* upon (or from) the body of the nourishing Big One, indeed going about his daily business umbilically attached to his provisional Savior without Whom he cannot "shine" or "bear fruit" or even stay alive. The believer's homeopathic, magical identity, the alternate self that accompanies him on his biological journey, is based imagistically, emotionally, and psychologically upon the central feeding arrangement of life's initial stages.

As for the intimate connection between abiding *in* Christ and arousing the Holy Spirit, which is to say, arousing implicit recollection of the early symbiotic relationship on which the idea of the Holy Spirit is founded in the first place, the Reverend Billy Graham discloses it for us in an invaluable passage: " 'Abide in Me,' " writes Graham, quoting Scripture, and then, "by that is meant we are to have the closest, most intimate relationship with Christ, with nothing coming between us. . . . Also, this tells us that we can *only* bear spiritual fruit if we abide in Christ: 'Apart from Me you can do nothing' "[66] Graham proceeds to declare—and here are the decisive words,

> We can see, then, how crucial it is to be filled with the Spirit, and we are being filled as we abide in Christ, the vine. . . . Cut me off from this vine and I will wither away and become useless. Without the vine the branch can do nothing. So it is with our lives. As long as I strain and work to produce the fruit of the Spirit from within myself, I will end up fruitless and frustrated. But as I abide in Christ—as I maintain a close, obedient, dependent relationship with him—the Holy Spirit works in my life, creating in me the fruit of the Spirit.
>
> (pp. 242–43)

Clearly then, one *feels* the Holy Spirit working in his life when one *feels* himself *in* a close, dependent relationship with his provider, his *feeder*, his nourisher, his *vine*. As in Eucharistic rite, when boundaries blur, when the separated biological self conjures up the symbiotic, dependent self of the early period, when one *acts all this out imitatively* through his inward, emotional commitment to Christian teachings, one awakens in one's own mind-brain the delicious mnemonic residues of one's original life-or-death attachment to the biological caregiver and thus luxuriates in the certainty of Christianity's supernatural claims. What the worshiper wants desperately (to be *in* not out, to have someone *there* at all times as Inner Companion) but cannot discover directly or sufficiently through his own natural existence is magically provided to him through his religious participations. The Christian who *seeks* will certainly *find* because what it is that he is seeking emerges from his own head when he indulges himself in specific magical behaviors. As *God Speaks: Devotional* advises, "Put your trust in God. Cry out to Him for a *lifeline*. He will meet you right where you are, in the moment of your need."[67] In other words, postulate faithfully the existence of a supernatural, parental Big One and then cry out to that Big One as a helpless, dependent, supplicating little one, and you will receive your *lifeline*, your *cord*, your umbilical attachment, the magical connection that makes you feel all right again, soothed and reassured as you were soothed and reassured over and over again, thousands of times, when you cried out during your career as a biological infant and child. *Infantilize yourself*, in short, and you will discover once again through your implicit recollection of your own biological past the security and comfort you passionately crave.

## Obedience, Will, and Control

Obedience is another major facet of the Christian's homeopathic, magical behavior. Reborn as Christ's "little child," substituting Jesus explicitly for his biological progenitors, praying to Him regularly for assistance as His needy, helpless follower, ingesting Him on a regular basis so as to accomplish merger or interfusion (*in* Christ), relying utterly upon Him at all times through a "moment-to-moment relationship of dependency," indeed regarding Him as the Vine, the Root, from which one draws umbilically his very life, his very being—thus does the Christian forge his alternate self, the magical other with which he identifies as he goes about his business on the planet. The chief internal, culturally proffered, and ultimately self-imposed result of such behavioral infantilization is, as we have seen, the arrival of the mysterious Holy Spirit, that elusive, airborne entity that turns out to be, quite logically, the powerful, affective, implicit recollection of the very biological experiences that are aroused neurologically as the necromantic, infantilizing practices and beliefs of the religion go forward at the conscious level of the worshiper's existence. If one *acts* like a little child, one is apt to *feel* like a little child, which means in this particular mythic, religious framework or context, to *feel* oneself attached to and secure in the continuous, inward presence of a parental caregiver or companion, one's *Abba*, one's Father, the Lord of one's "Mother" or Church. Can it come as a surprise in the face of all this that the Father's "little children" are expected and instructed to be good little girls and boys 100 percent of the time, always to submit to the *will* and the *control* of the Big One, always, in short, *to do exactly as they're told*? Of course not.

Significantly, Jesus lays down the law in the very same passage in which He declares Himself to be the follower's *vine*, the follower's nourisher, the umbilical source of the follower's life and being (John 15:3–14). "As the Father hath loved me, so have I loved you: continue ye in my love. If ye keep my commandments, ye shall abide in my love; even as I have kept my Father's commandments, and abide in his love." He then "commands" His followers to "love one another": there shall be no divisiveness, no debilitating rivalries and hatreds among those who comprise His little sect, or cult. Indeed, Jesus makes it perfectly (and chillingly) clear that He expects His devotees to be willing to *die* for each other, just as He is willing to *die* for them. How often have we heard such sentiments from charismatic cultic leaders as they draw their credulous followers and themselves toward mortal danger. Here are the decisive words: "Greater love hath no man than this, that a man lay down his life for his friends. Ye are my friends, if ye do *whatsoever I command you*" (John 15:13–14, my emphasis). In this way, "abiding" in Christ's "love," being "friends" with Christ, being able to *depend* upon Christ from "moment-to-moment" means *obeying* Christ at all times, doing "whatsoever" He "commands" *or else*. The Savior's friendship, the Savior's love, the Savior's bestowal of life upon His devotees is *conditional*, not unconditional. Let's turn that last sentence around to better see its conditional structure: "*If* ye do whatsoever I command you, ye are my friends" (my emphasis). Like all compelling sectarian/cultic leaders, like all narcissistic personalities in the grip of their own putative divinity, their own unique grasp of all truth and all right as they place themselves directly at the center of the universe, the "good shepherd" Jesus (John 10:14) lets His "sheep" know the score: do my bidding or out you go. You must get along with each other and prove yourselves willing to die for the cause, or I reject you; I am no longer your "friend," your "vine," your source of life and being. The extent to which such conditional commitment enhances the process of infantilization is considerable.

When the godly Big One commands the "little child" to do exactly as He says or He won't "love" him anymore, won't be his "friend" anymore (his enemy, then?), the Big One awakens in the little one the primal anxiety of the early period, the anxiety of separation and loss, abandonment and isolation, the sickening prospect of being *out there*, entirely on one's own, without the support and affection that comprise the little one's entire symbiotic universe. Has not the Christian been baptized, or confirmed, or reborn? Is He not Christ's little child, and is Christ not his newly discovered *Abba*, replacing explicitly the biological caregiver (Matt. 10:35)? Does he not cry out routinely to his all-powerful Lord in a petitionary, supplicatory state of helplessness and submission? Is he not continuously *asking* in the hope of continuously *receiving*? Does he not regularly go into the Big One's body and vice versa through Eucharistic rite? Does he not exist, now, in a state of "moment-to-moment dependency" upon his nourishing *vine*, his Creator, his Savior, without Whom "He can do nothing," not even remain existent? And might all this be taken away, reversed, negated? Might Jesus reject His "little child" *if* His little child is not "good," dutiful, controllable, and *obedient*? True, Jesus tells His followers in certain places that He will never "leave" them (John 14:18), and the New Testament echoes this promise forcefully through Paul's Epistles (Rom. 8:38), but this only *deepens* the infantilizing process we're exploring here.

I mean, by playing it both ways, by ambiguously controlling its devotees, Christianity exposes its "little children" to something *all children* experience at one time or another as they develop from the primal stages of the early period (years 1–3) toward the subsequent stages of early childhood (years 3–5), namely, the "*bad object*," the ambivalent or dichotomous quality of the caregiver's loving ministrations, the two-sided nature of the parent's devotion, the big one's capacity to both succor and threaten the little one in his or her care. On the one hand, the big one says, I love you and will always love you; on the other hand, the big one says, be good or you're *out*! Here is the perfect formula for tightening the little one's anxious grip on his benefactor. The more the child is threatened with something akin to Jesus's words "*If* you do whatsoever I command," the more desperately does the little one cling to the big one's neck, or thigh. Within the homeopathic, magical world of Christian behavior, such dichotomous ministration translates quite straightforwardly into *more regression*, more implicit mnemonic arousal of the early time, more affective sensations of dependency, all of which lead, in turn or cyclically, to more *control*, more negation of one's own *will*, and more *obedience* to the purveyors of the specific religious code, the religious doctrine, the religious outlook as a whole. Indeed, the posture of unquestioning obedience as it is associated with the centerpiece of love is capable of arousing the entire magical system of imitative compliance, infantilization in short. As the little one is apprehensive or even frightened on the inside, so is he prone to do the bidding of the Savior, to adopt and to stick with his own sorry self-identification as a helpless, needy dependent who "can do nothing" on his own.

I'm not suggesting for a moment, of course, that such compliant behavior does not have its positive, rewarding, adaptational aspect. The vast majority of human beings underwent, and implicitly recall, the basic, primal pleasure of mama's continuous, unwavering control, of going about securely in daddy's directional care, hand-in-hand with the guiding big one. In fact, such control, such direction, and the feeling of security they engender are frequently mistaken in *maturity* for *love*, with disastrous consequences. Because the adult commander's commands are unconsciously linked in the mind of the subordinate partner to the caregiver's dominant role during life's opening stages, the vulnerable adult gets hopelessly lost in what turns out to be a dangerous, abusive relationship. One strives to behave as a grown-up when one functions inside as a helpless, dependent child. We recognize an offshoot of this emotive configuration in Christianity past and present when the follower of Christ becomes rigid, severe, compulsive, fanatical, even self-punitive in his obedient devotion to the Redeemer. Do not the history books offer us a motley crowd of harsh inquisitors, determined self-flagellators, and skeletal ascetics? Do we not have at least a hint of all this here, in the New Testament, as Jesus suggests to his devotees that they be willing to *die* for the cause, just as He is willing to *die* for them?

Everywhere in the literature of the Christian religion such infantilizing emotional patterns play themselves out. Blackaby and King commence their section titled "His Will Is Always Best" with the assertion (from I John 4:16) "God is love."[68] They follow this immediately with the startling equivocation, "this does not say that God loves, though He does love with perfect, unconditional love" (p. 17). Scripture declares, they continue, making matters worse, that "God's very nature is love. God can never function contrary to His own nature [love]. Never in your life will God express His will toward you except that it is an expression of perfect love. He can't!" (p. 17). Surely at this point one has the right to ask, what's going on? God is love [noun], yet doesn't necessarily love [love as a verb]. However, God will never "express" [verb] anything toward you "except" perfect love. But if that is the case, then He certainly loves [love as verb], does He not? A moment later, in the next series of sentences, Blackaby and King inform us that God is prone to direct His "wrath" toward those who don't "obey" Him, those who rebel and sin. Still, He loves us so much "that He gave us His only begotten Son, and by this we know love" (p. 17). Indeed, God's "punishments" themselves are based on "love," just as His "commands" are "for your good." As the big ones used to tell us when we were little guys and gals, God "knows what is best for you" (pp. 18–19). The upshot is clear: "If you love Him," you will obey Him! If you do not obey Him, *you do not really love him* (p. 22, my italics for that old cliché of manipulative parenting). You must "respond to Him in simple, childlike trust," and as you do so "your life will be fulfilling. You will never have to sense an emptiness or lack of purpose. He always fills your life with Himself" [separation overcome through the inner companion; symbiosis restored] (p. 25). When you declare, "I have no will of my own," and view yourself as "God's obedient child," you will "know" the "Holy Spirit" is "speaking to you," is "touching your heart," is "leading" you to a "love relationship" with the Almighty [implicit recollection of one's primal experience as a helpless little one] (p. 173). Can even the most dubious, resistant reader fail to see what is occurring here? Blackaby and King's mixed message, namely, that God "is" perfect, endless, unconditional "love" yet responds with "wrath" when His followers are disobedient, recalcitrant, "bad," echoes precisely Christ's *conditional* injunction, "Ye are my friends, if ye do whatsoever I command" (John 15:14). The Big One is *there*, just as he was *there* early on when the little one navigated the behavioral challenges of his fresh biological existence, yet the Big One's presence, love, support, provision, and ministration may *not* be *there*, may *no longer* be *there*, if the little one's *obedience*, the little one's submission and will-lessness, is not evident at all times. The nourishing "vine" nourishes *only* when the "branches" manifest their unqualified dependency; or, to express the matter in the light of Christianity's homeopathic, imitative core, the religious magic works *only* when the worshiper *acts out* the essential nature of his early, developmental interactions with the caregiver.

God will never "leave me," never "forsake me," asserts Anderson in his volume *Who I Am in Christ*.[69] Then, adding a crucial rider, a crucial afterthought to the initial, comforting assertions, Anderson declares, "As long as I obey God, I will live in harmony with Him" (p. 27). Backing this up with the words of Jesus Himself, Anderson quotes the New Testament as follows: "If anyone loves me, he will obey my teaching" (John 14:23). Here we have again the manipulative, conditional style of parenting, of *controlling* the "little children," that we discovered in Blackaby and King a few sentences earlier: Are you naughty? Are you bad? Are you rebellious and disobedient? Well, that proves you don't love me! To make his position perfectly clear, Anderson treats us to this infantilizing ditty, the sort of rhyme one might put to kindergartners:

Trust and obey,
For there's no other way
To be happy in Jesus,
But to trust and obey.

(p. 27)

Thus, "obedience" *becomes the condition* upon which the "little child's" happiness rests. "I come to You as Your child," cries Anderson in heartfelt supplication; "I no longer put any confidence in myself," he pitiably maintains; "my confidence is in You. . . . I now accept myself as a child of God" (p. 29). Employing for us the crucial notion of "abiding in" Jesus (John 15:3) from which the thesis of this section originally arose, Anderson notes in a passage titled "What God Requires" that only "the one who keeps His commandments abides in Him and He in him." Indeed, pronounces Anderson, "abiding *is* obedience" (p. 209, my emphasis). The conclusion is inescapable: one's submission, one's will-lessness, one's dependency, one's obedience to the Big One *means in*, *means* attachment, *means* holding, *means* security, and to turn the coin over, one's obedience to the Big One *prevents* separation, *prevents* loss, *prevents* betrayal and abandonment, *prevents* the very problem or issue or preoccupation with which Anderson *opened* his discussion, "Will God leave Me?" (p. 27). We've come full circle then: the Christian's *ultimate* concern is separation, being *out* as opposed to *in*, in the body of the Big One, the feeder, the vine, the supernatural umbilicus rooted neurologically in the worshiper's implicit mnemonic and emotional structure, hippocampus and amygdala, which hold at the level of unconscious memory the primal anxiety and the primal fusion of the early period. Accordingly, the religion's manipulation of the worshiper through the *condition* of obedience is not effectuated for its own sake, for its "power" or "force," but for the manner in which the *condition* recalls the early time, and through such recollection summons the Holy Spirit, the implicit, affective, feeling-level memory of the parental tie upon which the little one utterly depended during the course of his primary years. The whole scheme of vine, branch, abiding, commanding, and *obeying* is designed magically to recreate the past, the time of symbiosis and submission, the time of parental *control*, and insert it into the present. The Big One, by which I mean here the leader of the sect or cult, is finally inextricable from the merger and security one *seeks*, the sacred *in*, the divine *entry* into the Body of the God, the attachment to the vine, the umbilicus: "I don't want to be self-sufficient" declares Anderson ever so pitiably again; I want to "abide in Christ"; I want to be his "child," to "submit" and through such "submission" to feel the "Holy Spirit indwelling" within me: "I commit myself to be obedient to Your will" (p. 212).[70] Oh, what a friend we have in Jesus, Anderson notes (p. 33), echoing the famous hymn by that name, to which I would add, yes indeed, *if* we mind Him, as a little one minds his mommy and daddy. Then and *only* then is He our "friend." Otherwise, by His own New Testamental implications, He's *not*.

Here's Rev. Schuller summing things up for us through the words of a specific parishioner, an active, representative Christian worshiper who attends Schuller's famed Crystal Cathedral in Garden Grove, California:

> I feel that all the values the Lord has laid down for us are really for our own benefit. And if we think that we want to do something contrary to those values, well, that's fine, but we're only going to be hurting ourselves if we give in. God knows the future, and He knows why He set down certain rules. I feel that the Lord is just. Like He says, He's our Father and He's looking out for us. So long as I can remember that God's rules are only for my good and for my own happiness, and that He knows better than I do, then they are easy to adhere to.[71]

Could there be a more striking, transparent instance of a Christian believer *transferring* to the Parent-God, the Father, the *Abba*, or "daddy" precisely the thoughts and attitudes that characterize her own early, developmental interactions with the caregiver? According to Schuller, "Lisa" (whose words he's just cited) "knows the secret to happiness" (p. 81), which turns out to be, in *our* terms, permitting herself to be infantilized in a manner that restores her to the period of *childhood* during which her behavior was entirely *controlled* by an omnipotent Big One to whose *will* she completely subordinated herself as a little one. As Lisa *acts this out*, as she goes about *behaving* this way, she births the alternative, magical identity or self through which Christianity exerts its hold upon its followers, its subscribers, its "spiritual seekers," by which I mean those countless millions who relish the sensation of a soothing, reassuring implicit memory called "Holy Spirit" suffusing their inner lives.

Presenting the essentials in two "steps" termed "sanctification" and "submission," Graham not only makes plain for us the tie between abiding and obedience, between minding the Big One and existing *in* the Big One, he also discloses the causal connection between arousing the implicit memory of one's early, dependent years and experiencing the comforting presence of the putative Holy Spirit. In short, Graham captures for us Christianity's magical nature with a few brief sentences as follows: "The word 'sanctification' comes from the Greek word which means to be 'separate' or 'set apart for a purpose.' Paul speaks of the believer as having been 'sanctified by the Holy Spirit' (Rom. 15:16). He wrote to the Corinthians saying that they, *having been sanctified*, are called to be saints (I Cor. 1:2)."[72] Graham continues, "We Christians are to be 'progressively sanctified' or 'made righteous' in holiness as we daily abide in Christ—and obey His Word. Abiding and obedience are the keys to a successful Spirit-dominated life" (p. 99). And finally, "We are as much sanctified [through our obedience] as we are possessed by the Holy Spirit. It is never a question of how much you and I have of the Spirit, but how much He has of us" (p. 99). Clearly then, we are "sanctified" or "abiding in" Christ only to the extent that we follow the rules set down for us by the supernaturals. The magical system is neurologically grounded and virtually automatic: as we adopt the infantilized posture of unquestioning obedience to the Parent-God, we apprehend the implicit, feeling recollection of our primal bonding with the biological caregiver. The putative Holy Spirit "has us" in His addictive *control*.

The "second step in being filled by the Holy Spirit," declares Graham, "is what we might term *submission*. What do I mean by this? By submission I mean that we renounce our own way and seek above all else to submit to Christ as Lord and be ruled by Him in every area of our lives" (p. 140). And then,

> the essence of sin is self-will—placing ourselves at the center of our lives instead of Christ. The way to be filled—controlled and dominated—by the Spirit is to place Christ at the center of our lives, instead of self. This only happens as we submit to Him—as we allow Him to become Lord of our lives.
>
> (p. 140)

Graham insists that "nothing is excluded. We can hold nothing back. . . . He must control and dominate us in the whole and the part. . . . This *surrender* is a definite and conscious act on our part in obedience to the Word of God, . . . a complete and final act of submission" (pp. 143–44). Here again is the essence of the homeopathic magical system: we choose to follow after a self-styled cultic/sectarian Leader ("Follow me," says Jesus to the "fishers," and they "follow" [Matt. 4:19]); we become the Big One's "little children," dependent upon Him from "moment-to-moment" for security and love; we reject our self-determination, our self-sufficiency; we participate in patently magical actions such as the Eucharist and prayer; we entirely give over to the Leader the direction, the *control* of our lives, and presto chango we possess an alternate identity, an alternate self upon which we can rely amid the stern, unchanging realities of our separate, limited, mortal condition on the planet. Once again within the protective cocoon of the Big One, once again *in* as opposed to *out*, merged as opposed to separated, special as opposed to ordinary (we are now "saints"), and finally, immune to the harrowing awareness of biological mortality, we cleave unto our "Shepherd" in a sheep-like trance state, leaving everything ultimately up to Him (more of this particular metaphor in the next major section). The psychological weirdness of the Christian religion, its strange, cultic, eerie nature, derives overwhelmingly from this two-sided magical arrangement. On the one hand, Christians walk about as grown-up men and women, participating straightforwardly in their society, their culture, just like everyone else. On the other hand, they walk about immersed in a fog of regressive behaviors and beliefs, thoroughly infantilized even to the extent of turning their volition, their self-determination, their very perception and comprehension of the universe in which they exist over to an invisible, tripartite parental presence who leads them doctrinally around as helpless dependents. Because they can't *see* directly the implicit biological memories that validate emotionally the claims, the perspectives, of the creed, because the neuropsychological underpinnings of "faith" lie obscured in the realm we now usually call the unconscious, Christian worshipers are readily drawn into the welcoming Body of Jesus, into the Church and its many soothing infantilizations, not to mention, of course, the normative social interactions that enrich the congregant's day-to-day involvement in his environmental surroundings.

A major facet of the submission, the will-lessness, toward which Graham urges his readers resides in the sexual sphere and highlights the importance of *abstinence*. In a section titled "The Battle with the Flesh," Graham quotes St. Paul as follows: "For the flesh sets its desire against the Spirit, and the Spirit against the flesh; for these are in opposition to one another" [Gal. 5:17] (p. 103). He then declares,

This indicates what the real conflict is in the heart of every true believer. The flesh wants one thing and the Spirit wants another. The black dog and the white dog are often fighting. As long as there is not the surrender of mind and body every moment of the day, the old nature will assert itself.

(p. 103)

Graham spells out what he has in mind explicitly when he refers to "any kind of impurity in thought or deed, . . . lust, . . . modern films, pornographic literature, . . . wantonness or debauchery, . . . lewdness and sensuality of any kind" (p. 106). He sums things up with, "By faith we turn over our lives totally and completely and without reservation to the Holy Spirit" (p. 113). This is, of course, a well-flogged, inescapable, even notorious theme in Christianity past and present, as witnessed most famously perhaps by Friedrich Nietzsche's lively tract *The Antichrist* in which the author pens what he calls the "eternal indictment of Christianity" as "*against life itself,*" as "contemptuous" of "the body . . . through the concept of sin."[73] Nietzsche asks in his best rhetorical style,

Really, how can one put a book in the hands of children and women which contains the dictum: "to avoid fornication, let every man have his own wife, and let every woman have her own husband. . . . It is better to marry than to burn."? And how can one be a Christian as long as the notion of the *immaculate conception* Christianizes, that is, *dirties*, the origin of man?

(pp. 642–43)

However, what we recognize at this stage of our discussion through specifically Graham's use of Paul's words, "the flesh sets its desire against the Spirit, and the Spirit against the flesh," is that Christianity's condemnation of sensuality emanates *not* from its hatred of "life" and the "body" but from its intuitive recognition that sexual behavior *interferes with the process of infantilization upon which the entire magical edifice of the religion as a whole is reared.*

As we have seen, it is the implicit recollection of the early period, the period of *prepubescence*, that is connected inextricably to the emergence of the putative Holy Spirit, and it is, in turn, the emergence of the Holy Spirit within the worshiper that convinces him of the creed's validity. If and only if potential believers are transformed through the teachings of Jesus from ordinary men and women into helpless, dependent, obedient "little children" (Matt. 18:3) will the Holy Spirit work its miraculous, salvational change, a change that cannot occur while ordinary men and women are acting out their sexual impulses. Indeed, human sexuality (outside of its dutiful, procreative presence in marriage) is anomalous to the infantilizing process. How can

Christianity produce the "little children" it requires when its prospective converts or struggling practitioners are carried away by their aroused and eager sexual organs? People who are mating or thumbing through pornographic magazines are hardly the helpless babies Christianity needs to fill its ranks of will-less, obedient worshipers. When Nietzsche writes elsewhere that the "priest" leads "humanity by the nose" through the concept of "morality" (p. 621), he fails to take us to the heart of the matter: it is not "morality" in some sexual sense that Christianity ultimately advocates; it is obedience, will-lessness, submission, control; it is *these* precisely that reside at the foundation from which the notion of "morality" arises. Accordingly, Christianity does not condemn "life" or the "body." It condemns grown-up "life," grown-up biology, grown-up participation in the world. It lovingly promulgates *infantile life, infantile biology, infantile participation in the world* because in the process of infantilization it discovers not merely the power to control but the potential to gratify its followers who will rest fully content *only in* the Savior, *only in* the regressive, symbiotic merger with the Big One, *only in* the magical, homeopathic return to the period in which being separate, being out there on one's own, *has not yet occurred.* As in every sphere of human conduct with which it concerns itself, Christianity's aim in respect to sexuality is to play it both ways, to deal over here with the ordinary, grown-up men and women it requires in its worldly ranks in order to gain fresh followers from each generation, and over there with the regressed, needy "little children" it strives to produce through its infantilizing doctrines and rites, its postulation of an explicitly parental Deity upon Whom its submissive, obedient devotees must entirely depend.

From the perspective of the last few paragraphs, including the brief discussion of Nietzsche's famous treatise, we begin to spy the underlying quality of what we might think of as the Devout Christian Practitioner, the dedicated Christian soul who has rendered himself or herself up to the Church's teachings, to the Way of the Savior, to the religious essence of the inspirational creed. And what we behold in our mind's eye as we picture this, as we recall perhaps the sweet, compassionate face of the Christian expositor on television, the softly smiling mouth, the concerned, gentle eyes, the exalted, soothing message of mercy and forgiveness and love, is not a hater of life and the body, a despiser of the world and the flesh, but an infantilized human being who has fallen under the spell of a cultic, magical system of thought and conduct dedicated to the notion that all men and women are created as the "little children" of an omnipotent, infallible, invisible Parent-God, a Big One Who commands that His devotees exist submissively as little ones for all their days on earth and for all their eternities in heaven. We have in the Devout

Christian Practitioner what Rev. Anderson captures for us perfectly when he cries out in his devotional handbook over and over again, "I no longer put any confidence in myself; my confidence is in You" (p. 29);[74] "I come to You as Your child" (p. 51); "I commit my body to God as a living sacrifice" (p. 51); "I belong to You" (p. 59); "I was incomplete without You" (p. 100); "I renounce my self-sufficiency" (p. 154); "I declare my dependency upon You" (p. 204); "apart from You, I can do nothing" (p. 204); "I don't want to be self-sufficient" (p. 212); "I was given weakness, that I might feel the need for God" (p. 244). From such material emerges the quintessential Christian, the infantilized one, the dependent one, the pitiable one, or perhaps as we used to say in the 1970s and 1980s when we employed psychological thinking informally in our thoughts and in our everyday interactions with others, the castrated one eagerly pursuing his path toward "sainthood" (I Cor. 1:2), toward the inward, salvational condition he may confidently expect as Jesus's obedient disciple, as one who attaches himself firmly to the umbilical Vine from which comes not only his nourishment, but his very existence itself.

To what may we naturalistically attribute this remarkable expression of our basic human nature? I've been suggesting that from this book's inception: the powerful, persistent anxiety engendered neurologically in a neotenous animal born into an extended period (ages 1–6) of biological helplessness and dependency, and eventually (adolescence onward) into a profound, inescapable awareness of its own inevitable demise and disappearance from the world (dust to dust). Such dependency and such awareness of death (both of which trigger the elemental fear of separation) have been with us for millennia and were thoroughly established within the human psyche by the time a Galilean faith healer named Jesus began regarding himself out loud as the long-awaited Biblical Messiah and wandering as such about the land of Israel.

## Love: Neurological Catalyst of the Holy Spirit

That Christianity ties God's love to obedience in one place doesn't mean it can't allow love to stand alone, as unconditional, as absolutely certain, as the unqualified expression of the Deity's active, fundamental nature, in another place. Indeed, Christianity feels perfectly comfortable saying one thing over here when that one thing serves an immediate purpose, and another thing over there when circumstances change. What is essential for Christianity in one era may not be essential in another. The religion as a whole, historically, geographically, and intraculturally is wholeheartedly in sympathy with Ralph Waldo Emerson's famous definition of consistency as the hobgoblin of little minds. As long as a particular theological doctrine or perspective (religious dualism, for example) does not attack the very pith of the creed and thus threaten destruction of the overall theological message, it may well have, one day, an opportunity to fly.

Love is the *sine qua non* of human infancy and childhood. Without it, normal development is at risk. It isn't enough that babies and children are fed and clothed and bathed and changed. They must be lovingly held and stroked and cooed and smooched, over and over again, without end, for happiness to take root. And the street is, of course, two-way: from the parent the baby gets his full-blown life, his existence as a person, his *joie de vivre*; and from the baby the parent gets precious, gratifying maturation toward sexual and interpersonal fulfillment. We're talking here about the very core of human experience, at least when humans come together as biological progenitors of the species to which they belong. To read the New Testament or the literature of Christianity, to watch Christian television or the ardent preacher at work in the meetinghouse on Sunday, makes it obvious that love is also the *sine qua non* of the Christian religion. Christians are told continuously that Jesus loves them, and this is in itself sufficient to awaken the Holy Spirit within. Through baptism, which produces little Christian children; through prayer, which thrives on helpless, dependent followers who believe that merely to cry out is to receive; through the Eucharist in which Christians reenter the body of their creator; through obedience wherein Christians discover the umbilical Vine on which they feed and flourish; through this infantilizing context as a whole, to hear of God's infinite, unconditional, salvational, and personal love for each and every one of His individual offspring is more than enough to arouse the implicit recollection of one's own personal, loving bond with the biological caregiver and thus produce for the Christian worshiper the unchallengeable inward perception of a loving, protecting, providing parental presence, the mysterious, sanctifying spirit of the beneficent Father and His tender Son. As the old Beatles' tune has it, "all you need is love." No matter how wounded, disappointed, defeated, disheartened, or lonely the condition in which one discovers himself on his worldly journey, this may do the trick. Can we not see, now, why Christianity insists the Holy Spirit is a *person*? For the theological assertion of God's all-encompassing love to work fully, that love itself must be tied intellectually and emotionally to an actual human being, not simply to Jesus as the parental substitute (Matt. 10:35–38), but to the biological caregivers themselves, to the ones who were *actually there as people, as bodies*, and who are *still* there as people, as bodies in the implicit mnemonic foundations of one's affective, emotional life.

"It wasn't an argument that saved me," declares Mark Chironna on the Trinity Broadcasting Network as he recounts his voyage from sin to salvation; it was "the love of a Savior Who would never let me go."[75] How many times has one heard something exactly like this enunciated on the radio or the television set, or expressed in a devotional handbook or pamphlet? Nor does the love of God have only to be received, recorded, and accepted as *there*, to work its homeopathic magic. The affective, memorial system operates equally well when the worshiper's devotion is openly affirmed, when the worshiper says to his Parent-God as he said over and over again through his sounds and words and gestures to his biological mommy and daddy as a little one, "I love you." This is, of course, why Christians are encouraged to tell the Big One of their love, to lavish that love upon Him, to preserve, in short, the emotional foundation of their own biological lives so that it may serve as the magical foundation of their putative "spiritual" lives. To actualize our love for God, states Stafford, we must express it openly, all the time. We must say to the Lord, "Father, I don't know what this means or where it will lead, but I have to tell you I love you."[76] When we do this, "when that step is taken," claims Stafford, "something happens." We hear "the sound of the door closing behind us. We are in this relationship now. There is no way to back out. . . . The courtship is over. We belong to him" (pp. 45–46). It is the "Holy Spirit," the "Person," declares Stafford, Who

> plants this seed of love in us. By Him we cry *"Abba*, Father." The Spirit himself testifies with our spirit that we are God's children (Romans 8:15–16). There is nothing irrational about calling out to God as "Daddy": we are like small children before God. But only the spirit enables us to love Him for it.
>
> (p. 45)

In this way, in this *magical* way rooted neurologically in our implicit memorial structure, "we go in and are never expected to back out. Why would we? Inside, we find love and joy. In Christ, through the Holy Spirit, we live in love" (p. 54). Surely the gist of our theoretic, psychological position in this book as a whole is pellucid at precisely this juncture: the aim of the Christian religion is to find one's way back *in*, to be *in* again, not *out*, to be safe and secure *inside* the body of the loving Big One, not *out there* in that anxious, scary world of separation, smallness, and death. There is no need to cavil over the exact ordering of the implicit mnemonic processes that trigger the magical goings-on in their entirety, the forging of the alternative, homeopathic identity of "little one" that exists alongside one's ordinary biological nature. To *hear* of God's love may be enough to awaken the Person of the Holy Spirit; or the implicit recollection of the early period as it is aroused by a variety of ritualistic and doctrinal cues such as baptism, prayer, the Eucharist, or specific key images discoverable in Scripture (the umbilical vine, for example) may be sufficient to prompt the avowal of the believer's "love of God," an avowal that will reinforce through a kind of neurological chain reaction the unconscious affective memory of the loving biological exchanges that stand directly behind the fashioning of the Holy Spirit itself as an integral aspect of the tripartite Godhead. "God, who is altogether person, expects and demands that avowal of love," writes Stafford, and then, "He also gives us vows of His own" (p. 54). The Holy Spirit exists and functions at both ends of this dynamic, mnemonic continuum.

"We cannot do anything to qualify for unconditional and voluntary love," asserts Anderson in his volume *Who I Am in Christ*; "we labor under the false assumption that if we live perfectly everybody will accept us, while there was One who lived His life perfectly, and everybody rejected Him."[77] Anderson goes on to declare,

> I know who I am now. I'm a child of God, and the basis of my acceptance is in Him, not in man. . . . Understanding and receiving God's unconditional love is foundational for all future growth. We don't have to do things so God will someday accept us. We are accepted by God completely as we are.
>
> (pp. 21–22)

And then, relying on the terminology that calls to mind explicitly the early stages of our human existence from which the magical potential of all this directly springs, Anderson states,

> When you know who you are in Christ, you no longer need to be threatened by people or compete with them, because you are already secure and loved. . . . Like babies, we are newborn in Christ, and we are to long for the pure milk of the Word. . . . Let me encourage you as a newborn babe in Christ to long for the pure milk of the Word.
>
> (p. 23)

Anderson concludes his devotional treatise with this prayer to the Almighty: "I love You with all my heart, soul and strength. You are the Lord of the universe, and the Lord of my life, now and forever." For the reader he has, "Can you be content with His will in any situation? Yes, because He is there with you, and you are in Him" (pp. 276–77). Surely the reader, with that, will be inclined to breathe, Amen.

Through this rich, lush imagery of loving parental care and infantile feeding and bonding we are taken once again to the heart of Christian magic, to the way in which the religion's supernatural edifice reawakens the strong, originative time when the devoted biological caregiver was *there* for the helpless, dependent little one, when the newcomer's very survival hinged directly upon remaining in orbit, in the gravitational field of the primary provider. "There, there," says Anderson's book in effect to its readers, to the "newborn babes" taking in the "milk" of Jesus's Word, "everything is going to be all right. Don't fret. You're not *out there* anymore. You're back *in*, back again in the arms of the Big One who loves you unconditionally and will never let you go." Can we not appreciate from this perspective the full psychological significance of the following definition of "Heaven" in that ever-popular paperback volume *Chicken Soup for the Christian Soul*: "Heaven is a great big hug that lasts forever"?[78] Here is Christianity in nine simple words that boil down straightforwardly to the alternate, magical reality in which Christians choose to position themselves as they cleave unto the word: perfect loving security upon the bosom of the Parent-God, the *Abba*-Daddy and the tender Son who want nothing more than to love their little ones to pieces, personally and forever. How could the vast, mysterious, surrounding world possibly appear more benign than this to a vulnerable primate whose limitations and mortality are always resounding in his mature, symbol-making mind?

What is the Christian's "secret to happiness," asks Rev. Schuller who chooses to answer through one of his parishioners (Lisa) whose following words he considers to be "psychologically and theologically sound":

> [Happiness comes] from knowing that I am loved no matter what, and that I don't have to perform and I don't have to be a good person. I don't even have to follow the Lord's laws to be loved. It's just total grace and it's all mercy. It's knowing that I'm loved just because He created me. So if I blow it, I blow it, but Jesus is still standing here with open arms. And if I do good He's standing there to commend me. When you know you're totally accepted for who you are, it's a lot easier to be yourself with others. If they accept me, that's great, but if they don't that's okay too, because then I'll just run home to Daddy—to Jesus, to my Heavenly Father.[79]

Could there be a more vivid, striking exemplification of implicit memorial materials from life's opening stages drifting into the mnemonic operations of the grown-up such that the total, unconditional, loving acceptance of the little one by the Big One may be transferred unconsciously to the "Daddy" of the putative supernatural realm, a realm that is cognitively and emotionally fabricated ab initio for the express purpose of providing the vulnerable, mortal human creature with an alternate identity, an alternate world in which he may enjoy the limitless perfections of the symbiotic stage of development during the course of which his existence transpired *within* the organic, emotional field of ministering other? Listen again to the key phrases: "I'm loved just because he created me." There is only one natural, empiric precedent for *that* sentiment. "I'll just run home to Daddy—to Jesus, to my Heavenly Father." Surely the reader can see the early, developmental period from which those words derive. "I'm loved no matter what." Here is the positive, inner conviction harbored by people whose parents did a reasonably decent job during the formative years. As for the employment of the image of "home" specifically, its widespread usage in the literature of Christianity warrants further consideration.

Saxophonist Ron Brown joins Pat Robertson on the 700 Club in May 2006 to recount for the television audience both his descent into the snake pit of drug addiction and his ascent into the refuge of faith. From marijuana to cocaine to heroin, Ron becomes hopelessly addicted until one day, in the midst of suicidal ruminations, a "miracle" occurs. Somewhere in his tormented mind Ron begins to hear the voice of his Savior, Jesus Christ, saying to him again and again, "You are my child. Come home to me." This is the turning point. Rendering his life up to the Lord, Ron "goes home" at last. After listening intently to Ron's story, Pat turns to his viewers with the words, "This is the journey home for which each of us was created."[80] A year or so later, in August 2007, Robertson is once again ministering to his television audience. As he approaches the conclusion of his inspirational message he maintains with a concerned yet tender expression and with a firm yet soothing voice that the Gospel's ultimate message is not "avoid sin," or "follow the rules," or "prepare for heaven," but simply this: "come home."[81]

Let's keep firmly in mind as we go that Jesus's devotees do not "come home" in just any old way, anymore than they pray in just any old way. The French philosopher Gaston Bachelard notes that "all really inhabited space bears the essence of the notion of home,"[82] to which I would immediately add that every notion of home bears the essence of the notion of mother, father, parent, or some combination thereof. Coming home for the Christian is operationally intertwined with the Christian having become God's "little child," newly born through baptismal rite, attached to the umbilical "Vine," feeding on the body and blood of the Redeemer, taking in the "milk" of the "Word," existing in a state of "moment-to-moment dependency" on the Big One, praying regularly as the needy offspring of the omnipotent Deity, obediently performing "whatsoever" the Big One "commands" for the filial Christian's "own good," and looking forward to the endless, loving "hug" that is commensurate with Christianity's death-denying notion of "heaven," eternal union with the original Parent-Creator.[83] As Lisa puts it in Schuller's psychologically and theologically "sound" presentation of the creed, no matter what happens to the Christian during the course of his earthly days, he always has the option of "running home to Daddy" (p. 83), just as Rev. Robertson declares that he should. In this way, the entire journey "home" transpires in a doctrinal, ritualistic context of infantilization through which the worshiper is psychologically, mnemonically, and emotionally restored to the opening stages of his existence, the stages during which the ministering caregiver is always, somehow, *there*. What else would we expect? Surely a religion that devotes itself to reentering the parental body, to going back *in*, must lead finally to the place (or Bachelard's "space") where all the infantile, childish behaviors were *acted out* on the naturalistic, biological level and internalized memorially to become the basis of the religious magic and hence of the Holy Spirit's personification, the Holy Spirit's "reality" in the mind and body of the religious seeker, namely *home*. If, as *God Speaks: Devotional* informs us, the Parent-God's message to His "children" is, "I love you. I love you. I love you,"[84] then surely that love will be connected inextricably to the notion of "home," to the actual place in which such "love" was expressed between real people to lay the foundations of Christian necromancy and thus rear up the "supernatural," "spiritual" enclosure wherein Christians indulge their timeless longing for eternal union with an ever-faithful, loving Provider. When Robertson breathes out the word "home," he discloses for us the immediate, conscious goal of Christianity because this word precisely will trigger, or cue, the whole mnemonic context of retrieval upon which, as I've just stated, the edifice of religious magic is constructed, and, in particular, the idea of the *person* of the Holy Spirit. The way this goes in the New Testament and in the related Christian literature is psychologically arresting, or, dare I say, revelational.

When Jesus is informed in one place (Matt. 12:47–50) that His mother and brothers are nearby and wish to speak with Him, He replies as follows: "Who is my mother? and who are my brethren?" He then "stretche[s] forth his hand toward his disciples" and says, "Behold my mother and my brethren! For whosoever shall do the will of my Father which is in heaven, the same is my brother, and sister, and mother." Here are Stafford's interpretative comments on the passage: "A person's family is the context he has come from: the father and mother who bore him, his brothers and sisters, aunts and uncles, and cousins." With "Jesus," Stafford goes on,

> this is reversed: he is the context out of which his family must spring. . . . "Pointing to his disciples, he said, Here are my mother and my brother" (Matt. 12:49). Paul, following this example, called Christians the adopted children of God. He also called the church the "body of Christ." In the church we

find the down-to-earth focus of Jesus' personality. Jesus is invisible to us, but through his family [his body/church] he makes himself known.[85]

Stafford declares that "those who quickly become participants in Jesus' family grow in faith" and live

> active, fruitful lives. The reason for this vitality is obvious, if we think about faith as a personal relationship to Jesus. His flesh and blood carry more of his personality than a set of bloodless ideas. If we know Jesus' family, we are not far from knowing Jesus as a person.
>
> (p. 83)

Accordingly, when we are *in* Jesus's "family" we are *in* Jesus's "church," and when we are *in* Jesus's church we are *in* Jesus's "body," *in* His "flesh and blood" *as* His "flesh and blood," the terms people use diurnally to describe their *biological kin*. "We will feel his life flowing to us [the umbilical Vine] through his own body," concludes Stafford (p. 88). The psychological implications are transparent.

God's message of love, for Christians, is linked integrally to home and to family, both of which are linked in turn to Jesus's body, to His "flesh" and His "blood," which are also His "church," His followers, His "mother," and His "brethren." To "come home," as Robertson advises us to do in keeping with Christianity's ultimate wisdom, is to come *into* the "body of Jesus," *into* His "flesh" and His "blood," His "Person" as He is manifested in His sacred "church." The whole religion at its magical foundations is thus rooted in our biological foundations, our families, our parental bodies, the flesh and blood we actually knew and internalized into the neurological ground of our memorial makeup that is implicitly awakened again and again through doctrine and through rite to lend emotional support, indeed emotional conviction to the supernatural claims of the creed. The putative "Holy Spirit," as I've suggested from the outset, is neither more nor less than our feeling recollection of those actual people who were lovingly, caringly *there* when, as helpless little ones, we needed them to stay alive. When Jesus makes the connection between His mother and His family and His church, He allows us to do so, too. And when Paul makes the connection between Jesus's church and Jesus's body, he shrewdly invites us *into* that body (through the Eucharist, for example) and into the originative symbiosis it recalls. "Salvation comes from God alone," asserts the *Catechism of the Catholic Church*; "but because we receive the life of faith through the Church, she is our mother. 'We believe the Church as the mother of our new birth.'"[86] And again, this time with explicit reference to adults undergoing baptismal rite and becoming thereby

Jesus's "little children": "'With love and solicitude mother Church already embraces them as her own'" (p. 319). Thomas Wolfe maintained in his famous novelistic title that *You Can't Go Home Again*; and when he did so, he meant *really*, not *magically*. Within the realm of Christian magic you can leave home and not leave home, you can say goodbye to "daddy" and then run home to "daddy," you can separate from the matrix and not separate from the matrix, all at the same time as time holds both the present and the past. That indeed is Christianity, through the stirrings of the Spirit: *into* the body of Christ through the wound in His side; *into* His body forever to stay as His "little child" of love. Such is the inward shape of what we've chosen to call here infantilization.

Were we obligated to suggest the most compelling link in the overall magical setup, it would have to be, from the neurobiological angle at least, the link between love and the reversal of separation—by which I mean the separation of the child from the parent and the final separation of the individual from the world and everyone in it through death. No facet of human existence drives the magic of Christianity more relentlessly than separation in both of these fundamental senses. Indeed, the religion as a whole must be regarded as a mythic veiling and finally a denying of separation's role in our lives. *Into* the loving body of Christ *means* into the permanent shelter, into the permanent security, of symbiotic interfusion with the immortal, parental Big One. Faithful, bona fide Christians, then, are allowed to play it both ways: they put the invisible Deity in the parent's place and thus move away from biological union with its threats of incestuous dependency; at the same time, as they gravitate toward the Deity, they become "little children" again; they find the early period again; they gratify their thirst for infantile dependency again, feeding on the body, the Vine, of the umbilical Provider. Psychologically, Christians are like crabs, moving forward and backward all at the same time. Let's sample a vivid, characteristic instance of mythological veiling and comprehensive denial.[87]

In "Becoming One of God's Children," *The Watchtower* notes "how family members rejoice when they find one another after being separated and lost! The Bible describes how humans were tragically separated from God's family. It also tells how they are now joyfully united."[88] Here's the specific "story" that veils the biological realities and sets the stage for wholesale supernatural denial:

When God's first human son, Adam, rebelled, . . . the human race was painfully separated from its loving Father and Creator [the developmental separation of the child from the parent, internalized implicitly into the memorial system during years 1–4]. This is because through his rebellion, Adam forfeited for himself and his yet unborn offspring the privilege of being children of God. Through his servant Moses, God described the consequences of what had happened: "They have acted ruinously on their own part; they are not God's children, the defect is their own." The defect, or sinful nature, alienated humans from God, who is holy and perfect in every way. In a sense, then, mankind became lost, fatherless.—Ephesians 2:12. ["In a sense, then" marks the struggle of the myth maker to turn the story toward our own biological development: "lost, fatherless," etc.]

(p. 8)

*The Watchtower* goes on,

> To emphasize the extent, of mankind's isolation, the Bible refers to those outside God's family as "enemies." (Romans 5:8, 10) Separated from God, humankind has suffered under the harsh rule of Satan and the deadly effects of inherited sin and imperfection [death as a biological reality of human existence]. Can sinful humans become part of God's family [enter the unconscious longing for resumption of primal symbiotic interaction with a parental presence]? Can imperfect creatures [separate and anxious] become children of God in the fullest sense, the way Adam and Eve were before they sinned? [In other words, can the biological facts of human existence be reversed so as to create a world free of primal anxiety, primal terror, the brute animal detection of separation, smallness or vulnerability, and death?]

(p. 9)

*The Watchtower* forges ahead this way in a section titled perfectly for our purposes "Gathering Separated Children"; note the tie between love and separation's magical defeat:

> Lovingly, God made provisions for the benefit of imperfect people who love him. (I Corinthians 2:9) The apostle Paul explains: "God was by means of Christ reconciling a world to himself, not reckoning to them their trespasses," (2 Corinthians 5:19) God provides Jesus Christ as a ransom for our sins. (Matt. 20:28) With appreciation, the apostle John wrote: "See what sort of love the Father has given us, so that we should be called children of God." (I John 3:1) Thus, a way was opened for obedient mankind to become part of God's family once again. . . . All who respond to God's love will be progressively restored to the perfection of life that Adam lost [union with the Creator, the perfect symbiosis of the early time, or the Garden]. Even the dead will be raised [the denial of death]. Thus God will fulfill his promise.

(p. 9)

When we are told in *The Watchtower*'s companion pamphlet, *Awake*, that such "good news, . . . preached to all the nations (Matt. 24:14) . . . strikes a responsive chord in honesthearted individuals" and "instills conviction,"[89] we think to ourselves, "you bet it does!" For the "responsive chord" that "instills conviction" is none other than the putative Holy Spirit, the implicit memorial recognition of the biological experiences upon which the mythological material is ultimately constructed. To express it another way, as the Christian or potential Christian begins to perceive the "good news," as he begins to feel it awakening the early period of loving symbiosis with the big one, he *maps* the original caregiving arrangement onto the supernatural tale and thereby experiences its "truthful" nature. Recognizing neurologically the foundational *pattern* on which his own biological existence is based, he doesn't hold back; he goes with it. In precisely this way is the believer or the convert an "honesthearted individual" who "wants to worship God" in accordance with the gospel of John (10:4, 27). His search for replacement, his "want" in short, is coming to an end.

Again and again the New Testament breaks the "good news." Again and again Jesus assures the "lost sheep" of "Israel" that He will always be there for them as their good shepherd and guide (Matt. 10:6). "I am with you always," He declares, "even unto the end of the world" (Matt. 28:20). "I will not leave you comfortless; I will come to you" (John 14:18). "I will never leave thee, nor forsake thee" (Heb. 13:5). In what is perhaps the New Testament's most intense, most passionate passage, the utterance that underscores once and for all Christianity's supreme promise, supreme commitment, first as a fledgling sect or cult and subsequently as a full-fledged religion, Paul writes in his Epistle to the Romans,

> For I am persuaded, that neither death, nor life, nor angels, nor principalities, nor powers, nor things present, nor things to come, Nor height, nor depth, nor any other creature, shall be able to separate us from the love of God, which is in Christ Jesus, our Lord.
>
> (Rom. 8:38–39)

Nothing, then, absolutely nothing, including the realities of the biological world (death above all), the powers of the societal sphere, and the figments of the supernatural domain, will interrupt or cancel the parent-child bond between the loving Father, the ministering *Abba*, and the "little children" who have entered *into* his sacred body through the intercessions of Jesus Christ, the merciful Redeemer. Separation as life's bugbear is simply erased from the universe, and as it is erased, Christianity's chief psychological purpose for each and every individual who gravitates toward its emotional blandishments is accomplished. All Christians are *in*, not *out*. Indeed, for Christians there *is* no *out*. The faithful worshiper is forevermore the Deity's special, immortal darling, resting his head on the bosom of the Big One Who is eternally present, eternally *there*.

As we would expect, everywhere in the literature of Christianity this grati-fying, transformational "news" is proclaimed. "We will never be cast away by our heavenly Father," declares Anderson. "He has promised to never leave us or forsake us. Let me encourage you as a newborn babe in Christ to long for the pure milk of the Word" (p. 23). "It is thrilling to note," writes Graham,

> that Jesus says believers will not be left alone. Through the Holy Spirit whom He and the Father sent, He will never leave us or forsake us (Heb. 13:5). He will remain with every believer right to the end. This thought has encouraged me a thousand times in these dark days when satanic forces are at work in so many parts of the world.[90]

Graham's daughter, Anne Graham Lotz, presents her heartfelt comments on this theme as follows:

> There have been times in my spiritual journey when my feelings have crowded out any awareness of God's presence in my life. I have felt abandoned by Him. At such times of weakness I have needed a clear vision of Jesus—a vision that He has given me through His Word, which distinctly promises, "Never will I leave you; never will I forsake you."

And what does Jesus *say* to Lotz when He is "there," when he is "present" once again "in her heart"? It goes like this: " 'I love you.' "[91] The faithful Christian, asserts theologian Niebuhr,

> trusts in the loyalty of the Transcendent One and in His power, being certain in his mind that nothing can separate men from the love of God. He trusts God for himself, for his nation, for mankind. This trust is wholly personal. He has the assurance that God will never forsake him, that God seeks and saves the lost.[92]

Thus are we back again through Christ to the "lost sheep" of "Israel."

Surely the reader can discern in the foregoing citations Christianity's magical system of thought and the central role of separation therein. Everything is at hand. The worshiper becomes the Parent-God's "newborn babe" (Anderson), and as he does so, he gravitates mnemonically toward the early period of his life and the implicit, feeling recollection of the big ones who "encouraged" him in the beginning (Graham's "Holy Spirit"); he feels their loving presence as they whisper "I love you" to him (Lotz); and he feels their reliability, their trustwor-thiness, and the inward assurance that they will never "forsake" him, let him go

(Niebuhr)—*precipitate separation*, in short. Mapping this pattern of care onto his current, separate condition in the world (biological autonomy accomplished with concomitant awareness of death), creating an idealized, flawless version of parental ministration and devotion personally for himself through the Parent-God of the putative supernatural sphere, the worshiper magically resolves the "dark, satanic" imperfections of his mortal existence: He is now *in* the body of the Lord, loved, protected, sheltered, and secured forevermore, world without end. As Niebuhr renders it in the theological language of the creed, "Christ is the personal companion who has been engrafted into my personal existence so that I cannot and do not live except in this companionship. . . . He does not let me go" (pp. 104–5).

* * * * * *

Let's move on, now, to the second part of this central chapter. There, I'll strive to expand my neuropsychological analyses into what I hope will become a fruitful evolutionary view of the manner in which Christianity works in the mind and in the body. Where the behavior of human beings is concerned, the neuropsychological and the evolutionary proceed inseparably, and it's time we started putting them together.

## Notes

1. Joseph Ratzinger, ed., *Catechism of the Catholic Church* (Liquori, MO: Liquori Publications, 1994), p. 312.

2. Robert H. Schuller, *The Be (Happy) Attitudes* (Dallas: Word Publishing, 1985), pp. 115, 227.

3. Neil T. Anderson, *Who I Am in Christ* (Ventura, CA: Regal Books, 1984), p. 9.

4. Tim Stafford, *Knowing the Face of God* (Colorado Springs, CO: Navpress, 1986), p. 50.

5. Throughout this book, as stated in the notes to Chapter 1, I'm using the King James Version of the Bible.

6. See note 5 above.

7. G. P. Fisher, *A History of Christian Doctrine* (Philadelphia: Fortress Press, 1978), p. 348.

8. Ratzinger, ed., *Catechism of the Catholic Church*, pp. 330–31.

9. See note 3 above.

10. Friedrich Heiler, *Prayer: A Study in the History and Psychology of Religion* (Oxford: Oxford University Press, 1997).

11. Ibid., p. 123.

12. Romano Guardini, *Prayer in Practice*, trans. L. Loewenstein-Wertheim (London: Burns and Oates, 1957), p. 209.

13. Ole Hallesby, *Prayer*, trans. C. Carlsen (Leicester, England: Intervarsity Press, 1979), p. 24.

14. C. H. Spurgeon, quoted in Richard S. Foster, *Prayer: Finding the Heart's True Home* (New York: HarperCollins, 1992), p. 179.

15. Patrick Cotter, *How to Pray* (Boca Raton, FL: Globe Communications, 1999), p. 13.

16. James Pruitt, *Healed by Prayer* (New York: Avon Books, 2000), p. 1.

17. Walter A. Elwell, ed., *Evangelical Dictionary of Biblical Theology* (Grand Rapids, MI: Baker Books, 1996), p. 622.

18. Timothy Jones, *The Art of Prayer: A Simple Guide* (New York: Ballantine Books, 1997), p. 108.

19. Huldrych Zwingli, quoted in Heiler, *Prayer: A Study in the History and Psychology of Religion*, p. 271.

20. Elwell, *Evangelical Dictionary of Biblical Theology*, p. 622.

21. Hallesby, *Prayer*, p. 22.

22. Guardini, *Prayer in Practice*, p. 63.

23. Gordon Lindsay, *Prayer That Moves Mountains* (Dallas: Christ for the Nations, 1996), p. 37.

24. Joshua David Stone, *Soul Psychology* (New York: Ballantine Books, 1999), p. 168.

25. Foster, *Prayer: Finding the Heart's True Home*, p. 179.

26. Cotter, *How to Pray*, p. 14.

27. Jones, *The Art of Prayer*, p. 110.

28. Larry Dossey, *Healing Words: The Power of Prayer and the Practice of Medicine* (San Francisco: Harper San Francisco, 1993), pp. 100–101.

29. Stephen Winward, *Teach Yourself to Pray* (London: English Universities Press, 1961), p. 46.

30. George Arthur Buttrick, *So We Believe, So We Pray* (New York: Abingdon-Cokesbury, 1994), p. 30.

31. See Tony Castle, ed., *The New Book of Christian Prayers* (New York: Crossroad, 1986), p. 61.

32. Walter Burkert, *Creation of the Sacred: Tracks of Biology in Early Religions* (Cambridge, MA: Harvard University Press, 1996), p. 75.

33. Cited in Leonard Roy Frank, ed., *Quotationary* (New York: Random House, 1998), p. 636.

34. Christopher Bollas, *The Shadow of the Object: Psychoanalysis of the Unthought Known* (London: Free Association Books, 1987), pp. 13, 33.

35. William James, *The Varieties of Religious Experience* (New York: Library of America, [1902] 1987), p. 69.

36. Bollas, *The Shadow of the Object*, p. 33.

37. Terry Lynn Taylor, *The Alchemy of Prayer* (Tiburon, CA: H. J. Kramer, Inc., 1996), p. 15.

38. Bollas, *The Shadow of the Object*, pp. 14–15.

39. The terms Holy Ghost and Holy Spirit were interchangeable among Christians until the inception of the twentieth century when Ghost was dropped because of its associations with magic and the paranormal.

40. It is worth noting here that Billy Graham considers the personhood of the Holy Spirit to be a mysterious and "terribly difficult subject." See Billy Graham, *The Holy Spirit* (New York: Thomas Nelson, Inc., 1978), p. 10.

41. See note 30 above.

42. Ratzinger, ed., *Catechism of the Catholic Church*, p. 334.

43. Stafford, *Knowing the Face of God*, p. 94.

44. Cited in Fisher, *A History of Christian Doctrine*, p. 321.

45. Perhaps one day in the not-so-distant future scientific experiment will allow us to see the memorial regions of the brain light up when Christians are suffused with the putative Holy Spirit by virtue of their participation in Christian thought and practice.

46. See John 16:7 for the Holy Spirit as "the Comforter."

47. Fisher, *A History of Christian Doctrine*, p. 406. Interestingly, on p. 409, Fisher suggests that the modern scientific view of matter as energy may eventually obviate the controversy over the nature of the bread and the wine. If the bread and the wine are Christ, then His energy is in them; if they represent Christ, then they may, as energy, still hold Him. Energy, in this way of thinking, is very close to spirit.

48. For the Church as Christ's body, see Graham, *The Holy Spirit*, p. 73. The "body of Christ," holds Graham, "is the Church." See also I Cor. 6:15 and 12:11–12.

49. Gerhard O. Forde, *Where God Meets Man: Luther's Down-to-Earth Approach to the Gospel* (Minneapolis, MN: Augsburg Publishing House, 1972), p. 87.

50. H. Richard Niebuhr, *Faith on Earth* (New Haven, CT: Yale University Press, 1989), p. 104.

51. Stafford, *Knowing the Face of God*, p. 94.

52. Louise Kendall and R. T. Kendall, eds., *Great Christian Prayers* (London: Hodder and Stoughton, 2000).

53. See Ratzinger, ed., *Catechism of the Catholic Church*, pp. 355, 516.

54. Maurice Wiles, "What Christians Believe," in *The Oxford Illustrated History of Christianity*, ed. John Mc Manners (New York: Oxford University Press, 1990), pp. 553–71. My citation is on p. 570.

55. Ratzinger, ed., *Catechism of the Catholic Church*, p. 484.

56. Henry T. Blackaby and Claude V. King, *Experiencing God* (Nashville, TN: Broadman and Holman Publishers, 1998), pp. 25, 30.

57. Henry Cloud and John Townsend, *God Will Make a Way* (Nashville, TN: Integrity Publishers, 2002), p. 98.

58. Schuller, *Be (Happy) Attitudes*, p. 17.

59. Anderson, *Who I Am in Christ*, p. 9.

60. Stafford, *Knowing the Face of God*, p. 31.

61. Anne Graham Lotz, *I Saw the Lord* (Grand Rapids, MI: Zodervan, 2006), pp. 90–97.

62. Darcey Steinke, "Divine Intervention." *Los Angeles Times Book Review*, February 24, 2008, p. R2.

63. Niebuhr, *Faith on Earth*, p. 104.

64. See Paul Tillich, *A History of Christian Thought* (New York: Harper and Row, 1968), pp. 100–101.

65. Ibid., p. 101.

66. Graham, *The Holy Spirit*, p. 242.

67. N.A., *God Speaks: Devotional* (Tulsa, OK: Honor Books, 2007), p. 87.

68. Blackaby and King, *Experiencing God*, p. 17.

69. Anderson, *Who I Am In Christ*, p. 27.

70. Houston Smith writes, "It is obedience to the will of the Father that is the 'food of Jesus,' and it is obedience which is to be characteristic of his Body, his Bride, which is the Church." See Houston Smith, *The Soul of Christianity: Restoring the Great Tradition* (San Francisco: Harper San Francisco, 2005), p. 133.

71. Schuller, *Be (Happy) Attitudes*, p. 81.

72. Graham, *The Holy Spirit*, p. 99.

73. Friedrich Nietzsche, "The Antichrist," in *The Portable Nietzsche*, trans. and ed. Walter Kaufman (New York: Penguin Books, 1976), pp. 656, 642.

74. See note 69 above.

75. *The Gospel Hour*, Trinity Broadcasting Network, September 6, 2006, 7:00 p.m., Channel 40, Orange County, California.

76. Stafford, *Knowing the Face of God*, p. 45.

77. Anderson, *Who I Am in Christ*, p. 20.

78. Jack Canfield, *Chicken Soup for the Christian Soul* (Deerfield Beach, FL: Health Communications, Inc. 1997), p. 294.

79. Schuller, *Be (Happy) Attitudes*, p. 83.

80. *The 700 Club*, Christian Broadcasting Network, May 9, 2006, 9:00 a.m., Channel 40, Orange County, California.

81. ———, Christian Broadcasting Network, August 7, 2007, 9:00 a.m., Channel 40, Orange County, California.

82. Gaston Bachelard, *The Poetics of Space* (Boston: Beacon Press, 1969), p. 5.

83. Christianity has through the ages offered us many versions of heaven, of course. Yet heaven as one's eternal home with a loving Parent-God at the center is certainly chief among them. See Colleen Mc Dannell and Bernhard Lang, *Heaven: A History* (New Haven, CT: Yale University Press, 1988), pp. 14–37.

84. N.A., *God Speaks: Devotional* (Tulsa, OK: Honor Books, 2000), p. 16.

85. Stafford, *Knowing the Face of God*, p. 81.

86. Ratzinger, ed., *Catechism of the Catholic Church*, p. 46.

87. My initial allusions to the mythological aspect of Christianity occur earlier in this chapter, during my discussion of the Eucharist.

88. N.A., *The Watchtower* (New York: Watchtower Bible and Tract Society, March 1, 2008), Vol. 129, No. 5, p. 8.

89. N.A., *Awake* (New York: Watchtower Bible and Tract Society, March 1, 2008), Vol. 89, No. 3, pp. 8–9.

90. Graham, *The Holy Spirit*, p. 10.

91. Lotz, *I Saw the Lord*, pp. 88–90.

92. Niebuhr, *Faith on Earth*, pp. 94–95.

# PART TWO

# Tracking the Parent-God: The Pastoral Metaphor

Edward O. Wilson provides us with the broad evolutionary framework we require when he characterizes religion (and thus Christianity) as "an environmental tracking device."[1] Let's pay close attention to his way of working up to that. Believe me, it's worth it if our goal is to understand Christianity right down to its biological roots. "Social behavior, like all other forms of biological response," writes Wilson (p. 74)

> is a set of devices for tracking changes in the environment. No organism is ever perfectly adapted. Nearly all the relevant parameters of its environment shift constantly. Some of the changes are periodic and predictable, such as the light-dark cycles and the seasons. But most are episodic and capricious, including fluctuations in the number of food items, nest sites and predators, random alterations of temperature and rainfall within seasons, and others. The organism must track these parts of its environment with some precision, yet it can never hope to respond correctly to every one of the multifactoral twists and turns—only to come close enough to survive for a little while and to reproduce as well as most.

Organisms solve the problem, Wilson goes on,

> with an immensely complex, multi-level tracking system. At the cellular level, perturbations are damped and homeostasis maintained by biochemical reactions that commonly take place in less than a second. . . . Higher organismic tracking devices, including social behaviors, require anywhere from a fraction of a second to a generation or slightly more for completion.

It is among humans, Wilson contends, that we discover the "highest grade" of "adaptational, organismic response" to the environment, namely, "the generalized learner" (pp. 74, 77).

In a series of key conceptual utterances that we'll have in mind from this point forward, Wilson observes,

> The organism has a brain large enough to carry a wide range of memories, some of which possess only a low probability of ever proving useful. Insight learning may be performed, yielding the capacity to generalize from one pattern to another and to juxtapose patterns in ways that are adaptively useful. . . . The process of socialization in this highest grade of organisms is prolonged and complex. Its details vary greatly among individuals. The key social feature of the grade, which is represented by man, the chimpanzee, baboons, macaques, and perhaps some other Old World primates, is a perception of history. The organism's knowledge is not limited to particular individuals and places with attractive or aversive associations. It also remembers relationships and incidents through time, and it can engineer improvements in its social status by relatively sophisticated choices of threat, conciliation, and alliances. It seems to be able to project mentally into the future, and in a few, extreme cases deliberate deception is practiced.
>
> (p. 77)

What evolves, then, "is the directedness of learning—the relative ease with which certain associations are made and acts are learned, and others bypassed even in the face of a strong reinforcement" (p. 79). In this way (and I will italicize the words that are absolutely vital to our purpose), "culture, including the more resplendent manifestations of ritual and religion, can be interpreted as a hierarchical system of environmental tracking devices. . . . To the extent that the specific details of culture are not genetic, *they can be decoupled from the biological system and arrayed beside it as an auxiliary system*" (p. 284). Here, then, is the overall perspective that enables us to integrate the neuropsychological and evolutionary approaches to Christianity's magical enactments, and in so doing, to deepen and enrich the contextual observations that have carried us to this juncture.

To understand Christianity as both "social behavior" and "biological response," we must include the *first society* in which and through which all human beings discover themselves as people "in the beginning" (Gen. 1:1), namely, the society of neonate and caregiver. For several crucial years (1–5) the infant and small child *track* the parent, and the parent *tracks* the infant and small child in an adaptive, life-sustaining mutuality (or symbiosis) upon which the survival of both individual and species entirely depends.

Homeostasis for the newly born human animal is inextricably bound up with this *environmental tracking system* that is memorialized into the emerging mind-brain and recalled implicitly, and to a lesser extent explicitly, for the duration of that animal's existence on the planet. At one level of environmental tracking, homeostasis is maintained by parental reaction that commonly takes place (I will echo Wilson as closely as I can) in a few seconds (response to the child's pain or hunger); other organismic tracking behaviors involving bodily training and what we think of as "manners" (adaptive integration into the familial unit and wider communal group) require anywhere from days to weeks to months to years for completion. The *directedness* of this internalized learning is clear. The little one cries out, calls, mouths his primal syntactic speech (mama, come), or otherwise indicates through bodily movement and gesture his biological, emotional urge to gratify his needs, and the big one responds accordingly, thus fulfilling her or his role in the *tracking arrangement*. To employ the Christian terminology, associated primarily with the act of supplication as we've seen, the little one *asks* and the big one sees to it that he *receives* (Luke 11:9–10).

As the little one develops mnemonically through such directional learning, he *remembers* not merely individuals and places with attractive or aversive associations; he remembers *relationships through time*, and this yields the capacity to generalize from one pattern of relationship (mama/daddy) to another pattern of relationship (the God who watches over him [tracks him]/mother church)—in short, to *juxtapose patterns* in modes that are adaptively useful. He comes to Christianity *with a perception of history*, with the contextual knowledge of his first *salvational experience* in the hands (quite literally) of his transformational ("magical"), loving, omnipotent provider who comprised for many crucial years his principal *environment*, his *world*. Thus, he comes to Christianity with the concomitant ability *to project into the future*, to *use* his past experience in his efforts to deal with the world in which he discovers himself. Because these manifold, two-way (child/parent), biological adaptations are not strictly genetical, they can *be decoupled from the biological system and arrayed beside it as an auxiliary system for tracking the environment*, the magical system of Christianity, for example, which is designed explicitly to cope with problems that resemble, indeed that inevitably call to mind and to body, the problems with which the little one coped "in the beginning." Was he small and vulnerable in the beginning? Well, *he still is* as he confronts the unpredictable, overwhelming forces of nature and culture that surround him: accident, illness, injustice, enemies, floods, earthquakes, droughts, and starvation. Was he afraid of separation in the beginning? Was he anxious about finding himself alone? Well, *he still is* (especially in our anomic, modern social order) as he copes with the cessation of parental care, with "growing up," with the sheer physical and emotional recognition that he *is*, in fact, alone, or "on his own" in the world around him. Was he instinctually, organically afraid of cessation, of death? Of course he was, like all creatures great and small. Well, *he still is*, and afraid not only instinctually but consciously, perceptually, and existentially. As a "grown-up" he must confront cessation not only in his body but in his mind, his imagination; he must *contemplate* his end (dust to dust), and in such contemplation ("Alas, poor Yorick!") he must confront the primal terror that all human beings confront through their symbol-making capacity, through their "higher consciousness." It hardly needs to be added, of course, that all of this taken together, smallness, separation, and death, holds the potential to engender considerable anxiety, not to say genuine emotive malaise, in the normal, everyday human creature as he goes about his business on the planet. So what does the creature do?

Predictably, adaptively, and to a certain degree shrewdly, *he falls back on what worked*. Tracking the parental big one worked early on, so let's juxtapose patterns, decouple the strictly biological from the purely inventive, and do the same thing all over again in our predicament, when we find ourselves coping with dangers and discomforts during a later stage of our development. Let's become "little children" *again*; let's follow a Big One *again* (lead us not into temptation), depend on a Big One, ask of a Big One, feed on a Big One (Jesus as umbilical Vine), go *into* a Big One (the Eucharist), and thus, precisely thus, we'll find ourselves "delivered" again. We'll feel attached, secure, empowered, and last but certainly not least, immortal (O death, where is thy sting?). In other words, we'll escape our primal fears, our primal anxieties, and by so doing we'll *function better*, more adaptively, more homeostatically, as we deal with the challenges, the demands, the sorrows, and the pleasures that greet us along the way. Through the magical system of Christianity we'll fashion another, alternative identity (a version of the original one we experienced), and place it alongside the problematical, biological one with which our development has saddled us. We'll become *two people*, one in the natural, physical, "fallen" world of smallness, separation, and mortality, and the other in the "spiritual" domain of eternal bonding, eternal security, eternal innocence, first as the creational Garden is restored to us (the new Adam) and subsequently as Heaven opens its magnificent, pearly portals. No matter that our infancy and early childhood were imperfect, had their flaws, even perhaps their miseries. They were, in the last analysis, "good enough" (Winnicott, p. 12). They *worked*, and that's all we need. We can idealize and refashion as much as we wish, now; we can luxuriate fully in contemplation of a perfect, flawless, loving Parental-Presence who is *there*, always and forever *there*, with no exceptions whatsoever (I am with you always, even unto the end of the world). We're *on track* again.

Finally, *as* we track the Big One, *as* we discover His salvational presence in our lives and being, something deep inside (implicit mnemonic retrieval of the original, unitary, biological tracking system) tells us directly, intimately, and feelingly that He is *actually there*, actually present in our hearts, and in everything that exists (the "Holy Spirit," an integral facet of the doctrinal Godhead). To return once again to our theoretical position as described in the opening paragraphs of this section, we have here what evolutionist Gerald M. Edelman would call a "teleonomic system," or a "prediction of the past."[2] Edelman writes, "Brains are selective recognition systems," and "recognition" is "a kind of adaptive matching of animals to their environments. . . . We are driven by a recategorical memory under the influence of dynamic changes of value." Memory, "the key element in consciousness," allows us to achieve meaning through "reentry," through mapping previous experience onto the present in a manner that leads us to adaptive, or selective, behavior. Accordingly, Edelman goes on,

> Evolution can select animals in such a way that they have general goals, purposes, and values. . . . The past experience of natural selection adjusts the set points of value systems . . . that are adaptive for survival. In our case, the brain of a conscious human being, serving as a somatic selective system, uses value constraints to project the future in terms of categories [parent/child] and goals [security].

In reference to religion specifically, Edelman remarks, "Of course . . . we must admit the possibility of an almost total denial of biological values on the part of those organisms we call martyrs and saints. Only creatures endowed with higher-order consciousness can so transcend the dictates of biology."[3] The ultimate adaptive aim of Christianity's magical system of behavior, then, is to deny the very "dictates of biology" that trigger its "Creation" in the first place. The ultimate *reality* of the infantilized Christian is a *spirit* that confirms the existence of a *supernatural* Parent-God.

We come now to a watershed: at the metaphorical heart of the Judeo-Christian tradition in general and the Christian religion in particular is an "environmental tracking device," or tracking system, in which a helpless, dependent little one (the sheep) tracks an all-powerful, provisional Big One (the shepherd) Who in turn watches over, or keeps an eye on, His charge, His creation, His child. Because the metaphor is designed to capture the ideal essence of the human being's relationship with the Almighty, and because that relationship is rendered in terms of absolute dependency, absolute trust, absolute submission, and sustainment, the pastoral configuration of care as a whole creates in the worshiper a striking memorial echo of his own biological development, an echo from which emanates, for Christians, that mysterious, validating, comforting entity known officially as the "Holy Spirit."

"*Follow* me," says Jesus to his first disciples, Andrew and Peter, as He discovers them "casting a net into the sea" (Matt. 4–19, my emphasis).[4] "And they straightway left their nets, and *followed* him." (I italicize the words that commence the theme of tracking.) "And going on from thence, he saw two other brethren," James and John, "And they immediately left the ship and their father, and *followed* him" (Matt. 4:22). Eventually, as Jesus's "fame" (Matt. 4:24) begins to spread in earnest, "there *followed* him great multitudes of people from Galilee, and from Decapolis, and from Jerusalem . . . " (Matt. 4:25). When Jesus perceives fully these "multitudes" approaching Him for guidance and succor, He is "moved with compassion on them" because (here the pastoral metaphor explicitly commences) "they fainted, and were scattered abroad, as sheep having no shepherd" (Matt. 9:36). Instructing His disciples to go about the land with His sacred, salvational message, Jesus declares, "go . . . to the lost sheep of the house of Israel. And as ye go, preach, saying, the kingdom of heaven is at hand" (Matt. 10:6–7). Let us note carefully that it is here, in the 10th chapter of Matthew and in precisely this emergent metaphorical context of following or tracking, of lost sheep, and of the shepherd who guides the flock, that Jesus announces to His disciples His intention of "set[ting] a man at variance against his father, and the daughter against her mother" (Matt. 10:35). Indeed, says Christ, "he that loveth father or mother more than me is not worthy of me; and he that loveth son or daughter more than me is not worthy of me. And he that taketh not his cross, and *followeth after me*, is not worthy of me" (Matt. 10:37). Clearly, Jesus in the guise of the ministering shepherd is bent upon taking the place of the parent in the worshiper's life; and if the worshiper is a parent already, then his or her "love" must be directed most powerfully, most passionately, toward his or her salvational guide as opposed to the natural offspring of the biological family. The devotees of God's Son and Heir will follow after Him, will track Him and only Him, and if they themselves are tracked by their mortal offspring, then they must subordinate such tracking to their loving affiliation with the Redeemer. The only tracking acceptable to Jesus is tracking after Him. He is the Shepherd, and everyone else without exception is sheep.

It is to the Pharisees that Jesus crystallizes through the pastoral metaphor the nature of His sacred purpose in the world, His intention for mankind, and His relationship with the Father in heaven. As He goes about His explanatory business, Jesus makes plain for *us* the evolutional, adaptive significance of the Christian religion, the way it works in the minds and bodies of those who become *followers*. It is no matter that the parable of the "sheepfold" falls on hostile, deaf ears where the Pharisees are concerned (they want to stone Him when He's finished). Our analytical ears, and eyes, are wide open, and we are grateful for the information.

> Verily, verily, I say unto you, He that entereth not by the door into the sheepfold, but climbeth up some other way, the same is a thief and a robber.
>
> But he that entereth in by the door is the shepherd of the sheep.
>
> To him the porter openeth; and the sheep hear his voice: and he calleth his own sheep by name, and leadeth them out.
>
> And when he putteth forth his own sheep, he goeth before them, and the sheep follow him: for they know his voice.
>
> And a stranger they will not follow, but will flee from him: for they know not the voice of strangers.
>
> (John 10:1–5)

Working to refine His meaning for those who attend, Jesus continues,

> Verily, verily, I say unto you, I am the door of the sheep.
>
> All that ever came before me are thieves and robbers; but the sheep did not hear them.
>
> I am the door: by me if any man enter in, he shall be saved, and shall go in and out, and find pasture.
>
> The thief cometh not, but for to steal, and to kill, and to destroy; I am come that they may have life, and that they might have it more abundantly.
>
> I am the good shepherd: the good shepherd giveth his life for the sheep.
>
> (John 7–11)

Finally, declares Christ,

> My sheep hear my voice, and I know them, and they follow me:
>
> And I give unto them eternal life; and they shall never perish, neither shall any man pluck them out of my hand.
>
> I and my Father are one.
>
> (John 27–30)

Here, within the pastoral metaphor through which Christ delivers his pivotal explanation of what becomes doctrinally the Christian religion itself, is the early period of our biological lives, down to a tee: the helpless little ones are ensconced in their special place, their nook, their gated room; vulnerable, at risk, ultimately within reach of the world's "evil," its dangers, its corruptions, its thievery and murder; dependent entirely on the big one who watches over them, protects them, feeds them (in "pasture"), ensures that they have and will continue to have the "life" they naturally crave. Just as the infant is instinctively attracted to the parent's "voice" (and "face" as we shall see very soon), so the little ones in the "sheepfold" know the "voice" of their provider and "follow" after it (track it) when they hear it. Not only do they balk at following after strangers; they "flee" from them when they hear their unfamiliar voices, just as human infants and small children anxiously shy away from those to whom they are not instinctually and/or socially connected. And, of course, the shepherd "names" his sheep and "calls them out by name," makes them his individual charges, members of his personal, pastoral family with whom he goes forward "hand in hand" (John 10:29). The "environmental tracking device" on which Wilson concentrated earlier from his evolutionary perspective is captured perfectly, finally, when Jesus declares that He will not only protect and provide for His charges but will ensure them "life more abundantly," which is to say, see to it that they receive from the "environment" everything they require to flourish. To render the issue from a homeostatic angle, to track after Jesus is to get all one needs, just as the infant/child gets all he needs by following after the biological provider (the human animal's original *tracking device*).

Let's bear in mind that the "sheep" of Christ's "parable" are explicitly His "little children" (Matt. 18:3), made so, or soon to be made so, through baptismal rite, through spiritual "rebirth." Indeed, *only* as Christ's "little children" can the followers or trackers find their way to the eternal "pasture" of "salvation," or the "kingdom of heaven" that is now "at hand." Too, the "sheep" have established themselves as "worthy" followers of Jesus by "loving" Him "more" than they love their natural, biological parents (Matt. 10:37), by putting *Him* in the parent's place. Jesus, the Shepherd after Whom the sheep track, has become explicitly a *parental presence*. At the end of His "parable," Christ firmly declares, "I and my Father are one" (John 10:30), which is to say, Jesus is now to be identified equally with the "Father" as the *creator* of the flock, as the divine progenitor of the *followers*, the *trackers* who look to *Him* for their existence, their lives, and well-being. And like all good parents who love their children overwhelmingly, unconditionally, Jesus affirms His willingness to *die* for His offspring, for His "little ones," for those who follow dependently after Him when He calls them forth by name from their shady nook—a wishful, idealized echo of the biological provider whose devotion to his little guy or gal is total, limitless, and complete. As for the "biological dictate" of mortality, the one dire earthy given that no one gets around, even *that* Christ Jesus defeats, or as Edelman would say, denies. To track *Him* is to live forever, to know the "pasture" forever, to experience what might be termed "eternal adaptation" or "eternal homeostasis." The collapse of organic integrity, the blunt fact of biological decay and extinction (Yorick's skull) is *ultimately canceled* as Christianity restores the worshiper through the infantilization process to the period of biological life that obtained *before* one became conscious of separation from the matrix, *before* one gained awareness of his eventual biologic disappearance from the world. The magical "shepherd" transforms his "sheep," his grown-up followers, into perfectly secure "little children," offspring as they *were* "in the beginning," in Eden, in the Garden days of flawless, timeless symbiotic merger with the Big One. Thus we see in the parable of the "sheepfold" the overall aim of the Christian religion, or how it works in the mind and the body. Christ's worshipers, Christ's devotees, Christ's trackers are returned through implicit recollection to the primal stage during which eternal union and eternal life were emotively or affectively *real*: death and separation did not yet conceptually exist. In this way, the actual biological program (or tracking system) of the infant and caregiver is decoupled from its biological foundation and arrayed metaphorically alongside the "cultural institution" or "religion" where it can awaken mnemonically the original "pattern" and thus restore the primal adaptation, the primal security, the primal homeostasis upon which each of us relied as we sought to get under way "in the beginning." The pastoral metaphor, to employ Edelman's terminology, seeks to fashion through memory "a perceptual identity between present and past objects."[5] As we've contended all along, it is precisely the mnemonic resuscitation of such affect, such feeling, such emotion that catalyzes the appearance of the wondrous "Holy Spirit" in the worshiper's endogenous perceptual field, an appearance that triggers in turn his heartfelt belief in the veracity of the Christian "story," its mythologized version of our origins and destiny that to this very day enchants the countless millions who seek to reverse, for perfectly understandable reasons, the stern "dictates" of our biological existence.

The centrality and frequency of pastoral metaphors in the Judeo-Christian tradition is randomly attributed to the ubiquity of pastoral life in the ancient Near East.[6] "Pastor" in the religious sense derives ultimately from "pastor" in the Biblical sense of "shepherd." But to let it go at that, to adhere exclusively to a historical exegesis (as is usually the case), would be arrantly superficial. The pastoral metaphor is everywhere, and frequently at the center of decisive doctrinal exposition, because the pastoral situation in and of itself, with controller, caregiver, and guide in charge of helpless, dependent trackers or followers, lends unerring metaphorical expression to the inward essence of Christianity, its psychological/neurological foundations in the early period of our lives, the period during which the original biological tracking arrangement between caregiver and neonate is implemented for years and internalized deeply into the mind-brain of the potential believer, the worshiper and follower of the explicitly parental Deity Who watches over his explicit "little children." During but one stage of our participation in the natural order of things did we know perfect or relatively perfect security and perfect or relatively perfect love as we luxuriated in the hands of the ministering big one. Christianity's chief aim, from which comes its appeal, is to restore the faithful to precisely that situation on the supernatural (magical) level and thereby to remove from their existence on the earth the natural, biological imperfections that all of us inherit simply by virtue of our having been born. If "metaphor" is "the currency of the mind," as Edelman maintains in his evolutionary writings, and if "memory" is "the key element in consciousness" or in what Edelman calls "the remembered present,"[7] then the pastoral metaphor as it is consciously employed in the Judeo-Christian tradition purchases our admission to the psychological/neurological analysis in which we may behold the wishful, emotional roots of present-day Christian thought and practice. Just listen to the commentators as they pin the matter down for us.

"Learning to listen to God's voice is critical if you and I want to maintain the fire of our personal revival," writes Anne Graham Lotz.[8]

> Jesus taught that listening to His voice is one of the fundamental principles of discipleship. He described Himself as the Good Shepherd and you and me as His sheep when He taught, "the sheep listen to his [the Shepherd's] voice. He calls his own sheep by name and leads them out. . . . His sheep follow Him because they know his voice."

Lotz goes on,

> In Western civilization, the concept of a personal shepherd is relatively meaningless. When an epidemic of hoof-and-mouth disease was reported in the news a few years ago, we saw sheep ranches flashed on the news and sheep pens pictured on the front page of our morning newspaper, making the public aware of a little-noticed but vital industry. Sheep today graze in carefully fenced-in pastures and are guarded by specially bred dogs and identified by a number tattooed in their ears.
>
> (p. 140)

And then, in the crucial utterance,

> But the eastern shepherd was, and in many parts of the world still is, very different. He raised his sheep from the time they were lambs and maintained responsibility for them twenty-four hours a day, seven days a week, year in and year out, for their entire lifetime. There were no dogs or fences or tattoos.
>
> The Eastern Shepherd of Jesus's day raised his sheep primarily in the Judean uplands. The countryside was rocky, hilly, and filled with deep crevices and ravines. Patches of grass were sparse. So the shepherd had to establish a personal, working relationship with each sheep, developing its love and trust in him in order to lead it to where the path was smoothest, the pasture was the greenest, the water was the cleanest, and the nights were the safest. The shepherd always *led* the sheep. He knew their names, and when he called them, they recognized his voice, following him like a swarm of little chicks follow the mother hen. When he stopped, the sheep huddled closely around him, pressing against his legs. Their personal relationship with him was based on his voice, which they knew and trusted.
>
> (p. 141)

"In this parable," concludes Lotz, "you and I are the sheep, the Good Shepherd is Jesus, and the voice of the Good Shepherd is the Word of God. Our Shepherd speaks to us through the written words of our Bible, and His words are personal" (p. 141). The psychological/neurological gist of all this could hardly be plainer.

The "Eastern shepherd" attends to his sheep in a manner that strikingly recalls the manner in which human parents attend to their own little "lambs," maintaining their parental responsibility "twenty-four hours a day," establishing a climate of "trust" and "love," guiding their offspring toward the "smoothest paths," the "greenest pastures," the "safest" locations for rest and sleep. Lotz even offers us an actual "tracking device" that explicitly reflects the essence of the tracking arrangement among humans during the early period when she alludes to a "swarm" of "chicks" following after their mama hen. But we don't need Lotz's chicks and hens to fathom the significance of the pastoral metaphor in Christian thought and practice. We have our own human experience, our own early stage of biological existence that provides us not only with the nature of Christianity's appeal to the human subconscious but with the mnemonic mechanism through which arises the mysterious Holy Spirit when the Christian practitioner finds himself convinced by the overall mythologic configuration to which he is exposed as he involves himself in the magical enactments of the creed (baptism, prayer, the

Eucharist, and the Scriptural metaphors of vine and shepherd). "You and I are the sheep," and "the Good Shepherd is Jesus," declares our theological expert (Lotz, p. 141). As for the most decisive and revealing utterance in the whole of Lotz's rendition of Christianity through the pastoral metaphor, it resides in her remark that the shepherd "maintained his responsibility" for his sheep "twenty-four hours a day, seven days a week, year in and year out, *for their entire lifetime*" (my emphasis). Here is the very *crossroads* of the *human tracking systems* both biological and symbolic in a single sentence, if the reader will allow the pun. I mean, human beings do *not* receive from their caregivers, their "shepherds," *all* that the docile, ever-dependent sheep receive. They are *not* led about (or allowed to follow after) for the entire length of their lives. In contrast to the ovine little ones, the human "lambs" must *separate* from the caregiver/shepherd as their earthly existence goes forward; they must *relinquish* their dependent reliance upon the big one, go out on their own, confront the future with its dangers and challenges, including, of course, the future's final culmination (and termination) in *death*. So what do the humans *do* when through their higher consciousness (ultimately a *tracking* feature) they find themselves staring straight at the "biological dictates" of separation, smallness, and morality? Well, what millions of them do in our modern Western culture about which I am writing here is precisely what this book has been suggesting they do from its inception: they discover through the Christian religion that awaits them with open arms a way to keep the original tracking arrangement alive by relocating it on the symbolic, supernatural plane (Christianity's infantilizing process); they subscribe to a theological "story" about a spiritual "Shepherd," a Parent-God, who continues to love and watch over them (track them) "for their entire lifetime," long after the separation stage of their development has transpired. In this way, they simply remove, or deny, the problematic biological dictates, thereby diminishing the uncertainty and anxiety that attends them in their vulnerable, separated state, or alternatively, increasing their adaptation to the environment in which they reside and function. Christianity, the "environmental tracking device" (Wilson, p. 284), has spied the destabilizing dangers. Human beings are *not* separate, says the Christian creed; they are *not* alone, and small, and vulnerable; they do *not* face a future that leads ineluctably to death, extinction, and removal from the world and from all the loved ones that world contains. On the contrary, human beings will be *shepherded* for all eternity, led by the hand, in the care of a perfect parental presence through whom they will know *only* security, love, and everlasting life.

Neil T. Anderson, in a section titled "God's Love Reaches into the Future,"[9] makes the matter crystal clear. "With God," he writes, we have an eternal relationship that cannot be overcome by the temporal calamities of life.... Our heavenly Father is the Lord of Eternity. We should have no fear of tomorrow, death, demons, or eternity. The shepherd of our souls says, "My sheep listen to my voice; I know them, and they follow me. I give them eternal life, and they shall never perish; no one can snatch them out of my Father's hand (John 10:27–29)."

(p. 135)

Anderson concludes with the assertion "our relationship with God is not a question of our ability to hang on to Him. It really isn't within our own personal power to do that anyway. The fact is, God holds on to us, and He has the power to keep us securely and safely in His hand" (p. 135). Can we fail to perceive the upshot? Powerless, utterly dependent, led by the hand like a little child who is apt to get lost, the Christian "lamb" follows after the Shepherd into a psychological/neurological realm of perfect "security" and perfect "safety" both of which are his to enjoy forevermore. There is no separation, no vulnerability, no *future* in the anxiety-inducing sense of ordinary time leading to one's ultimate extinction. As in the early period of symbiotic merger with the caregiver, the period during which the organ relationship of parent and newcomer places the child within the emotional orbit of his natural controller and guide, the infantilized Christian is *ultimately removed* from the reach of "biological dictates" with the potential to upset his adaptational equilibrium. "No organism," wrote Wilson in the materials with which we opened this section, "is ever perfectly adapted" (p. 74). Christianity, by fashioning another, supernatural "environment" in which its adherents may track after an omnipotent Parent-God with the capacity to dispense "eternal" security and safety, strives to give Wilson's realistic, earthly observation *the lie*.

## Applications: The Pastoral Metaphor at Work

To track the pastoral metaphor to its psychological/neurological origins in the early period allows us fully to perceive, fully to understand, a veritable host of Christian materials that are otherwise obscured by conventional and ultimately fatuous significations. Write Blackaby and King,

God is far more interested in a love relationship with you than He is in what you can do for Him. His desire is for you to love Him.... You can trust Him to guide you and provide for you.... Agree with God that you will follow Him [track Him] one day at a time. Agree to follow Him even when He does not spell out all the details. Agree that you will let Him be your Way.[10]

Pray to God thusly, instruct Blackaby and King at this juncture: "Lord, I will do anything that your kingdom requires of me. Wherever You want me to be, I'll go. Whatever the circumstances, I'm willing to follow. If You want to meet a need through my life, I am your servant; and I will do whatever is required" (p. 37). Rather than abandon such material to whatever it happens to signify for whoever happens to read it or utter it or think it—it can mean, simply, anything—we must recognize its specific power and appeal within the framework of Christianity's infantilizing process. Blackaby and King are looking to recapture a "love relationship" they once knew and deeply internalized as they "trusted" and "followed" after the big one during the period of their lives when the caregiver's "way" was the only trustworthy, loving, gratifying way and when the follower's will was entirely bound up with the will of the omnipotent parental presence, the proverbial lord of the nursery. In other words, *it makes no difference* to the Christian what the particulars of his or her following are—to work for the Salvation Army, to forgive the family members he or she rejected as a youth, to go off as a missionary in the outback of Australia, to stay at home and raise the kids, or a thousand other things. What ultimately matters is that one returns psychologically or inwardly to the "love relationship," the putative will-lessness, the "trust," the sense of tracking and union that one knew "in the beginning." The worshiper feels loved, secured, guided, and bonded when he gets back to this arrangement with a big one, and he gets back to it precisely (how else?) by mentally becoming a will-less, trusting, loving, and tracking "infant" once again. The Christian religion always works for those who become "little children" because whatever it is that one is doing, he gains a sense of connection through his implicit mnemonic rediscovery of the little one's "way" (Blackaby and King, p. 37), the little one's inner world. The magical identity with its promise of loving union and eternal security lessens or even removes the anxiety, or perhaps the existential discomfort, that attends the biological identity of separate, vulnerable, time-bound mortal man or woman.

Here are a few more citations from Blackaby and King that tell us why "a love relationship with God" is so important: "He loves you. He knows what is best for you [if the reader had a childhood he'll remember *that* one]. Only He can guide you to invest your life in worthwhile ways. The guidance will come as you walk with Him and listen to Him [track and recognize His "voice" as in John 10:4]" (p. 91). Or again,

> God wants us to adjust our lives to Him so He can do through us what He wants to do. . . . We are His servants, and we adjust our lives to what He is

about to do and to His ways of doing it. If we will not submit God will let us follow our own device [that is, allow us not to track Him].

(p. 106)

Or still again, this time through a heartfelt supplication titled *My Surrender to God's Invitation*:

> God, when You invite me to join You in Your work, I will respond immediately. I will adjust my life to You. Show me how to respond to what You lovingly reveal to me. It is an awesome privilege to be in a love relationship with You and have You trust me to join in Your work. I am ready to join You. Show me Your timing. Make clear to me what You are doing. I praise You that You have promised to complete whatever You start. I surrender to Your invitation. Lead me to where I should begin.

(pp. 129–30)

Clearly, the tracking metaphor, the "following," the "guidance," the "walking with God," the "obedience" and "surrender"—all of this—is paramount in a context that is *left wide open*. What does it *mean* to "walk with" or "listen to" God, to "adjust" one's life to what God wants one to do, to "submit" to His "will," to be "led" to "where one should begin," and all the rest of it? Over and over again we hear this sort of thing on television, or in church; over and over again we read such declarations in the Christian literature, as here. The answer is, it means whatever the Christian wants it to mean, whatever he happens to consider godly in his moment of inspiration, for whatever reasons he manufactures through his consciousness and his subconsciousness, the latter of which is not available to him when his putative will-lessness gives way to his desired goal. The specifics do not matter. What matters, as I've suggested, is the magical sense that one is *back in* the dependent, symbiotic relationship of trust, and love, and uninterrupted tracking in which one luxuriated early on. When the Christian arouses through his implicit recollection the feeling of being *in* as opposed to out, the "way" of the Lord, whatever it happens to be, has made itself known.

Does the Holy Spirit, perchance, have a hand in all this? Of course it does, for the Holy Spirit is itself but a magical metaphor of the addictive recollection one craves as he strives to track the Big One's commanding presence or "voice" in his life. "Is it important to know when the Holy Spirit is speaking to you," ask Blackaby and King? They immediately reply, "Yes!" Then come the words, "How do you know what the Holy Spirit is saying" (p. 176)? An excellent question! Here is the answer, to which we must pay very close attention: "I cannot give you a formula," writes Blackaby, now speaking for both himself and his co-author;

I can tell you that you will know His voice when He speaks (John 10:4). You must decide that you only want His will. You must dismiss any selfish or fleshy desire of your own. Then as you start to pray, the Spirit of God starts to touch your heart and cause you to pray in the direction of God's will. "It is God who works in you both to will and to do for His good pleasure" (Phil. 2:13). . . . When you pray, anticipate that the Holy Spirit already knows what God has ready for your life.

(p. 176)

Through precisely this methodology for contacting the Holy Spirit does the underlying, appetitive psychology of "doing God's work," or "following God's way," emerge within the framework of Christianity's infantilizing process. The worshiper is instructed to *act out*, to *imitate* (homeopathic magic) the assertion of John 10:4 that "the sheep follow him: for they know his voice" through the ritual of prayer, a ritual, as we previously established, in which the supplicant adopts specifically the role of the helpless, dependent little one crying out to the loving, omnipotent Big One for succor and support. If this behavior awakens the implicit recollection of parental ministration and care, then the putative "Holy Spirit," right on schedule, will prompt one's "heart" to pray "in the direction of God's will," and we are back to Blackaby and King's opening assertion, the significance of which is now in full view, that "God is far more interested in a love relationship with you than He is in what you can do for Him. His desire is for you to love Him" (p. 36). Accordingly, the tracker, the follower, the worshipful lamb whose will now belongs entirely to the Shepherd and whose "fleshly" or *adult* "desires" have now been entirely "dismissed" reaches his ultimate, magical goal, namely, symbiotic union with the Lord. No longer "lost" in the biological world, which means existing without a "love relationship" with the Big One, but doing the Almighty's "work" on the spiritual plane, which means doing whatever one's mind has happened to create as a worthy goal, the believer has come full circle, from the early period of security and innocence to anxiety-inducing separation (including the awareness of death) and back again to the realm of eternal provision and care. The "formula" here, needless to say, is the formula for the Christian religion as a whole; Blackaby and King's extended discussion of how one goes about learning to "follow" God's "way," or to do "God's work," is merely one more facet of the infantilizing procedure. What are those concluding lines of Charles Wesley's wishful prayer cited earlier?

Concealed in the cleft of thy side,
Eternally held in thy heart.[11]

This, in the final analysis, is all a Christian really wants.

We no longer have to wonder, then, what the word "lost" signifies when theologian H. Richard Niebuhr tells us in a prototypical Christian moment that Jesus "seeks and saves the lost."[12] We have the pastoral metaphor, the "lost sheep of Israel," to inform our understanding as we derive psychological/neurological specificity as opposed to flaccid generality from the utterance. Although its precise emotional, circumstantial denotation will differ in each and every case (no two snowflakes are exactly alike, etc.), "lost" signifies in the Christian context separate, alone, isolated, abandoned, on one's own, or, to turn the coin over, not merged, not bonded, not joined to a big one, not contained symbiotically in the body of salvational Jesus—in short, not receiving the adaptational sensation one receives as he enjoys the deep-seated, implicit recollection of the loving, ministering parental presence (the "Holy Spirit"). It is when the Christian's participation in the creed's infantilizing magic allows him to *follow* his memorial capacities all the way back to the "beginning," to his original security-inducing interactions with the nurturing biological caregiver, that he finds his "way," which means his escape from the dreaded biological dictates of his natural, mortal existence on a "fallen" planet.

The reader may be thinking, wait a minute! Surely within a Christian context "lost" may have a moral denotation, may indicate the seeker's failure to lead a moral life, one based on Christian principles, one grounded in the decent, chaste, substance-free treatment of oneself and others. Is not Christianity ultimately a moral system, a moral guide to human conduct? The answer, of course, is that Christian morality does not stand apart from Christianity's infantilizing process. The two go together, in powerful combination. To be a good, obedient Christian, to respect Christianity's moral teachings, is *also* to be in a bonded relationship with the Savior as His "little child," His "sheep," His helpless, dependent follower, as one He will never "forsake" or "abandon": follow Christ "as dear children," not as "children of disobedience," instructs the New Testament (Eph. 5:1, 6). Accordingly, to be "bad," disobedient, unlawful, unchaste, unwholesome, alcohol or drug addicted, or even selfish and insincere is for the Christian to feel "lost," alone, "out in the cold," without the sense of parental connection to a big one, to a loving source of security and succor—a grievous, painful, extreme version of the very feelings of biological separation that goad the bond to Jesus into life in the first place. When the drunk, or the drug addict, or the prostitute on the street, or the bank robber on parole finds Jesus and begins to participate in Christianity's infantilizing rites and narratives, to do the magic in short, he or she also discovers the long-forgotten inward sensation of being valued, and cherished, and held. *That* is what impels him or her to stay the course.

"Go out there again" (note the word "out" as opposed to "in"), the reformed Christian asks himself? "Lose this feeling of self-love and self-worth based upon my Christian faith? Not a chance"! As human beings, we don't need the supernatural to achieve morality. The moral impulse can take vigorous root within the natural, secular realm. What resides at the foundation of Christianity's moral directives is the emotional, psychological tie to the supernatural Big One Who, on the plane of magic, holds His "dear child" forever in His heart of hearts.

With our increasingly rich, perhaps newly found awareness of what resides at the psychological/neurological ground of the pastoral metaphor, its developmental, emotional relationship to the engendering experiences upon which our lives as biological organisms move forward "in the beginning," let's sample a few excerpts from famous Christian prayers both past and present. Let's get a feeling for what Christians are actually saying and seeking beneath the surface imagery of certain heartfelt expressions of their faith.

Here is Saint Augustine:

> I thank thee, O my Light, that Thou didst shine upon me; that Thou didst teach my soul what Thou wouldst be to me, and didst incline Thy face in pity unto me; Thou, Lord, hast become my Hope, my comfort, my Strength, my All. In Thee doth my soul rejoice. . . . When I loved darkness, I knew Thee not, but wandered on from night to night. But Thou didst lead me out of that blindness. Thou didst take me by the hand and call me to thee, and now I can thank Thee, and Thy mighty voice which hath penetrated to my inmost heart.[13]

We do not know, and we cannot know, what Augustine refers to when he writes of his "blindness," of the "darkness" through which he "wanders," lost and miserable. Perhaps he refers to his youthful absorption in Zoroastrianism, or to his powerful, unruly sexual nature against which he struggled for many years. It doesn't matter. Each reader will apply Augustine's supplication to his own experience. What does matter here is the invariant Christian solution to the dilemma, whatever it happens to be, namely, becoming the Almighty's dutiful "little child," putting one's "hand" into the hand of the Big One, listening to God's mighty "voice" as in the pastoral metaphor explicitly—in short, *tracking after the Lord* (as an "environmental tracking device") and thus refinding a version of the homeostasis or equilibrium one enjoyed early on through one's dependent, symbiotic interaction with the biological provider. When the confused, insecure, miserable human creature submits to Christianity's infantilizing process, he transforms himself into a contented, even joyous member of the species by awakening his implicit recollection of the time in which he *actually knew* the guidance and the loving security he craves.

"Thank you, Father, for your love," writes Corrie ten Boom, and then,

> Thank you for hearing our prayers and giving us that which You know is best for us. We thank You that we need never walk in darkness, because you are leading us and showing us the way, step by step. Teach us, Lord, to be obedient. . . . Show us in what way we still hold on to our own will and desires, and give us the courage to leave all in Your hands, Thank you, Father, that You will always speak to us when we come to You with a heart which is willing to hear and willing to do as You say.
>
> (p. 23)

Once again, whatever the dilemma the supplicator confronts, its solution resides in *tracking the Big One* Who "knows what is best" for His sheep, Who leads them and shows them the way, step by baby step, as in the opening stages of their biological lives. The prayer beseeches the Deity to instruct her not merely in "obedience" but in "leaving" her "desires" and her "will" entirely His hands, an accomplishment that can occur *only* within the realm of implicit recollection, the memorial trace (or phenomenology) of the early period when the "will" and the "desires" of the newcomer are inextricably intertwined with the direction of the omnipotent biological provider. Simply to brush one's teeth and comb one's hair negates in reality the notion of "leaving" everything in "God's hands" unless one behaves with an inward sense of the Big One's overarching participation in one's activities, a sense that drifts toward consciousness from the implicit memorial realm as it is aroused by Christianity's infantilizing beliefs and practices.

"Lord what can I say?" asks Oswald Chambers at the commencement of his heartfelt supplication. He goes on,

> Keep me simply Thine. To body, soul and spirit come with the influx of life. Lord, through all the multitudinous duties keep me calm, ennoble by Thy touch and tenderness. O Lord, it is Thee I want, strong and mighty and pure. Settle me and quieten me down in Thee. Thy word says, "Casting all your cares upon Him, for He careth for you." What a wonder those words are! Lord, I look to thee that I may be renewed in the spirit of my mind. How entirely I look to Thee! Unto Thee do I come in great and glad expectancy. Cleanse me from flurry, and keep me purely and calmly Thine. Gather me into concentrated peace in Thee.
>
> (p. 57)

Chambers captures for us unmistakably the loving, symbiotic union of parent and little one during the opening stages of our biological lives. We're returned to the time during which the "tender touch" of the caregiver "settled" and "quieted down" the agitated, exhausted newcomer. Note above all the way in which the little one's relief transpires "in" the Big One: "quieten me down *in* Thee" (my emphasis). The symbiotic interaction of the early period is as much emotional as it is physical, as much a matter of *feeding* the newcomer with loving care as with bodily nourishment. We never learn from Chambers (as we never learn from Augustine) the specific nature of his trials, his discomforts, his "multitudinous duties" because the only thing that matters to him, as to Christians generally, is the invariant solution as follows: "Gather me into concentrated peace in Thee." To be *in* the body/spirit of the Big One, calm, secure, a perfectly *adapted* babe in arms, as it were, is the Christian's ultimate goal. Were we to "translate" Chamber's supplication into the underlying infantile feelings that serve finally as its emotional inspiration we would have the Big One saying to the little one in a soothing voice, "There, there; hush now; shh; everything is going to fine; there, there." Christians who follow after the Shepherd are seeking, one and all, such tender, parental reassurance as they go about their stressful, biosocial lives.

Observe the lack of homeostasis, of soothing adaptation to the stressful environment, that confronts the Christian who fails to track after the Deity. "Oh blessed Lord!" begins Longfellow,

> How much I need
> Thy light to guide me on my way!
> So many hands, that without heed,
> Still touch Thy wounds and make them bleed,
> So many feet that day by day
> Still wander from thy fold astray!
> Feeble at best in my endeavor!
> I see but cannot reach the height
> That lies for ever in the light;
> And yet for ever and for ever,
> When seeming just within my grasp,
> I feel my feeble hands unclasp,
> And sink discouraged into night—
> For Thine own purpose Thou has sent
> The strife and the discouragement.
>                                    (p. 56)

Here is a "sheep" not only "wandering" from the "fold" but feeling miserable about it. We don't know the nature of the "night" into which Longfellow "sinks" anymore than we know the nature of Augustine's "darkness" or

Chambers's "duties," but we do know what Longfellow is *missing* without his "guide" to lead him on his "way": the adaptational feeling of comfort and security that arises through symbiotic bonding with the Deity. The supplicator tries to make the best of his inability to *grasp* and *hold onto* the "height" that represents the Big One by characterizing his "strife and discouragement" as some sort of divine lesson, or test. What we're left with, however, is a vivid expression of the inner torment and hopelessness that may arise in those who, for whatever reason, cannot conjure up the alternative, magical identity that emerges through Christianity's infantilizing process.

Here is George Matheson:

> When Thou sayst that I must, my heart says, "I can." My strength is proportional to the strength of those cords that bind me. I am never so unrestrained as when I am constrained by Thy love. Evermore, Thou Divine Spirit, guide me by this instinct of the right. Put round about my heart the cord of Thy captivating love, and draw me wither in my own light I would not go. Bind me to Thyself as thou bindest the planets to the sun, that it may become the very law of my nature to be led by Thee. May I be content to know that goodness and mercy shall *follow* me without waiting to see them in advance of me.
>
> (p. 101)

Could there be a more substantial, arresting confirmation of this book's thesis? The supplicator, with Psalm 23 explicitly in his mind ("The Lord is my shepherd. . . . Goodness and mercy shall follow me") asks to be "drawn" after the Big One by a "cord of captivating love," to be "bound" to the Big One ("Bind me to Thyself") as the "planets" are bound to the "sun" through its *controlling* gravitational power. Rather than go about the world as a grown-up "on his own," Matheson would be "led" by the omnipotent Deity, the "constrainer" whose "love" awakens within him a sense of freedom or unrestraint, by which we understand, of course, the "freedom" that wells up within the child when he feels himself utterly in the hands of the all-powerful, protective parent who "takes care of everything." Matheson's supplication provides us with what we can think of as a magical *map* through which the worshiper may negotiate or *track* the environment in which he discovers himself, thus assuring both his avoidance of those "biological dictates" (separation, vulnerability, and death) that engender anxiety, even terror, and his adherence to the necromantic, supernatural promises (continuous parental guidance and care and immortality) that remove the dreaded bugbears of his natural existence.

Within the natural as opposed to the supernatural realm the production of maps is integrally linked to locational memory and spatial orientation.

"Philosophers, scholars, and brain researchers," writes Hanspeter A. Mallot in his seminal paper "Finding Our Way," "have long suspected that spatial orientation is more than a special ability—it may be one evolutionary root of memory or thought itself."[14] For example, "Cordula Nitsch and her colleagues at the University of Basel in Switzerland showed in experiments with gerbils that increasing level of damage to the hippocampus, a deep and ancient brain structure, increasingly impaired both the animals' spatial orientation and memory retention in navigating a course they had previously mastered" (p. 77). Mallot goes on, "We see today that many of the idioms we use in daily speech have spatial roots: we 'get oriented' to new situations, try to 'find ways out' of our problems, and ask colleagues to 'walk us through' proposed plans" (p. 77). Finally, declares Mallot,

> It is not inconceivable that over the course of human evolution a memory structure developed for spatial orientation—one that was later employed for other cognitive functions. The uses to which lower animals apply spatial cognition implies as much. Or to put it more provocatively: in the animal kingdom, spatial cognition is the most widespread form of thought.
>
> (p. 77)

Within the magical realm of Christianity's infantilizing process, by contrast, the worshiper's *map* consists entirely of the Deity's spiritual body, the transcendent field of His divine *will*, or in neurological/psychological terms, the implicit memory of the "orientation" the worshiper experienced early on when his world, his universe, was intertwined integrally with the parental presence, the caregiver to whom he was *bound* as a helpless, dependent newcomer.

The advent of spatial awareness as we encounter it in Mallot's discussion commences in earnest only *after* the little one develops fully into childhood (ages 4–6) and toward adolescence, in other words, only as separation from the matrix and functional autonomy gain significant, irreversible momentum.[15] It is when the developing human begins to perceive himself "out there" and "on his own" that he may discover himself increasingly in need of *both* his map of "spatial orientation" (where I am; where I was) and his alternative, magical map of symbiotic interaction with the all-powerful protector and provider, the *otherworldly* map that complements (or even offsets) the natural one by positioning the believer within the *controlling field* of the Big One's will (Matheson's planet in the grip of the sun). Write Blackaby and King in their volume *Experiencing God*,

> As He fills you with His presence, He will guide you to do things. But even as you do those things, He will be the One at work through you to accomplish

His purposes. He is all you need. The Christ in you is your way. He is your "map." When you follow His leadership one day at a time, you will always be right in the middle of God's will for your life.[16]

To exist within the body, within the *will* of the supernatural Big One magically resolves the natural dilemmas of existing within one's own separate, vulnerable, mortal body, one's own fallible, earthly will, not to mention the wills of other imperfect human beings. "Sometimes," declares the handbook *Our Daily Bread*,

> life demands that we weather a storm. At other times it puts us to the test of tedium. We may feel stuck. What we want most is just out of reach. But whether we find ourselves in a crisis of circumstance or in a place where the spiritual wind has been taken out of our sails, we need to trust God for guidance. The Lord, who is sovereign over changing circumstances, will eventually guide us to our desired heaven.[17]

As in the supplications we've just finished examining, the exact nature of the "storm" or the "tedium" or the "crisis" is left wide open and does not ultimately matter. Of sole significance is the original *map* of one's existence as it remains available through the jogging of implicit memory, namely, feeling oneself in the sphere of the Big One's will, guided, protected, secure among the flock, and on the way to the Shepherd's "haven." When we are "led by the Spirit," asserts *Our Daily Bread* in another place,[18] "our lives will be characterized by joy, peace, and self-control," which is to say, we will have *found our way* magically to an emotional/spiritual "orientation" in which the all-powerful, loving companion constitutes the very ground of our experience.

I'll leave it to the Christians themselves to bring all this together in a couple of vivid, unforgettable passages. Note, in particular, the way actual and magical maps coalesce as they come into play. Remember, too, that we're still on the track of the pastoral metaphor's ultimate significance. When James Hewett found God, we learn from *God Speaks: Devotional*,

> It seemed as though life was rather like a bike ride, but it was a tandem bike. God was in the back helping me pedal. I don't know just when it was that He suggested we change places, but life has not been the same since. When He took the lead, it was all I could do to hang on! He took me down delightful paths, up mountains, and through rocky places— at breakneck speeds.
>
> I was worried and anxious, and asked, "Where are you taking me"? He laughed and didn't answer, and I started to learn trust. I forgot my boring life and entered into adventure. When I'd say, "I'm scared," He'd lean back and

touch my hand. At first I did not trust Him to be in control of my life. I thought He'd wreck it, but He knows bike secrets—how to make it lean to take sharp corners, dodge large rocks, and speed through scary passages. I'm beginning to enjoy the view and the cool breeze on my face with my delightful, constant Companion.[19]

*God Speaks: Devotional* titles the section containing Hewett's testimonial "Let's Do Life.—God" (p. 148), and the title takes us to the heart of Christianity's map for its followers. Going about on one's own, apart from the idealized parental Deity, is no way to live. One requires a "constant Companion," a Big One who is always *there*, not merely to show one the way through Scripture and supplication, but to remove the sense of emptiness, listlessness, and "boredom" that comes from one's own company. When one returns to the old, carefree days of "adventure," the days in which one ran outside to play knowing the big ones, mom and dad, were *there* to look after one, to "touch one's hand" if one becomes "scared," *then* does one discover "life," or the delight of one's existence. For countless millions, the journey, the road, the map is fully acceptable *only* "in tandem," only *in* the sphere of the Big One's tender, loving *will*, the Big One's ultimate *control* of "everything."

"It's human nature to fear the future," maintains *God Speaks: Devotional* in another place, and then,

> After all, none of us knows what's around the next bend. Life is a series of hills and valleys, sharp turns and bumpy roads. Sometimes we'll be sailing down an interstate highway, enjoying the scenery, when we hit an unexpected detour that takes us miles away from our destination. What if we make a wrong turn and get lost?
>
> Don't worry. God's already been there before you. He knows where all the ruts and potholes and speed traps are. If you open His map book—the Bible —He'll show you the best route to take to avoid the worst roads. You can trust God to lead you every step of the way. He knows the beginning and the end, as well as the middle of the journey. He will walk right by your side through every circumstance of life. And He will never leave you. There is nothing to fear when you are walking with Him. There is one catch. You actually have to listen and let Him teach you. You'll wander around lost if you refuse to read the map or ask for directions [that is, pray]. So trust Him to lead you in The right direction. All you have to do is ask! . . .
>
> God knows all your secrets, your hidden fears, your desperate needs, and even your innermost thoughts. He loves you anyway. Ask for his help to get your life back on track.
>
> (pp. 39–41)

The formula here is reading Scripture (explicitly a map, as Christ is a map in Blackaby and King) *and prayer*: "ask and ye shall receive" (Matt. 7:8). What we must recall from our earlier discussion of supplication is the psychological "orientation" required for its successful usage. To pray fruitfully, to find God, is to adopt an attitude of helplessness and dependency, to approach the Lord as the small child approaches the parent—in a word, to act out the ubiquitous asking and receiving of the biological beginning through homeopathic magic. As one does this, as one *asks*, one "automatically" *receives*, which is to say, the magical behavior conjures up memorially the period during which the care-giver was *there* to meet one's needs, to guide one, to comfort one, to hold one, thus removing adaptationally sources of stress, or disequilibrium, by providing the reassurance of symbiotic bonding. And this is, of course, what the *Devotional* strives to accomplish by providing the believer with the infantilizing map of Scripture and supplication. *The nature of the problem doesn't matter.* The *Devotional* makes this perfectly clear: "God's already been there." What matters is to sit with the Good Book, to go down on one's knees as God's "little child," and to savor the implicit mnemonic sensation that someone is "right by one's side," leading one "every step of the way," Some-one Who will "never leave you," Who is entirely "trustworthy," Who will show you "the best route," and above all, "Who loves you" unconditionally. In the final analysis, the maps of Scripture and supplication in this passage *equal* the "constant Companion" of the previous passage belonging to Hewett. All Christian roads, to echo the old Roman saying, lead to the body of Christ inside of which the worshiper discovers his ideal, stress-free loca-tion: "there is nothing to fear when you are walking with Him." He and His Word are one. *He* is the map.

Such passages help us to grasp analytically that mysterious enactment of Christianity (and other faiths) known generally as "the pilgrimage" wherein worshipers (the sheep) actually indulge themselves in *explicit bodily tracking behaviors*, actually *walking about* in search of some magical goal integrally tied to the Almighty (the Shepherd). With supplication, as we've just under-scored, believers *act out* the ubiquitous asking and receiving of the early period, thus awakening mnemonically the loving dependence in which they luxuriated as little ones. With the pilgrimage believers *act out* another major facet of their early days on earth, namely, their instinctual predilection to *fol-low after* the big one, the parental guide upon whose loving ministration they rely in what is literally a life-or-death biological context. The worshiper tracks, of course, for a variety of specific, magical purposes, two of which stand out: (1) to enhance his spiritual worthiness by concentrating on the *map* that guides him to the "holy place," the shrine or church or abbey or tomb (Christ in Jerusalem; Muhammad in Mecca) from which the Deity's magnetic power emanates or radiates, thus positioning the pilgrim directly in the "field" or the Big One's *will* or *control*, once again as Matheson expresses it in his analogy of the planet "bound" to and "led" by the sun, and once again as the newcomer maps his initial biological environment at the center of which resides the omnipotent parental figure; (2) to restore his health, or well-being, to pursue the Almighty's capacity to reverse the course of nature in general and the ravages of disease or injury in particular; just as the mama or the daddy kisses the boo-boo and "makes" the little one "all better" early on, so will the Big One, through His infinite, unconditional love, remove the affliction and restore His little one's soundness in the magical domain of supernatural convictions. Thousands of such trackings have transpired throughout history, and while we cannot, obviously, account for all of them, or designate nuances, we can discern the sameness of, the persistence of, the motivational core: to awaken the sensation of being *in* the "sheepfold," or "flock," or *home* with the loving, all-powerful Shepherd, not *out there* on one's own, small, vulnerable, mortal, "lost" in a dangerous and often merciless world from which one cannot expect anything in the way of unconditional parental affection and acceptance, let alone the removal of disease or the restoration of damaged organs or limbs. The pilgrimage, in short, relies upon the same infantilizing magic that we found in the baptismal rite, in prayer, in the Eucharist, in the metaphor of Vine and Shepherd, and in a dozen other aspects of the Christian religion and its inspirational guidebook or map, the New Testament.

"O God," writes D. Martyn Lloyd-Jones, "grant us to know that the one born of old in Bethlehem has also been born in our hearts." And then, "A living Christ within, never leaving us. O lord, *follow us* to our homes, our work, wherever we go and in whatever we do. May we know thou wilt never forsake us, and witness the sweet intimations of thy nearness and grace." And finally,

> Bless O God, those who long to know Thee better and the truth more truly. And now may the grace of our Lord and Saviour, Jesus Christ, the love of God, and the fellowship of the Holy Spirit abide with us throughout the remainder of *our short and uncertain earthly pilgrimage* and forever more.[20]

The whole of one's earthly existence, then, is metaphorically contextualized through *the pilgrimage*, through tracking behavior in which the worshiper follows the map that leads to the Big One's will, control, power, guidance, mercy, or alternatively, through tracking behaviors in which the Big One permanently "shepherds" His flock, following His little ones to home, to work, to wherever they go. Of overriding significance is the manner in which *separation* from the Big One, from the Parent-God, from *the matrix*, is apprehended and explicitly characterized as *forsaking*, renouncing, abandoning, as *taking away* parental nearness, the "sweetness" of primal union and security. Here precisely is the presentational utterance that discloses for us the neurological/psychological tie to the early period, *to the original separation and loss the reversal of which, or the denial of which, is the Christian religion's ultimate aim.*

The metaphor of the pilgrimage, like the acting out of the pilgrimage, mnemonically resuscitates at the feeling level *both* sides of the original symbiotic union, its compelling "sweetness" as big one and little one interfuse through an organic relationship designed to further the survival of the species, and as big one and little one experience not merely the imperfections of the early time, but the inevitable, selectional *separation* in which the original symbiosis culminates of necessity. The "pilgrim" wants the Big One to be "near," and the pilgrim also feels deep within his core the *anxiety* of his earthly, biological presence on the planet. He longs for the "fellowship" of the Holy Spirit, which means the sense of the Big One's "nearness" during the course of an "earthly pilgrimage" that is ultimately both "short" (mortality looming) and "uncertain" (anxiety at work in the worshiper at both the conscious and unconscious levels). Once again, the pilgrim longs to be *in*, not out, joined to the Big One, *watched over* or shepherded by the Big One as he goes about his business in the world, "at home, at work, wherever" he happens to be. The "motivation to be a pilgrim is complex," the experts tell us, but "one of the pilgrimage's features must be that the devotee sees in it something of the successful achievement of the whole of life including the successful arrival at one's final goal."[21] Surely we don't have to puzzle very long over what that "final goal" might be. Lloyd-Jones's supplication has made that perfectly clear, along with the context of this book: to feel the "intimations" (implicit recollections designated as the Holy Spirit) of the Big One's "nearness," to go about tied inwardly to the Parent-God, to the loving protector and guide Who will never "forsake," never renounce, never abandon the members of His flock. The "goal" is *union* as union cancels out the biological reality of separateness. According to Janet Collins in her recent article on the vogue of pilgrimages in society today, the heart of the "spiritual journey" is "the journey itself. . . . All spiritual roads lead to the same destination."[22] To *track*, to *follow*, or to attain the sense of being shepherded, being *watched over* by the Big One is what constitutes the "journey itself," the *acting out* of a basic, instinctual proclivity that, like the asking and receiving of prayer, recreates the adaptational, survival behaviors of the early, precarious stage of our natural existence.

Can a discussion of the pastoral metaphor culminate in any other way than in a presentation of Psalm 23, one of the most influential Biblical utterances for Jews and Christians alike? I don't think so.

(1) The Lord is my Shepherd; I shall not want.

(2) He maketh me to lie down in green pastures: he leadeth me beside the still waters.

(3) He restoreth my soul: he leadeth me in the paths of righteousness for his name's sake.

(4) Yea, though I walk through the valley of the shadow of death, I will fear no evil: for thou art with me; thy rod and thy staff they comfort me.

(5) Thou preparest a table before me in the presence of mine enemies: thou anointest my head with oil; my cup runneth over.

(6) Surely goodness and mercy shall follow me all the days of my life: and I will dwell in the house of the Lord for ever.

The worshiper, or the suppliant, views the Lord as his Shepherd, as his careful guide and protector. Immediately thereafter he strikes a blended maternal and paternal note: he shall not want; the Herdsman-Master will accord him everything he requires in the way of emotional and physical nourishment. Dependent, submissive, following along, he will be made to lie down in green pastures, a striking maternal image of lushness, of leisurely feeding, chewing, swallowing, digesting, and sleeping; he will be led to the still water, another vivid maternal image recalling both breast and womb, the peace of symbiosis, the mirror-like, fluid surface in which the self is birthed into awareness, existence, being. Such care, such provision, such recollection of delicious maternal engendering and love adaptationally restores the suppliant, pleases him soothingly in the innermost regions of his self-consciousness, his subjectivity, especially as those regions are ruffled by the tribulations of the journey. The suppliant returns to the paternal sphere. The Shepherd is morally fastidious; He keeps His flock on stable, solid paths of righteousness; He is covetous of His unimpeachable identity, His name, His reputation as entirely dependable and prudent in His decisions for the route of His flock. All of this, of course, is projectively reassuring to the one who prays, who worships through the psalm. Such reassurance continues unabated.

Although the worshiper, or the suppliant, must traverse the dark, harrowing valley of the shadow, although as a member of a mortal flock he must confront the final, terrifying separation of death, the reengulfment into the valley-womb whence he arose, he will be fearless because he will not be alone; the Shepherd will be there with His supportive staff, with His protective rod;

the suppliant will be heartened by the presence of his loyal, supernatural companion. Ultimately, there will be no separation. The employment of paternal and maternal themes goes forward as the overall pastoral framework fades off. The Lord will continue to nourish the suppliant even in the presence of those who stand against him. What a humiliation for his foes! The Lord will bless the suppliant, consecrate him, anoint his head with oil (primary narcissistic homeostasis). What more could the suppliant want? He cries out. His cup runneth over: both his inward emotional requirements and his external physical requirements will not only be met but met in abundance; the breast is moist, full, dripping with life-sustaining nectar. Accordingly, the suppliant's future is sure to go well (anxiety diminished), is sure to contain goodness and mercy that will now follow the suppliant to the end as the suppliant originally followed the Shepherd in the beginning. The suppliant will dwell in the house of the Lord, in the paternal temple, in the place of paternal worship, paternal power, and he will also dwell in the home, in that "house," in the maternal abode, in the place of rest and safety, in the protective womb of the elemental nourisher. Moreover, and finally, he will not dwell there for a limited period; he will not be forced to relinquish his "house," his home, his place of cohabitation with the parental presence; on the contrary, he will dwell in that location forever. Ultimately again, there will be no separation.

For the Christian the "house" or the home *in* which he will "dwell for ever" is not simply the Church, the congregation of his fellow worshipers, the wider world of Christian institutions as a whole, but supremely the body of the Savior whose sacrifice has precipitated the salvational triumph over death, the actual arrival of a world without end in the upper, heavenly reaches into which Jesus eventually ascends after his emergence from the tomb. Here, for a final time, are Wesley's unforgettable syllables that provide us with the fitting Christian conclusion to the illustrious Psalm 23:

Ah, show me that happiest place, The place of Thy people's
abode, Where saints in an ecstasy gaze, And hang on a
crucified God.

'Tis there I would always abide, And never a moment
depart, Concealed in the cleft of Thy side, Eternally held in
Thy heart.[23]

The "house of the Lord" for the Christian, then, is the "heart" of the "crucified God." To that destination precisely does the Shepherd guide the members of His flock. Where Judaism stops with the temple and the home,

Christianity pushes on to the interfusion of bodies, the intermixing of flesh and of blood, to the primal obliteration of boundaries. For the Christian, the body of Christ is the womb.

## The Longing for God's Face

Everywhere in the literature of Christianity we find worshipers longing to see the face of God, to gaze upon the countenance of the Almighty, to know Him by His face. What can this possibly mean? Does the Lord have a face, an actual face? What about the Holy Spirit? He's a person, we're informed, an actual person, and actual people have faces. We noted in Chapter 3, Part One Billy Graham's admission that the whole "subject" of the Holy Spirit is "terribly difficult" and "beyond the limit of our minds to grasp fully."[24] Does this include the "subject" of the Holy Spirit's face? Graham tells us that the Holy Spirit "hears," "speaks," and has a brain, or "intellect" (pp. 4–6). Does this mean the "person" of the Holy Spirit has ears, a mouth, and a head, as part of His countenance? What about Jesus? He probably existed near the Sea of Galilee in ancient Israel some 30–40 years before the common era, as we now call it in our secular society.[25] When the worshiper looks upon the face of Christ, does the worshiper see in his mind the features of a relatively young Hebraic male from that location and period of history, a young Jew in other words? Routinely in North America and Europe we see depictions of Jesus in magazines, pamphlets, and books and on posters, billboards, and on the television screen. Usually such items proffer an attractive, rather Anglo-Saxon countenance with light eyes and light hair, a small, straight nose, and a peaceful, gentle expression—a kind of movie star archetype if I may employ "movie star" adjectivally. Is this the sort of "face" Christians inwardly perceive in their moments of religious intensity? And what of the Almighty, the omnipotent, omniscient Creator of everything, by which I mean the infinite cosmos wherein we finite mortals are contained? Does He too have a "face," a physiognomy in the usual signification? Or is this the wrong way to go about the whole issue? Does "seeing the face of God," or "knowing the face of God," imply an intimate, subjective *sense* of the Lord's presence, or Christ's, or the Holy Spirit's as opposed to the actual sighting or beholding of a face? If so, why the reference to "face"? Why bring in "face" at all? Why not "presence" or "feeling" or "intimation" or "suggestion" or something like that? *The Eerdmans Bible Dictionary* tells us that the word "face" in the Old and New Testaments generally and in the Christian tradition particularly indicates "the presence of the Deity,"[26] and thus the question remains, why "face"? I believe there is a way to understand all this fully along naturalistic, psychological lines that go far beyond the "explanations" of our anthropomorphic predilections as a species and the prominent employment of the word "face" in the Scripture that obviously only begs the question. More specifically, I believe our analysis of the pastoral metaphor in the evolutionary context of mapping and tracking allows us to demystify *all* the religious usages and exegeses, and in the process, to obtain a clear, straightforward grasp of how this persistent verbal tendency works in the mind and body of the Christian faithful. Romano Guardini informs us in his famous book on prayer that God "has no face as we understand it."[27] Well then, let's get to work and enlarge our understanding.

Recent neurological/psychological studies suggest that facial recognition and facial tracking are instinctually implanted into human beings. Babies have "a predisposition to look at faces" because faces in general, and the face of the nurturer in particular, are inextricably bound up with their survival and well-being.[28] Accordingly, facial recognition and tracking constitute an "evolutionary adaptation" (or "survival mechanism") for an utterly helpless, infantile primate with nothing and no one to rely on *for years* besides the big one who is *there* watching over him or her.[29] Frederick V. Malmstrom sums the matter up for us as follows:

> Human facial recognition is a highly specialized ability, and it seems to be pre-wired before birth in specific, visual processing areas of the brain. However, the human newborn ability to distinguish between familiar and unfamiliar faces does not develop in infants until about two months of age. . . . An infant's inborn ability to recognize a generalized face is apparently evolutionarily quite primitive. According to this research, the infant begins with the prototype female "protoface" pre-wired visually into the midbrain, and then later utilizes the cortical areas to add additional visual recognition cues, such as the hairline and ear. . . . Obviously, one of the first and most frequent things a baby sees and commits to memory is its mother's face. . . . The infant's immediate recognition of a prototype female face, and especially that of its mother, is arguably an important survival advantage.[30]

The mother's face, then, is the infant's *first map of the world*. He awakens not to "creation" in some all-inclusive sense, but to *the face of the caregiver*, his anchor for survival.

" 'I'll draw His face'—that is a refrain I've heard spoken in many languages by children of Christian denominations." Thus observes Robert Coles in his seminal volume *The Spiritual Life of Children*.[31] Coles proceeds to point out that 90 percent of the 300 children he asked to draw a picture of God "drew pictures of His face" (p. 40). When Coles inquired of one sixth-grader,

" 'Would you want to go beyond the face?' . . . There was a pause, and no response." A moment later, writes the author, "I spelled out the question: 'Would you want to draw the body?' 'No.' Another pause and then: 'I don't think of God except for His face; I mean, when I picture Him, it's His face' " (pp. 40–41). Even children "who have pictured Jesus as a man and have seen Him pictured—walking, talking, eating with His friends and followers," Coles tells us, "are often reluctant to go beyond the representation of God's face" (p. 41). The faces of God created by Cole's subjects mirror those subjects' genetical background: white children drew Caucasian faces; black children drew negroid faces (p. 44). One child declares,

> When I look up to God, I think of Him looking down on me. . . . It's His eyes that are real special, I'm sure. I mean, *He's* as special as you can be, but it's the eyes that He uses, to see all of us down here! . . . That's all I see, His eyes mainly and His forehead, I guess. . . . He's looking down and I pray He'll smile on us.
>
> (p. 52)

Interestingly, one participant who pictures God's face in his mind wonders about the face of the " 'Holy Ghost' ": " 'I never figured It had a face' " (p. 63). For Coles, all of this material taken together reflects the principal reason people (Christians) turn to God or come to "believe in God" in the first place (p. 6). Following D. W. Winnicott and Ana-Maria Rizzuto, Coles suggests that people long for a God who can watch over them, assist them, succor them, listen to them when they pray or cry out—in a word, love them. Coles writes (and we must keep God's face in mind here), "a baby uses its eyes" in relation to its "longings," and "we adults, babes in the woods of a universe whose enormity and mystery and frustrations are only too obvious, do likewise." Shall we look again at George A. Buttrick's revelational comment cited in Chapter 3, Part One in our analysis of prayer? "God will be found," declares Buttrick, "by a response in prayer" to "One of whom we are dimly aware—as a child, half waking, responds to the mother who bends over him."[32] This is what it means at the deepest memorial, psychological, emotional level when Coles's young subjects declare the hope that God's face, when they behold it in their minds, will be smiling down upon them.

The upshot is apparent: to comprehend Guardini's observation that "God has no face as we understand it," we must *understand* the ubiquitous longing among Christians to "see the face of God" in the full context of Christianity's infantilizing agenda, of baptism in which Christ's *followers* or *trackers* become His "little children"; of the Eucharist in which the faithful are fed by and feed on their Vine, their ultimate source of nourishment, of life itself; of prayer in which the supplicator approaches his Lord as an utterly helpless little one permanently submitting to the will of his omnipotent Father; of moment-to-moment dependency in which the believer continuously acknowledges his ever-present, urgent need for his heavenly Creator's support; of the pastoral metaphor in which the worshiper's felicitous destiny is to *follow* his Creator to green pastures, to still waters, through the valley of the shadow of death, and finally to his permanent *home*, namely, the body of Jesus Christ. The Almighty's *face* is at the center of the creed because the parental face during the early time is the little one's chief tracking device, the little one's chief map of the world to which *for years* he emotionally, psychologically, and neurologically devotes himself in his life-or-death effort to survive and adapt to the environment in which, willy-nilly, he suddenly discovers himself.

As this face is gradually *taken away*, as this initial map or tracking device is *removed* through the process of biological separation from the matrix, the human creature searches for ways to get it back again, to restore his connection to the big one upon whom he depended overwhelmingly for his environmental adaptation and survival. The whole of Christianity in its infantilizing process is devoted to precisely this magical, homeopathic, or imitative accomplishment. Accordingly, the ubiquitous reference to God's *face* in Christianity is designed to arouse an implicit recollection of the early period and through such a recollection to awaken *the Comforter*, the Holy Spirit from Whom emanates inwardly the original, primal symbiosis, the original, primal *connection* through which the "little child" gained his feeling of security and well-being. God "has no face as we understand it" until we perceive God's face as the magical recreation of *a relationship* in which the human creature thrived and luxuriated as he strove to flourish in the world of his "creation," the first world, the first map, the first environment in which he endeavored *to find his way.* The face of the Almighty for the grown-up, practicing Christian ultimately emerges from the early, foundational synapses of his ceaselessly developing brain. Primal and primitive and emotionally magnetic, it begins to take shape as the nursing infant locks his eyes on the face of his empathetic provider, as he notes the caregiver's visage appearing above the edge of his crib or his playpen, as he opens his mouth in his high chair to receive another spoonful of plums from his nourisher, his adored and adoring parental presence. Over and over again, thousands upon thousands of times during the early period, the little one looks into the empathetic face of the big one, and the big one looks back. Over and over again the child internalizes into his brain this *countenance*, this *face*, as the bedrock of his own emerging identity, his trust in life, his very selfhood.

Permit me to recall a few points from this book's theoretical sections. The genesis and the formation of the self derive from the initial mirroring experience with the mother. For several decades this unique, remarkable aspect of our origins has been studied intensively by observers within the psychological/neurological community and has come to be regarded generally as a central structural occurrence of our normal development. And inborn tendency on the part of the infant prompts him to seek out his mother's gaze and to do so regularly and for extended periods. The mother sets about exploiting this mutual fact-gazing activity. As eye-to-eye contact becomes frequent, and easily observed by the investigator, the mother's continual inclination to change her facial expression, as well as the quality of her vocalizing, emerges with striking clarity. Usually she smiles, and nods, and coos; sometimes in response to an infant frown, she frowns. In virtually every instance, the mother's facial and vocal behavior comprises an imitation of the baby's. Accordingly, as the mother descends to the infant's level, she provides him or her with a particular kind of human mirror. She does not simply give the baby back his or her own self; she reinforces a portion of the baby's behavior in comparison with another portion. She gives the baby back not merely a part of what he or she is doing, but, in addition, something of her own. As Winnicott expresses the matter, "In individual . . . development the *precursor of the mirror is the mother's face*."[33] Of particular interest in this connection is Winnicott's answer to his own question, "What does the baby see when he or she looks at the mother's face" (p. 112)? He writes, "I am suggesting that, ordinarily, what the baby sees is himself or herself." In other words, the mother is looking at the baby and what she looks like *is related to what she sees there* (p. 112). Thus, the process that engenders one's selfhood appears to go, once again in Winnicott's aphoristic style, "when I look I am seen, so I exist" (p. 114). Have we a variation upon the cogito here? "I was seen, therefore I am"? Is it possible that René Descartes missed, in his notorious monistic formulation, the empathetic, relational origin of his and everyone else's existence? The point is, when one discovers God's *face* in the Christian realm, one discovers it as an extension of the caregiver one has seen and loved during the course of one's early experience, just as we have it in Coles. This is the personal, individual, subjective core of Christianity, and as the core it can never be sundered from the theology, no matter how sophisticated the theology may get. The Christian religion cannot be broken up, let alone gutted of its emotional foundation. The face of God is there for those who believe because the face of God is the implicit recollection of the loving parental provider, otherwise known as the "Holy Spirit."

We're reaching a perspective, now, from which we can appreciate the full psychological quality, the full psychological *tenor* of the Christian's all-consuming wish to behold the face of his God, the face of his Deity Who according to the experts *doesn't have a face* as we understand it ordinarily.[34] Listen to Tim Stafford as he excitedly pursues the possibilities in his volume *Knowing the Face of God*. "For us as human beings of God's creation," he writes,

> full personal intimacy comes when we are able not merely to talk, but to see face to face. . . . John, who twice says that no one has ever seen God, also says this: "Dear friends, now we are children of God, and what we will be has not yet been made known. But we know that when He appears, we shall be like Him, for we shall see Him as He is" (I John 3:2). And, says John, "His servants will . . . see His face" (Revelation 22:4). Paul ultimately foresees prophecies, tongues, and knowledge passing away. But the image of a face does not pass away. "Then we shall see face to face. Now I know in part; then I shall know fully, even as I am fully known" (I Corinthians 13:9–12). When the Bible speaks of the new age when we will be fully satisfied, when we will be intimate with God in a way that no one on earth has ever experienced, it speaks this way—in terms of seeing God's face.[35]

Stafford continues,

> What this means I confess I do not know; I am not convinced that anyone knows. Our metaphysical speculations are likely to carry little weight at the time when God clears up our confusion. . . . We must be transformed to see, and we will only be so transformed in the very act of seeing. Yet we have been told about it in advance. That is the crucial point, focusing our longing for God in the right direction. We hunger to know God personally, not merely to talk about Him but to experience Him as a living character. He is our father: *we long to feel His arms. He has broken down all barriers to love us; we hunger to be in His possession.* This hope drives us on, and it also frustrates us because we get only glimmers, nothing solid. . . . *I believe this longing can only be fulfilled when our eyes are opened on the loving and glorious face of God.* Such will someday be our joy.
>
> (p. 183, my emphasis)

And finally from Stafford,

> If Moses could not see what he wanted, if Paul and John admitted their global ignorance of the wonderful light to come, then we should not be too surprised at *our own sense of incompleteness.* Our longing, even our frustration, is nothing to be ashamed of. . . . We long to know Him completely because we have come to know Him in part. Now that we have come to know Him, *nothing will satisfy but the sight of His face. . . . We are not condemned to endless searching. God will find us.* He will not always be beyond our sight. *He will look into our eyes, and*

*all the frustrating limits will be purified out of us just by the searching of those eyes.*
It will be more than we dreamed of, more than we longed for.

(p. 184, my emphasis)

Christianity's primal cravings reverberate throughout these remarkable, representative passages.

Stafford "longs to feel" God's "arms" around him, longs to experience God's "intimacy" and "love," longs to be in the Almighty's "possession," to belong to Him symbiotically just as the little one belongs in the most intimate, loving way to the big one who watches over him. Driven by such "hope," Stafford is also "frustrated" by its truncation, by his sense of "incompleteness" (his most revealing word) that signifies, of course, his sense of *separation from the matrix*, his sense of being *out there on his own*, a "babe," as Coles expressed it, lost in the "woods" of an enormous, frustrating "universe." And speaking of Coles, can anyone miss the connection between the youngster in Coles's book who comments on the face and eyes of God and the passage from Stafford just cited? First the youngster:

> Everyone is special in God's eyes. It's *His* eyes that are real special, I'm sure. I mean *He's* as special as you can be, but it's the eyes that He uses to see all of us down here! . . . I'll pray to God and I'll think of Him, and then I'll see Him, His face, His eyes. That's all I see, His eyes, mainly, and His forehead, I guess, and His hair, not much else. He's looking down, and I pray He'll smile on us.
>
> (Coles, p. 52)

Now Stafford:

> We are not condemned to endless searching; God will find us. He will not always be beyond our sight. He will look into our eyes, and all the frustrating limits will be purified out of us just by the searching of those eyes. It will be more than we dreamed of, more than we longed for.
>
> (Stafford, p. 184)

Both Coles's youthful subject and author Stafford are now separated from the matrix, from the original and originative big one who lovingly nurtured them into human life and selfhood as we ordinarily employ those terms. Coles's subject is now separate as a child in actuality, while Stafford, a grown-up, is separated as a "little child" (Matt. 18:3) through Christianity's infantilizing process. Both are in search of mnemonic cues that will awaken within them the loving ministrations of the caregiver, the loving symbiotic attachments and interfusions of the early period that, in their implicit, feeling recollection, are officially designated by the creed as the "Holy Spirit." For both the boy and the man, the notion of God's "face" is paramount among just such mnemonic cues. We no longer have to scratch our heads over this putative "spiritual mystery." The psychological/neurological provenance of what is occurring here is unmistakable. Where would the *eyes* of this otherworldly and explicitly parental *face* have come from in this Christian context of longing for the Big One, for union as opposed to separation ("God will find us"), for the Parent-Deity whose presence makes one feel, at last, *complete* if not from our own biological lives as those lives took shape in and through *the mutual face-gazing activity of our opening years*? Alluding to the gift of God's love, *God Speaks: Devotional* advises its readers to "open the door of your heart today. Look up into God's loving face and smile at this blessing. Then close your eyes and imagine Him smiling back at you. God loves you!"[36] Here is the mnemonic, relational essence of the Christian faith.

Precisely this significance, this *inner meaning*, is available to us here as we note Thomas Merton's insistence that the cardinal aim of the Christian "mind" is "to see the face of its Creator."[37] It is available to us as we read Basil Hume's supplication (based on Psalm 27), "It is your face, Lord, that I seek. Hide not your face,"[38] as we imagine the church choir singing of its wish to "see the sweet compassion" of "God's face,"[39] as we peruse Saint Augustine's declaration, "Thy face, Lord, will I seek. . . . The darkness of affection is the real distance from Thy face,"[40] or as we listen to the all-male quartet on the Trinity Broadcasting Network warbling harmoniously,

> Lord, don't hide your face from me.
> Take my hand and let me stand
> Where no one stands alone.
> Lord, don't hide your face from me.[41]

For the Christian who manages through the Holy Spirit to "behold the face of God," presumably on a regular basis, separation is over. The memorial magic has worked. The worshiper will never again have to "stand alone." God's "compassion" will belong to him forever. He will be *in*, symbiotically *in*, the gravitational orbit of the Big One, face to face with his heavenly Lord.

It can hardly come as a surprise to learn at this juncture that Christianity's infantilizing process plays upon *both* our primal longings and fears by metaphorically equating the presence of God's "face" with *light* and the absence of God's "face" with *darkness*. To be *out* of the symbiotic orbit of mutual face gazing, in short, is to be *lost in the dark*. We've already had a sample of this through Augustine's declaration that to be in the "darkness" of fleshly thoughts and deeds is to be "far" from the "face" of the Lord.[42] The connection of the Almighty's countenance to the light derives principally from the Psalms where we find "Justice and judgment are the habitation of thy Throne: mercy and truth shall go before Thy face. Blessed is the people that know the joyful sound: They shall walk, O Lord, in the light of thy countenance" (Ps. 89:14–15). And again, "Make thy face to shine upon thy servant; save me for thy mercies' sake" (Ps. 31:16). And finally, "Turn us again, O God, and cause thy face to shine; and we shall be saved" (Ps. 80:3). (We must note here that the longing for God's "face" to "shine" already holds by implication the suggestion of darkness, or shining's *opposite*.) For God to "hide" His "face," to turn away from His servants, to "cast off" their "souls," is to leave them "in the dark," to prevent them from "knowing" His "righteousness" and His "wonder" (Ps. 88:12–15). In the eye of the Christian, of course, it is Jesus Himself Who embodies the "light" of "the world" (John 12:46). To follow Him is to live in the light; to reject Him is to reside in the darkness: "I am come a light into the world, that whosoever believeth on me should not abide in the darkness" (John 12:46). And again,

> Then Jesus said to them, yet a little while is the light with you. Walk while ye have the light, lest darkness come upon you; for he that walketh in darkness knoweth not wither he goest. While ye have light, believe in the light, that ye may be *the children of light*. These things spoke Jesus, and departed, and did *hide himself* from them.
>
> (John 12: 35–36, my emphasis)

(Note the reference to Jesus's followers as "children" and the link to the Psalms through the notion of "hiding.") Everywhere in the teachings and traditions of the creed we find this dichotomy underscored, with an emphasis on the "child" or the "children." Writes Saint Paul in his Epistle to the Ephesians, "For ye were sometimes darkness, but now are ye light in the Lord; walk as children of light" (5:8). Prays Anderson in his volume *Who I Am in Christ*,

> Dear Heavenly Father, thank You for rescuing me from the domain of darkness. Because of your great grace, I announce that I am no longer a child of darkness but a child of light, and I choose to walk in the light and ask that you would enable me to do so.[43]

Note this remarkable passage from *God Speaks: Devotional* that makes perfectly clear the manner in which Christianity employs this theme as part of the infantilizing process, including the face of the Lord, indeed the very *eyes* of the Lord, watching over His little boys and girls, just as "Mom and Dad" do:

> Almost every kid has experienced the excitement and intrigue of a backyard camp out. . . . If you've been on one of these daring adventures, you know the one thing no one counts on is the darkness. The trees in the yard, so innocent by day, cast menacing shadows at night. Unfamiliar sounds, impossible to identify in the dark, begin to wear away at your resolve. The whole thing starts to feel pretty scary. Just when you're about to bolt for the house, you look up and see Mom and Dad watching from the window, ready to rescue you at a moment's notice. The world can be a dark, scary place. It can cast long, menacing shadows over our lives that leave us feeling alone and fearful. That's when we need to look up and see our heavenly Father watching, ready to chase away our fears and give us the courage to make it through the night.[44]

*God Speaks: Devotional* concludes the passage with these words from I Pet. 3:12, "The Lord is watching His children." Surely the psychological/neurological significance of all this is apparent.

Just as the *presence* of God's "face" mnemonically awakens the symbiotic interaction of the early period, the mutual face-gazing activity through which the little one finds his "map," his direction, his security in the environment in which he discovers himself, so does the *absence* of God's "face," the "hiding" of God's "face," the notion of the Big One leaving his *children* "in the dark" (Ps. 88:12) awaken the *primal anxiety* of the opening years, the fear of *separation*, the inward desolation of the "little child" when no one is *there*, when he's *on his own*. Christianity's infantilizing magic operates vigorously from *both* sides of the "facial" dichotomy, the presence of God's "face" calling up the Holy Spirit, or the conviction of the truth of the creed, the absence of God's "face" arousing elemental fears and through such painful arousal the desire to join in with the flock, to track after the Shepherd, to enter the body of Christ, the orbit of the Almighty's gravitational power. As that grand old American hymn *O God, I Cried, No Dark Disguise* has it, "The soul can split the sky in two/And let the face of God shine through."[45] It is time now to reject *both* sides of the "facial" dichotomy, to say no to both the infantilizing longings and the infantilizing fears, to grow up, indeed to *face up* to the realities of our separateness, our smallness in the immensity of the cosmos, and our own temporal, transient, mortal natures. No matter what the adaptational benefits of Christianity's magical procedures may be, the price we pay for them in the distortion of our basic perception of the world around us is too high. To put it somewhat differently, it is time now to say "Boo!" boo to the mysterious faces and spirits and ghosts and presences, boo to all the denizens of the putative supernatural realm, boo to every *thing*, including the "darkness," that would lead us away from the light of our reason, our rationality, our empiricism, our skepticism in the *face* of extraordinary claims—in short, our trust in our own down-to-earth perceptions as we experience them, and critically examine them, each and every worthwhile day of our lives.

## Speaking in Tongues: Origins of the Holy Spirit

Nothing discloses Christianity's primitive, magical nature more vividly than the burgeoning Pentecostal movement and the rite by which it is known, namely, speaking in tongues, or as it is alternatively called, glossolalia. Here is Webster's definition, which may help to give the reader some idea of the behavior in question: "speaking in tongues: a form of glossolalia in which a person experiencing religious ecstasy utters incomprehensible sounds that the speaker believes are a language spoken through him or her by a deity."[46] For glossolalia Webster has "incomprehensible speech in an imaginary language, sometimes occurring in a trance state, an episode of religious ecstacy."[47] Also for glossolalia, Webster suggests the reader take a look at the definitions for the word "schizophrenia." Of particular significance for our discussion here is the inextricable connection between speaking in tongues and descent of the Holy Spirit into the minds and hearts of the Apostles.

We've been discussing and alluding to the Holy Spirit for many pages in an attempt to demonstrate the manner in which credence or conviction suffuses the worshiper through the arousal of his deep, implicit recollection of the period during which he existed as a "little child" in the care of a big one, cherished, secure, following after the parental guide, feeding by means of parental provision, and taking the whole pattern into his developing mind-brain, for years, as a helpless, dependent newcomer to the world. It is no coincidence, we've suggested, that the Holy Spirit comes to the individual practitioner at the time of his *baptism*, the time at which he is ritually *born again* as the "little child" of Jesus Christ toward Whom he must now look for *everything*, his life (Jesus as Vine), his guidance upon the earth (Jesus as Shepherd), and his eternal salvation (Jesus as the vanquisher of death, the ultimate *separation*). Not only must the practitioner do "whatsoever" Jesus tells him to do (John 15:14), he must love his Savior more than he loves his own biological parents. He must become, centrally, a child of the Lord. We recognize immediately the neurological/psychological potential of such *doctrines* to reevoke the actual biological infancy and childhood of the worshiper, to conjure up, as it were, the infantile model of his own original experience: the Christian can't explicitly recall the early period but he can feel it reverberating compellingly below the surface of his consciousness such that Christianity's mirror-like version of those early interactional events resonates inwardly as *true*. The result is twofold: heartfelt conviction, frequently joyous or ecstatic because the believer or convert feels once again secure and unconditionally loved; and a sensation of the mysterious divine because the actual source or causation of the change is concealed forever in the realm of infantile amnesia, disclosed yet hidden, manifest yet unseen, powerfully and explicitly directive or intentional, yet powerfully and implicitly suggestive. Does not the Lord work in mysterious ways? Accordingly, if baptism and the Holy Spirit require correlation as marking the commencement of Christianity's infantilizing process, so glosso-lalia and the Holy Spirit require similar treatment as marking the Holy Spirit's entry into the *proselytizers*, the Apostles, whose *mission* is *to generate the creed*, to bring Christ's *parentage* and Christ's *doctrine* to everyone on the planet. Those who have become "little children" themselves will now go about finding more potential "little children" to swell the flock, the followers or trackers of the sacred Shepherd Whose map will lead everyone *home* to the sheepfold.

The Scriptural foundation and inspiration for the phenomenon of speaking in tongues derives from the New Testament, specifically the *Acts of the Apostles*:

And when the day of Pentecost was fully come, they [the Apostles] were all with one accord in one place.

And suddenly there came a sound from heaven as of a rushing mighty wind, and it filled all the house where they were sitting.

And then appeared unto them cloven tongues like as of fire, and it sat upon each of them.

And they were all filled with the Holy Ghost, and began to speak with other tongues, as the Spirit gave them utterance.

And there were dwelling at Jerusalem Jews, devout men, out of every nation under heaven.

Now when this was noised abroad, the multitude came together, and were confounded, because that every man heard them speak in his own language.

And they were all amazed and marveled, saying to one another, Behold, are not all these which speak Galilaeans?

And how hear we every man in our own tongue, wherein we were born?

Parthians and Medes, . . . Cretes and Arabians, we do hear them speak in our tongues the wonderful works of God. . . .

Peter, standing up with the eleven, lifted up his voice and said unto them . . . this is that which was spoken by the prophet Joel;

And it shall come to pass in the last days, saith God, I will pour out of my Spirit upon all flesh; . . .

> And it shall come to pass, that whosoever shall call on the name of the Lord shall be saved.
>
> (Acts 2:1–21)

Thus, 50 days after the resurrection of Christ (from the Greek *pentekoste*, literally 50th day) the Apostles receive from the Holy Spirit both the linguistic means and the inner resolve to go out into the world and preach the Gospel. What does this material signify from a naturalistic or realistic angle? We will never know, of course. In all likelihood, we have a tendentious, Scriptural rendering of some sort of hallucinatory, cultic contagion (or "enthusiasm") that transpired among Jesus's early followers as Christianity began to insert itself into the surrounding culture.

As for the Pentecostal movement transpiring around us today, it commenced toward the turn of the twentieth century, as follows (note the linkage between rebirth and the Holy Spirit): "On New Year's Day 1901 in Topeka, Kansas," write Andrew Newberg and Mark Robert Waldman,

> a young woman named Agnes Ozman, like Dorothy in *The Wizard of Oz*, was about to be transported to a strange wondrous place—not by a tornado, but through a born-again experience. She asked her teacher, Charles Parham, to lay his hands on her and pray, and when he did, she began to speak in a language no one had ever heard before. Some of the Bible students thought she was babbling, and others thought she was speaking Chinese, but they all agreed that she had been touched by the Holy Spirit and given the gift of "speaking in tongues." On that day was born the Pentecostal movement.[48]

The extent of the "movement's" current popularity and influence must not be underestimated. As a "spiritual" activity, glossolalia is reaching into all the major denominations of the creed, with millions of devotees either engaged directly or bearing pious, devotional witness to the practice. According to a recent Pew Forum poll, Pentecostalists (or "charismatics" or "renewalists" as they are also called) "are the fastest-growing religious group, approximately one-fourth of the world's two billion Christians," including approximately 23 percent of Christian Americans.[49] Since the 1960s, the movement has leapt from traditional Pentecostal denominations "to mainline Protestant and Catholic congregations. There are tongue-speaking Methodists, Presbyterians, Episcopalians, and Catholics" (p. 9d). There are, of course, dissenters, too, Christians who deem speaking in tongues "phony, weird, or even dangerous" (p. 9d); but at the moment, it seems, nothing is able to markedly diminish the enthusiasm. The "gift of tongues," writes Terry R. Baughman, pastor of The Pentecostals of Pleasanton (California), "is evidence of the spirit of God within us. . . .

We see it as filling a God-shaped hole in the heart of man" (p. 9d). In other words, to develop the pastor's metaphor, the whole business is related primarily to "man's" longing for emotional fulfillment, emotional connectedness, through some kind of merger or union with the Deity, a "spiritual" behavior that will *fill* the practitioner with the Godhead, end the separation, the loneliness, and the longing that comes inevitably to the human creature as he finds himself *out there on his own* as opposed to *in* there with the Big One.

What happens exactly, or perhaps one should say outwardly, when a speaker in tongues manifests his gift, his supernatural visitation from the Holy Spirit? We've had a brief taste of this already from Newberg and Waldman; here is further material from their text:

> What . . . is speaking in tongues? What does it sound like, and what does it mean? Even though the practice was widespread in the first half of the twentieth century, very few researchers took a strong interest in it, and not until 1977 did an ethnomusicologist, Jeff Titon, make a recording of this remarkable speech during a Pentecostal revival meeting. The following glossolalic passage, spelled out phonetically, was made from that recording (the phonetic symbol "?" refers to a guttural sound made in the back of the esophagus):
>
> > Kantasaborovo santolavo ilamasax rabaxo kalarabou. risadalabo pita rebasa toyen santoraba satrobaho satoya. rika salara santo labor "?" bokoli risantobo santayabadiante ikolorosi balso kolorianti
>
> In the early years of the apostolic faith missions, their publications often claimed that parishioners spoke in foreign languages that these people had never learned [thus echoing the New Testament]. Researchers call this form of tongue-speaking xenolalia or xenoglossia; but over the years, as linguists disproved such claims, belief in xenolalia died out. Instead, parishoners came to believe that glossolalics were speaking the language of God.
>
> (pp. 194–95)

Finally, assert Newberg and Waldman,

> Researchers who have studied glossolalia have not found linguistic evidence that any form of language is being spoken. Rather, the person is loosely stringing together and repeating familiar phonetic sounds. Nevertheless, in some churches, ministers and parishioners claim to be able to interpret the utterances, though in other groups it is only the speaker who privately intuits the meaning.
>
> (p. 195)

Here is another example, along with important commentary, from John P. Kildahl's volume *The Psychology of Speaking in Tongues*:

Standing at her sink, washing the breakfast dishes, Mrs. Rogers spoke out loud. She said, "Jana, Kanna, saree saree Kanai, Katai, akanna Kanai Karai Yahai, of saramai, saramoyai, iana Kanna." Mrs. Rogers was speaking in tongues—technically called glossolalia. She did not know what the words meant, but she felt a quiet contentment as she talked and sung the strange syllables. Some days she spoke only a word or two in this way before she changed to English, but that morning, she uttered the rhythmic sounds for about ten minutes and stopped only when she had finishing scouring . . . the frying pan. . . . Speaking in tongues still seemed strange to Mrs. Rogers, though she had been doing it for more than a year. She felt as if she had been given the ability to speak in a new language, without having to trouble too much about what the words actually meant. It was a pleasant, effortless thing to do and often filled her with a sense of well-being.[50]

It does not matter, then, whether or not the glossolalist is alone or in a group of fellow glossolalists, or in or out of a church setting.

He can speak in tongues while driving a car or swimming. He can do it silently in the midst of a party, or aloud before a large audience. The experience brings peace and joy and inner harmony. Glossolalists view it as an answer to prayer, an assurance of divine love and acceptance.

(p. 4)

Let's begin to develop this last aspect of the behavior, I mean the psychological/neurological direction from which feelings of "love" and "acceptance" well up in the glossolalist as he pronounces his nonsensical syllables.

We must bear in mind firmly as we go that the glossolalists with whom we are dealing are invariably *Christians*, which is to say individuals who have *already undergone Christianity's infantilizing process*, who regard themselves as the Almighty's "little children," who *depend* on their Shepherd/Savior for guidance, for sustenance, for protection, for affection—for everything they require as needful, vulnerable denizens of the planet. To put it another way, we must realize as we proceed that our glossolalists, our speakers, are looking to enhance their personal relationship with the Deity as it has been, and is, presented to them doctrinally by the overall magical formulations of the creed. As one of the glossolalists in Kildahl declares when asked what his activity has accomplished for him,

My life is radically changed as a result of this experience—a development *quite to be expected* [by a Christian] after a direct and personal encounter with the Holy Spirit. I know this from experience and so does every other *child of God* [every other Christian] who belongs to Him. Our speaking in tongues is our

seal to prove we belong to Him. Christ is alive in us. He leads and guides. . . .
He pulls us back from danger and covers us from unknown danger.

(p. 8, my emphasis)

We've heard all this before, of course, and may think of it as the Christian
*condition*: the speaker of the magical words is God's "child"; he "belongs" to
the Deity as the little one belongs to the parent; he perceives another being,
namely, Christ, "alive" in him, which means he perceives himself *united* with,
*merged* with, the Big One symbiotically such that he "walks" and "talks" with
another, supernatural entity (or internalized object, in psychological terms)
who "leads" him, "guides" him (the pastoral metaphor), protects him from
danger, indeed *covers him up* (the umbilical cocoon) from the anxiety-
inducing future of "unknown" threats. The aim of glossolalia, then, is to
intensify, to *deepen* the orthodox, infantilizing agenda of the Christian religion, and our business here is to understand in at least a preliminary way just
*how* such a deepening comes about.

A significant clue emerges as we observe investigators underscoring the
similarities between the glossolalist's productions and the babbling of infants
and small children. "What some authorities call 'infantile babble,' " writes
Kildahl, "is more scientifically described as similar to the second or parataxic
phase of an infant's attempts to communicate. During this period the toddler
repeats sounds which are meaningless to the listener but satisfying to the
child. Another speech pattern typical of this level of development," Kildahl
goes on,

> involves dual or collective monologues (Piaget). The youngster still does not
> make sense of his speech, but is stimulated by the presence of another person
> or persons who are not included in the monologue or expected to respond to
> it. Wayne E. Oates believes that this accurately describes the phenomenon of
> glossolalia. The distortions of speech which appear at the time are submerged
> by the child as he matures. According to Oates, these distortions reappear in
> tongue-speaking.
>
> (pp. 31–32)

Also significant is the section in Newberg and Waldman titled "The Pentecostal Brain in Action" (p. 197), wherein we discover at the experimental,
clinical level that speaking in tongues triggers a *decrease* in the activity of the
frontal lobes (p. 200). "This is a very unusual finding," according to these
authors, because the language that arises from the "glossolalic state" is always
"highly structured" and "filled with clearly articulated phrases" (p. 200).
Apparently, they contend, the language of the tongue-speaker is "being

generated in a different way," or "from someplace other than the normal processing centers of speech," as a kind of "incomplete speech" (p. 201). We're close, now, to the heart of the matter.

"When speaking in tongues," explain Newberg and Waldman,

> practitioners describe the experience as surrendering themselves to the spirit of God. In this sense, they are no longer attempting to control their thoughts, feelings, or bodily movements; such control is primarily a frontal lobe function. They are also deliberately suspending cognitive processes that are normally active in maintaining focused attention and awareness. In essence, they are surrendering their conscious will.
>
> (p. 201)

With "decreased activity in your frontal lobes," Newberg and Waldman continue, "you would have the conscious experience that 'something else' was running the show." Even "glossolalic people who were trained to speak a pseudo language also had the sense that they were being overtaken by an outside or foreign source" (p. 201). Accordingly, if the "goal" of the "Pentecostal tradition" is to "be transformed" through a "new religious experience" as Newberg and Waldman contend (p. 202), we may clearly perceive the psychological/neurological direction from which the "transformation" occurs by simply linking together the transformation's principal ingredients, namely, (1) infantile or child-like babbling, (2) decreased activity in the frontal lobes (decreased *cognition*), and (3) the sense of being "overtaken" (*taken over*) by an "outside" or "foreign" source. When all of this successfully transpires, in other words, when the speaker in tongues succeeds in *imitating* (homeopathic magic) the original relationship between the helpless, babbling, dependent little one and the all-controlling, all-directing, parental Deity, the infantilizing conduct arouses the cerebrally rooted, implicit recollection of the period during which the arrangement actually obtained. This is an arousal that Pentecostal Christianity invariably celebrates as confirmational, faith-bound visitation from the mysterious Holy Spirit (the "religious experience") Who just happens to be doctrinally not merely a spirit but a *person*, too. We may recall here, following Henry Cloud and John Townsend, that Christianity's deepest aim, deepest purpose, is to foster in the practitioner a "moment-to-moment relationship of dependency" between the worshiper and his loving Lord, Jesus Christ, and that it is the Holy Spirit specifically Who prompts the worshiper to "yield and follow," to permit the Deity to "control" and "guide" him throughout the course of his earthly existence.[51] Can one think of a better way to accomplish this orthodox purpose, startling as it is, than to babble like an infant, to inhibit the directional influence of one's "frontal lobes," and to consider oneself *usurped* by a "foreign source," or more specifically, by an omnipotent Parent-God?

In a section titled "The Dependency Syndrome," Kildahl points out that "tongue-speakers" in a group or congregational setting have "a strong need for external guidance" from a "trusted" figure of "authority," "a strong sense of leaning on someone more powerful than themselves," who gives them a sense of "security and direction in their lives" (the essentials of the pastoral metaphor). Followers feel "at peace," declares Kildahl, because they've "abandoned" themselves to the "control of someone else" (p. 51). Kildahl continues in a decisive utterance:

> A little girl walking down the street holding her daddy's hand feels serene and safe in a unique way. She holds his big, strong hand, and she rests joyfully in the belief that nothing can happen that her daddy cannot handle. She feels loved and she feels protected. Our research gave evidence that the believing tongue-speaker approaches this same feeling of euphoria. *He believes that he is in the hands of God.* He believes that he has proof of it because he can speak in tongues.
>
> (p. 51, my emphasis)

Glossolalia, then, constitutes "a reversion to an early level of maturity" during which the "rational way" of "relating to life" is "diminished." It is "more child-like" and "less critical" in "its nature" (p. 59). As for glossolalia's "magical quality," or the quality that aligns it with the other infantilizing facets of Christianity, it emerges unforgettably as Kildahl's study presents the glossolalist (1) crying out in prayer, "God, make me a puppet," as if the practitioner "believed almost literally that God would pull the strings and he as a puppet would respond" (p. 61), (2) declaring openly, "God now directs my tongue" and "He allows me to make these sounds" (p. 61), (3) asserting that God is actually "making his tongue move" (p. 61), or (4) claiming that his "tongue-speaking is caused by direct mechanical movement of the vocal chords by the Holy Spirit" (p. 71). As is always the case with Christianity's infantilizing doctrines and practices, the overarching psychological feature of all these astonishing utterances turns out to be the worshiper's eagerness to place himself *in* the gravitational field of the Big One's *will*, the Big One's *control*, which is to say, to re-create on the level of homeopathic magic the primal symbiotic interaction of the early time. The Holy Spirit enters upon the scene, or surges up within the emotional perceptions of the worshiper, when and only when such magical conduct awakens at the level of implicit recollection the actual biological substrate that underlies the whole of Christianity's magical goings-on. "The brain works by pattern matching, not by logic,"

Professor Jonathan Haidt reminds us,[52] as we explore the glossolalic world in which the *pattern* of infantile dependency and submission matches precisely the strange religious behavior we're exploring.

It will come as no surprise, we might add, that a "personal crisis of some kind" frequently precedes the Christian's initiation into the world of glossolalia where he may not only render himself up to the care and guidance of the supernatural Big One to Whose will he now utterly submits, but feel himself surrounded by other tongue-speakers with whom he shares both a mysterious gift and a sympathetic, reliable, social interaction. Pentecostals, notes Kildahl, "are often members of the affluent middle class, professionals or quasi-professionals suffering from the emotional deprivation common to our times. Sometimes individuals of this socio-economic level try to 'break through' their loneliness by means of alcohol or drugs." Speaking in tongues "provides a form of breaking through which allows the psychically ill to communicate their deep and too-long-repressed religious emotions in a socially acceptable form" (p. 33). This final point returns me to the theme I undertook at the conclusion of the previous section on the significance of the Godhead's face.

Extreme though it may be in its expressional features, speaking in tongues as we observe it today among burgeoning Pentecostal (and other) congregations harbors in its core the same infantilizing purpose that resides at the bedrock of the Christian faith as a whole. Accordingly, we have the analytical right to say, or to think to ourselves, here is Christianity; here is the Christian religion in all its magical splendor. What do we find in the studies we've just explored? Let's sum the matter up: (1) a "reversion" to "an early level of maturity," to a less "rational," more "child-like," way of "relating" to one's "life"; (2) a "decrease" in the "activity" of the "frontal lobes," a "less critical" perception of the world around one—in short, a shutting down of what we usually think of as our brainpower; (3) the "surrender" of one's "conscious will," the "euphoria" that comes over one as he feels himself "controlled" by, "led" by, the Big One, the supernatural "daddy" upon whom he depends every moment of his existence and into whose "hand" he places his own will (Christ instructs His "followers" to do "whatsoever" He "commands" [John 15:14]), to the point of becoming a symbiotic appendage, or "puppet," of the all-powerful Lord; (4) the tendency to adopt such an attitude, such a posture, when some sort of "crisis" or emergency enters into one's affairs, when the pressures of one's environment, one's "culture," make themselves vigorously known. All of this without exception resides at the very heart of the Christian code upon which countless millions of human beings everywhere construct their lives. As for the advent of the Holy Spirit as it is called, it surges up in one when all of this, or a significant measure of it, begins working in the worshiper, begins awakening implicitly and mnemonically the time of his earthly experience when he *was*, in fact, at "an early level of maturity," when he was, in fact, less "rational" and more "child-like," when his "frontal lobes" were, in fact, only partially developed, when he was, in fact, led around by a big one upon whom he wholly depended. And it is precisely, and sadly, these naturalistic, biological recollections, efficacious and unseen, that convince the worshiper of his religion's veracity, its "truth," and, of course, its guiding, salvational role in his existence (adaptational tracking). What is happening entirely on the *inside* is attributed psychologically and cognitively to a putative supernatural presence on the *outside*, as the fundamental misconception of the world goes solemnly or joyously forward.

Now that we grasp the infantilizing core of the Christian faith, now that we perceive its magical, wishful, reversional nature, its intention to rescue, to "save" its lost, mortal adherents by restoring them to the pattern, the map, of the pastoral metaphor, with the little one tracking after the Big One, we have no choice but to reject it once and for all as grown-up men and women. Indeed, the very suggestion that a human being can rely upon his "faith" as opposed to his mature, analytical, critical rationality for his guidance in the world is in and of itself an infantilizing move, an attempt to steer the adherent toward a "child-like" acceptance of supernatural, institutional claims as opposed to an uncompromising probe into their perceptional foundations. We made plain in a previous chapter that for Christianity faith is "prayer and nothing but prayer."[53] We also made plain that to pray successfully the Christian worshiper must adopt an utterly helpless, dependent, child-like attitude; he must turn to the Big One "as the child in distress turns to his mother."[54] In short, he must *act out* his "reversion" to an "early level of maturity" through an emotional performance of homeopathic magic, just as the glossolalic acts out his own babbling reversion through his own unforgettable, pitiable display. When it comes to such behavior, such conduct, such "faith," we must now say emphatically, *no*—not only to Christianity but to any religion or institution or organization or collection of lost souls looking for some way, any way, of adapting themselves to the relentless actualities of the natural universe around them. Already for millions of people on the planet the game is up; the long age of religious magic is over. Perhaps in some future era the majority of human beings, still under the spell of spirits and suchlike, will also be delivered, will also be released from the addictive trance state of infantilization. We can't know, of course, but we can hopefully anticipate, and while we're at it, work to diminish the world's religious confusion as much as we possibly can.

## Notes

1. Edward O. Wilson, *Sociobiology* (Cambridge, MA: Harvard University Press, 1975), p. 284.

2. Gerald M. Edelman, *Bright Air, Brilliant Fire: On the Matter of Mind* (New York: Basic Books, 1992), p. 161.

3. Ibid., pp. 79, 81, 152, 161, 163, 167.

4. I continue to employ the King James Version of Scripture, as I will do throughout the course of the book.

5. Edelman, *Bright Air, Brilliant Fire*, p. 182.

6. Alexander Cruden, *Cruden's Complete Concordance to the Old and New Testaments* (Philadelphia: John C. Winston Company, 1949), p. 483.

7. See Edelman, *Bright Air, Brilliant Fire*, p. 182. See also Gerald M. Edelman, *The Remembered Present: A Biological Theory of Consciousness* (New York: Basic Books, 1989).

8. Anne Graham Lotz, *I Saw the Lord* (Grand Rapids, MI: Zondervan, 2006), p. 140.

9. Neil T. Anderson, *Who I Am in Christ* (Ventura, CA: Regal Books, 1993), p. 134.

10. Henry T. Blackaby and Claude V. King, *Experiencing God* (Nashville, TN: Broadman and Holman Publishers, 1994, pp. 36–37.

11. Cited in G. P. Fisher, *A History of Christian Doctrine* (Philadelphia: Fortress Press, 1978), p. 321.

12. H. Richard Niebuhr, *Faith on Earth* (New Haven, CT: Yale University Press, 1989), p. 95.

13. Louise Kendall and R. T. Kendall, eds., *Great Christian Prayers* (London: Hodder and Stoughton, 2000), p. 3.

14. Hanspeter A. Mallot, "Finding Our Way," *Scientific American Mind* 16, no. 1 (May 2005): 70–77. This citation is on p. 77 of the article.

15. See David Roth and Sidney J. Blatt, "Spatial Representations of Psychopathology," *Journal of the American Psychoanalytic Association* 22 (1994): 871.

16. Blackaby and King, *Experiencing God*, p. 36 (see note 10).

17. Tim Gustafson, ed., *Our Daily Bread*, 51, nos. 3, 4, 5 (June, July, August 2006): 28. Published by RBC Ministries, USA.

18. Ibid., p. 35.

19. N.A., *God Speaks: Devotional* (Tulsa, OK: Honor Books, 2000), p. 149.

20. Kendall and Kendall, *Great Christian Prayers*, p. 360 (my emphasis). See note 4.

21. See John R. Hinnells, ed., *The Penguin Dictionary of Religions* (New York: Penguin Books, 1997), p. 383.

22. Janet Collins, "Spiritual Journeys," *Vancouver Sun*, May 26, 2007, p. G5.

23. See note 11.

24. Billy Graham, *The Holy Spirit* (New York: Thomas Nelson, Inc., 1978), p. 10.

25. See Berton L. Mack, *Who Wrote the New Testament? The Making of Christian Myth* (New York: HarperCollins, 1995), pp. 1–41. That Jesus actually existed is highly probable but not certain.

26. Allen C. Myers, *The Eerdmans Bible Dictionary* (Grand Rapids, MI: William B. Eerdmans Publishing Co., 1987), p. 373.

27. Romano Guardini, *Prayer in Practice*, trans. L. Loewenstein-Wertheim (London: Burns and Oates, 1957), p. 26.

28. James Shreeve, "Beyond the Brain," *National Geographic* 207, no. 3 (March 2005): 25.

29. Elizabeth Svodoba, "Faces, Faces Everywhere," *New York Times*, February 13, 2007, p. F6.

30. Frederick V. Malmstrom, "Close Encounters of the Facial Kind," *Skeptic* 11, no. 4 (2005): 45–47.

31. Robert Coles, *The Spiritual Life of Children* (Boston: Houghton Mifflin Company, 1990), p. 40.

32. George A. Buttrick, *So We Believe, So We Pray* (New York: Abingdon-Cokesbury, 1994), p. 30.

33. D. W. Winnicott, *Playing and Reality* (New York: Basic Books, 1971), p. 111.

34. See note 27 above.

35. Tim Stafford, *Knowing the Face of God* (Colorado Springs, CO: Navpress, 1996), pp. 182–83.

36. N.A., *God Speaks: Devotional*, p. 133.

37. Thomas Merton, *Contemplative Prayer* (New York: Doubleday, 1996), p. 51.

38. Kendall and Kendall, eds., *Great Christian Prayers*, p. 47.

39. Albert Christ-Janer, ed., *American Hymns Old and New* (New York: Columbia University Press, 1980), p. 663.

40. Saint Augustine, *The Confessions of Saint Augustine*, trans. Rex Warner (New York: Penguin Books, 2001), p. 21.

41. *The Gospel Hour*, Trinity Broadcasting Network, October 11, 2008, 7:00 p.m., Channel 40, Orange County, California.

42. See note 40 above.

43. Anderson, *Who I Am in Christ*, p. 94.

44. N.A., *God Speaks: Devotional*, p. 145.

45. Christ-Janer, *American Hymns Old and New*, p. 694.

46. *Webster's New Universal Unabridged Dictionary* (New York, Barnes and Noble, 1996), p. 1831.

47. Ibid., p. 813.

48. Andrew Newberg and Mark Robert Waldham, *Why We Believe What We Believe: Uncovering Our Biological Need for Meaning, Spirituality, and Truth* (New York: The Free Press, 2006), p. 191.

49. Kimberly Winston, "Faith's Language Barrier?" *USA Today*, May 24, 2007, p. 9d.

50. John P. Kildahl, *The Psychology of Speaking in Tongues* (New York: Harper and Row, 1972), p. 1.

51. Henry Cloud and John Townsend, *God Will Make a Way* (Nashville, TN: Integrity Publishers, 2002), pp. 96–99.

52. Jonathan Haidt, "Honey, I Shrunk the President," *Los Angeles Times*, December 16, 2007, p. M4.

53. Friedrich Heiler, *Prayer: A Study in the History and Psychology of Religion* (New York: Oxford University Press, [1932] 1997), p. xiii.

54. Guardini, *Prayer in Practice*, p. 77.

# CHAPTER 4

# Growing Up:
# A Concluding Word

My purpose as I conclude is to underscore forcefully, and expand upon, several of my contextual comments to the effect that Christianity, for all its soothing, adaptational capacities, ultimately exacts too high a price in sheer perceptual distortion to go unchallenged as a way of interpreting the world around us. In a word, Christianity must be rejected and set aside as a magical, prescientific mode of discourse. This is not, let me stress, to pick on Christianity in particular; as I've maintained throughout, it is rather to use Christianity as a vivid example of what is wrong with all supernatural creeds, with all supernatural rites and doctrines that move the human species backward into fallacious, cultic territory instead of forward into what is at least the possibility of an accurate, verifiable perception of things. However, it isn't merely Christianity's perceptual distortions that render it otiose and destructive. As the subtitle of this book declares, and as I have attempted to establish in detail for a couple hundred pages, Christianity also *infantilizes* its followers in several major mental and emotional ways not the least of which is urging them to rely for security and behavioral guidance on faith, on the existence and the perfection of overarching parental spirits from the beyond, as opposed to their own human reason and good sense.

Baptism, as we now appreciate,[1] constitutes the basis of the whole Christian life.[2] In the definitive words of the New Testament, or from the mouth of Jesus Himself, "Verily I say unto you, Except ye be converted, and become as little children ye shall not enter into the kingdom of heaven" (Matt. 18:3).[3] Everything in Christian rite and doctrine, everything without exception, is devoted to enhancing and deepening this "conversion," to completing the worshiper's transformation into the Savior's "little child." To render it in the terms we've been employing from the outset, with baptism Christianity's magical process of infantilization gets under way. The worshiper is instructed to love Jesus more than he loves his actual parents. He is instructed to "ask and receive," to call upon his Parent-God for guidance, for support, for sustenance and love as an utterly helpless, utterly dependent little one. Prayer for the Christian, *this* kind of prayer, becomes synonymous with faith itself. The worshiper is told by his theological mentors to adopt an attitude of moment-to-moment dependency on Christ as he goes about his business in the world; without Jesus Christ, Christian teaching informs him, "he can do nothing" (John 15:5). His entire life, at every instant of it, becomes a kind of behavioral prayer, an open acknowledgment of his total reliance on the Big One who watches over him. Through the pastoral metaphor that resides at the core of the Christian tradition, the worshiper is advised to regard his God as his Shepherd and himself as a sheep, following dutifully after the all-controlling, all-providing supernatural Guide who leads him to food, to water, to safety, to rest, and to the eternal home or "house" in which he will abide permanently without a hint of separation, or aloneness. "Heaven," we are informed in the popular Christian literature of today, "is a great big hug that lasts forever."[4] Through the Eucharist the worshiper participates in a transparently magical ceremony, a conjuration if there ever was one, wherein he actually or symbolically feeds upon the body of his Deity, ingests His blood and His flesh, mixes fluids and solids in sacred symbiosis, merging Jesus with himself and himself with Jesus who becomes his "bread of life." Finally for our purposes here, Jesus instructs His "little children" to obey Him at all times, to do "whatsoever" He "commands" them to do, and if they don't do that, if they don't become and remain good little girls and boys, then they run the risk of losing their precious Leader, for as Jesus makes plain, only those who obey Him may regard themselves as His "friend" (John 15:14). What we have in all this, obviously, is a vivid psychological-mythic presentation of the basic biological situation, a thinly disguised depiction of our earthly beginnings designed to arouse the worshiper's implicit recollection of his life-or-death involvement with his original caregivers such that he may feel within himself both the "truth" of the Christian narrative and an actual opportunity to reimmerse himself magically into an idealized version of his precious interpersonal, opening days. When this occurs and the worshiper adopts fully the particulars of his religion, he is said to have experienced a visitation from the "Holy Spirit."

Here is the point: as we come to *see* all this fully, to demystify the sacred rite and doctrine through realistic neuropsychological analysis, to fathom the magical process of infantilization in which the religion's power is ultimately rooted, we realize that Christianity provides us with precious, indeed invaluable understanding of what it means to mature as men and women, to accomplish precisely *the opposite* of a wishful return to an infantilized state of mind and emotion—in a word, *to grow up* and take our place as genuinely developed, contributing members of the human community. We begin the realistic process of growth by examining vigorously the cultural, institutional, social, or personal activities and behaviors in which we are engaged, or are invited to become engaged, for any trace, any suggestion, of magical content, and if and when we discover such content we reject it immediately and prepare ourselves to explain our rejection to anyone who may be interested. I do *not* have in mind here a trace of the "magic" by which we grow and thrive as we simply go about our business on the planet, our belief in ourselves, our healthy self-interest and self-confidence, in short, the kind of "magic" upon which Géza Róheim concentrates when he distinguishes a person's faith in his own "abilities" from the "omnipotence fantasies" of the "all-powerful sorcerer."[5] I have in mind, rather, the kind of magic that pervades the Christian religion, from baptism, to prayer, to the Eucharist, to glossolalia and the drawing down of the Holy Spirit. Such beliefs and behaviors are found throughout the world among an endless variety of religious sects, cults, and gatherings of all kind, from the mountains of Asia, to the sands of Africa, to the valleys and plains of the Americas and Europe; and in every case without exception such beliefs and behaviors infantilize participants, stunting their mental and emotional growth by playing down their reason and good sense, diminishing their capacity to recognize sound, verifiable information, distorting their intuitive and intellectual judgment of the communications to which they are exposed.

We continue our process of growth by acknowledging firmly and fully the biological facts of our existence on the planet, our separation from the maternal matrix, our smallness or vulnerability to the ever-present dangers of accident and illness, our mortality, our eventual demise and permanent disappearance from the universe. We view Christianity's magical affirmations (eternal union with a loving, omnipotent Parent-God whose divine plan includes everything that happens to us as individuals) as ultimately the veiling, or the denying, of the inescapable biological realities that not only mark us but define us as natural creatures in the world. We recognize the imperfections of scientific, evolutional approaches to our existence and our quality as living forms, yet we find such approaches more plausible and more potentially definitive than the imponderable, prescientific fantasies of the Christian faith. We don't believe in virgin births, in people walking about on the surface of the sea, or in dead folks emerging from the grave. If we cannot discover *some* ordinary, empiric, verifiable support for astonishing, preternatural claims, we reject them. When we read that "heaven is a great big hug that lasts forever,"[6] or hear Jack Van Impe declaring that "prayer is like calling home every day,"[7] we recognize the child-like dependency, the denial of separation, and the inappropriate infantilism that reside in such utterances when they are made by supposedly grown-up members of our species. We don't wish to be this way, to be involved in such retrograde states of mind and emotion. For us, "home" in this childish, wishful sense is simply gone. We're on our own now. When we find Anne Graham Lotz maintaining that Christ's ultimate message to us as He participates divinely in our earthly lives is "never will I leave you; never will I forsake you; . . . I love you,"[8] we feel precisely as we do when we read the earlier words on heaven and prayer: such utterances indicate a state of infantile neediness and all-absorbing, irrational fantasy that borders on the pathological. We see such states acted out routinely on the Christian television channels, of course: we see the rolling eyes and sweaty faces, the waving hands and trembling bodies; we see the open, shouting mouths; we hear the whoops and howls, the ecstatic cries, "He loves me! He loves me! He loves me!" Once again, we don't wish to be this way. Such conduct strikes us as pitiable. We regret that our fellow human beings allow themselves to be drawn in this infantile, irrational direction.

Our task of growing up moves forward as we repudiate any and all indications of the omnipotence of thought in ourselves or in others. Those who claim to have special, superhuman powers of perception, powers that afford them knowledge of the supernatural sphere, we immediately mark us backward-looking, retrograde personalities. We are familiar with the inextricable link between the omnipotence of thought and the grave narcissistic issues that reside deep within the individual who makes such extraordinary claims. Róheim's "all-powerful sorcerer"[9] is of interest to us *only* as a phenomenon to study, and we apply the very same evaluation to cult leaders, mystical wisemen, mediums, priests, pastors, and self-styled gurus of all sorts and fashions. Nor do we countenance those who claim to be the *blessed followers* of omnipotent supernatural entities, to be specially "chosen" by gods and spirits, and this includes, of course, the "converted," Christ's "little children," His newly appointed "saints" (I Cor. 1:2). All such claimants, all such individuals and groups, we regard as the blood relations, the not-so-distant cousins as it were, of Róheim's "all-powerful sorcerer." When Billy Graham, preoccupied as usual with images of omnipotence, insists that as Christians we are surrounded at all times by mighty guardian angels, hordes of them, in fact, who watch over us and protect us from harm,[10] we think to ourselves, there it is again, the religious denial of our smallness and vulnerability, Christianity's incapacity simply to accept the realities of our biological lives, its pathetic attempt to shore up the wounded narcissism and diminish the persistent anxiety of its worshipers by aligning them with spiritual giants. "You may think I'm just another barber trimming hair in this little shop, but as a Christian I'm connected to divine, all-powerful angels who look out for me."[11] What Graham and his followers need to be told, politely, should be perfectly clear at this point: grow up; stop the silly super-natural nonsense, and just grow up; surely it is time to do that now; we are all simply regular human beings attempting to thrive on the surface of the planet; there is no such thing as a guardian angel, okay?

Finally, we grow as we fully accept our mortality, as we refuse to indulge ourselves in what Ernest Becker calls in a famous phrase, "the denial of death."[12] We don't say to ourselves as we contemplate our biological cessa-tion, maybe I won't really die after all; or, maybe death is only a transition to another mode of being; or, I believe my soul will live on; or, I'll be with my loving Jesus forever; or, maybe I'll be reincarnated as a flamingo and go soaring off into the sunset, or some such. We consider Christianity's denial of death (Jesus arises from the grave; salvation is available through Christ) to be a major facet of its infantilizing process and the ultimate witness to its overall failure of nerve; for in the last analysis that is what Christianity boils down to as an approach to our human existence, a failure of nerve. There can be no *growing up* until one honestly *faces up* to the ineluctable reality of his or her demise and permanent disappearance from the universe. To put it in the paradoxical terms to which we're accustomed, to "be" dead is to "be" nonexistent. Moreover, we are supremely aware at this point in our develop-ment as thoughtful creatures that the denial of death is routinely acted out in myriad violent ways, most notably in the destruction of other living entities. For many human beings within a variety of sociocultural contexts, including war, homicide, and hunting, to kill is to experience deep within mind and body an exhilarating sense of one's aliveness and hence, a reduction of one's anxiety over death. Accordingly, as grown-ups, we will actively seek to explain and hopefully to diminish the denial of death whenever an opportunity to do so presents itself. And if all of this somehow hurts, if we undergo anxiety, and sadness, and anguish, and actual psychic and physical pain as we face up to the facts, well, so be it. We can say to ourselves, perhaps, something like this: better to have one moment of honest, face-to-face contact with things as they are, no matter how much death anxiety that engenders, than have a lifetime of comforting illusions.

Omar Khayyám writes in famous lines of verse,

Ah, love could you and I with Him conspire
To grasp this sorry scheme of things entire,
Would we not shatter it to bits—and then
Remold it nearer to the heart's desire?

(Rubáiyát, stanza 99)

Here is Christianity's magical program in unforgettable lucidity. Through magical doctrine and rite the worshiper "conspires" with "Him," the all-powerful Parent-God, to "grasp" or get hold of both mentally and physically the "fallen" or "sorry" state of the world in which he resides and then, once more through magical doctrine and rite, "shatter it to bits" and "remold it nearer to the heart's desire." There was separation from the matrix, the severance of mankind (Adam and Eve) from the paradisal Garden and its loving Creator; there was loss of paradisal ascendancy, the sudden advent of small-ness, of vulnerability to accident and illness, to the vagaries of postlapsarian existence; there was physical mortality as death entered creation, the utter cessation of life and being, the endless dust swirling about in the wind; there is now, however, the new Adam and Eve, eternal union with the omnipotent Provider, the protection of His loving presence (including, for Billy Graham, His mighty angels), and of course, the banishment of death, life everlasting in Heaven where the virtuous Christian has access to "a hug that lasts forever." All of this, needless to say, is exactly the opposite of what the grown-up Omar Khayyám has in mind. For the medieval Persian poet, the inescapable reality, the inescapable fact, *is* the "sorry scheme of things entire," *is* the way things are in the natural, biological world. We discover in Omar Khayyám the *acceptance* of our condition, the realization that we cannot change it, as much as we might like to through the putative efficacy of magical action (oh, that we could remold the world). For those who have attained acceptance and maturity, the bribe of magic, the bribe of Ali Baba, is a thing of the past, a childish fantasy, a poetical toy and nothing more. For Christianity, as we've seen, magic is the key, along with the infantilization (or irrationality) that makes magic a viable alternative to mature behavior. The magical perfection for which Omar Khayyám can only pine Christianity seriously extends to its infantilized followers (the sheep) who eagerly embrace it through their wishful longing to escape the facts of the human estate. In this way, Christianity's hand is ultimately joined with the hand of Ali Baba, and it will always be joined thus. For when Christianity drops the magical process of infantilization, it drops everything that resides within the very core of its theology.

## Notes

1. Baptism is discussed fully at the inception of Chapter 3, Part One.

2. See the *Catechism of the Catholic Church* (Liguori, MO: Liguori Publications, 1994), p. 312.

3. All the scriptural quotations in this book are from the King James Version of the Bible.

4. Jack Canfield, *Chicken Soup for the Christian Soul* (Deerfield Beach, FL: Heath Communications, 1997), p. 294.

5. Géza Róheim, *Magic and Schizophrenia* (Bloomington: Indiana University Press, 1955), pp. 45–46. For an additional interesting discussion of these matters, see Marcia Cavell, "Self Knowledge and Self-Understanding," *American Imago* 65, no. 3 (Fall 2008): 357–78.

6. See note 4 above.

7. *Jack Van Impe Presents*, Trinity Broadcasting Network, September 16, 2008, 7:00 p.m., Channel 40, Orange County, California.

8. Anne Graham Lotz, *I Saw the Lord* (Grand Rapids, MI: Zondervan, 2006), pp. 88–90.

9. See Roheim, note 5 above.

10. Billy Graham, *Angels: God's Secret Agents* (New York: Doubleday, 1954), pp. 72, 93.

11. The author's quotation.

12. Ernest Becker, *The Denial of Death* (New York: The Free Press, 1973).

# Index

## About the Author

**M. D. FABER** is Professor Emeritus of English Language and Literature, specializing in Literature and Psychology, at the University of Victoria, British Columbia, Canada. Formerly Special Fellow at the National Institute of Mental Health, Washington, D.C., Dr. Faber is the author of 10 books, including the widely acclaimed volumes *Synchronicity: C. G. Jung, Psychoanalysis, and Religion*; *The Magic of Prayer: An Introduction to the Psychology of Faith*; and *The Psychological Roots of Religious Belief: Searching for Angels and the Parent-God*.